ALSO BY RIC FLAIR

Ric Flair: To Be the Man (with Mark Madden)

ALSO BY BRIAN SHIELDS

30 Years of WrestleMania

Encyclopedia Updated & Expanded (with Kevin Sullivan)

DK Reader: WWE John Cena

DK Reader: WWE Triple H

WWE Encyclopedia—The Definitive Guide to World Wrestling Entertainment (with Kevin Sullivan)

Main Event: WWE in the Raging 80s

SEC
NAT

WWE

SECOND NATURE

THE LEGACY OF
RIC FLAIR
AND THE RISE OF
CHARLOTTE

RIC FLAIR AND CHARLOTTE

WITH BRIAN SHIELDS

ST. MARTIN'S PRESS ⊠ NEW YORK

SECOND NATURE. Copyright © 2017 by WWE. All rights reserved. Printed in the United States of America. For information, address St. Martin's Press, 175 Fifth Avenue, New York, N.Y. 10010.

www.stmartins.com

Designed by Steven Seighman

Photos on pages 18, 34, 44, 130, and 363 courtesy of *Pro Wrestling Illustrated*. Other photos courtesy of the WWE and the authors.

The Library of Congress Cataloging-in-Publication Data is available upon request.

ISBN 978-1-250-12057-1 (hardcover)
ISBN 978-1-250-15178-0 (signed edition)
ISBN 978-1-250-12058-8 (ebook)

Our books may be purchased in bulk for promotional, educational, or business use. Please contact your local bookseller or the Macmillan Corporate and Premium Sales Department at 1-800-221-7945, extension 5442, or by email at MacmillanSpecialMarkets@macmillan.com.

First Edition: September 2017

10 9 8 7 6 5 4 3 2 1

CONTENTS

PART IV: REUNITED

PART V: DEDICATIONS

RIC'S ACKNOWLEDGMENTS

Thank you to my agent, attorney, and best friend, Melinda Morris Zanoni, Esq. Thanks for your loyalty, disarming nature, quick wit, odd ability to find my keys from an airplane, keeping me busy working so I stay out of trouble, and dedication to my legacy over the last twenty years. This book would not exist without you and your team's vision and hard work at Legacy Talent and Entertainment and Apollo Sports & Entertainment Law Group. All my respect.

I want to say thank you to the McMahon family, Triple H, and all my friends at WWE for being there for me through it all. I owe you my life . . . . and maybe a case of beer or two. A sincere thank-you for your irreplaceable friendship and passion. Without you, I wouldn't be the Limousine-ridin', Jet-flyin', Kiss-stealin', Wheelin' -dealin', Son of a Gun. WOOOOO!

Many thanks to Brian Shields for your collaborative efforts with the Flairs and writing one helluva book. Thanks also to the incredible team at St. Martin's Press.

To my fans. My blood, sweat, and tears (not just a saying in my case) all these years have been for each one of you. Thank you for your support, and for allowing me to do what I love the most for my entire adult life.

To the love of my life and partner in crime, Wendy Barlow, thank you for the good, bad, and wild times. I wouldn't trade our time together for the world. You have stood by my side at my lowest and darkest times. I am eternally grateful for your love.

I've saved the best for last. To my precious children: Megan, David, and Ashley. You all have given me so much joy throughout the years. Thank you for supporting me in all of my endeavors. Your never-failing encouragement and love keeps me going. It is the greatest honor of my life to be your father. Ashley, a special thank-you to the best coauthor a father could have. The Flair legacy will live on!

CHARLOTTE'S ACKNOWLEDGMENTS

When I think of who I am, where I am today, and where I hope to go, everything goes back to my family.

Thank you to my mom. Now, I have an understanding of what it required to raise two children while your spouse was on the road every week of the year: carpool, homework, meals, love and care, and being my biggest supporter. You always found a way to make things possible no matter what I needed. Those times are with me every day.

I want to thank my dad. For always being there for me and for teaching me to live every day like it's the last. For pushing me to be where I am today, and reminding me to go to sleep every night and "know who you are." I never thought I'd say this . . . thank you for being an amazing coauthor!

To my older sister, Megan, thank you for your endless loyalty and unconditional love. Please know how special you are to me. Our bond will last forever. A thank-you to my big brother, David, for always being there for me, and for providing the humor only the four Fliehr kids could understand. Every time I walk through that curtain I say to myself, "This is for you, Big Dave."

To my little brother, Reid, thank you for being my other half . . . for teaching me how to live, and the importance of never being afraid of who you are.

I never imagined being blessed with friends who became family. Thank you, Erin Lunde, for showing me no matter how far apart people may be in age, kindred spirits make you best friends.

To my Uncle Arn, you've been such an important part of my life. It warms my heart to be able to work with you, knowing that Reid idolized you. It's been emotional, but it's meant to be. You never let me off the hook and treat me like a daughter. You'll never know what this means to me.

Thank you, Brittany Zahn, for being my best friend, teaching me how to be an adult, and being right by my side.

To my best friend Becky Lynch, thank you for showing me the importance of being true to yourself. You're one of a kind!

To my oldest friend Jared Eppes. Thank you for always standing by me.

To my wonderful coaches: Suzie Sanocki, Kevin Brubaker, and Zoe Bell. The life lessons and discipline I learned from you have given me the tools I needed to be successful today. I think of you often.

Sincere appreciation to Bethany and Alex Diffey for getting me on the right track to Tampa.

My clients from Ciarla Fitness. I wonder sometimes if I would be where I am today without getting to know each you: Lynn Wray, Julie Yakobowski, Beth and Paul Hecimovich, Chavanne Scott, Regi King, Rudy Bartel, Kathy Greenhagen, Woody Fox, Mike and Alicia Gainey, Rich Magner, Dawn Campbell, Mary Ann Yeager, Kristin Thompson, Kim Radke, Lisa Walters. . . . you'll always have a special place in my heart.

My friends over the years: Britany Helms, Becca Moffett, Sara Holbrooks, Whitney Burton, and Ashley Heard. I'm always a text away.

Thank you to Joe Gomez, Mike and Ruffin Campbell, and Mel Finley . . . important in my life since childhood.

Sara Kamber and Linda Palonen. You are cherished women in my life whom I continue to look up to on a daily basis.

Thank you to Brian Shields for your commitment to making this book what it is. For believing my story will help others, and taking on this task with all of my tears. I appreciate you working around my schedule, the late nights, and most of all, for believing in me.

Rave reviews for the incredible team at St. Martin's Press. Thank you for your dedication to making this book a reality.

Thank you to the FCW crew for getting me on my way in this incredible business. Special thanks to Tyler, the Four Horsewomen, Emma, Dean Muhtadi, and Ryan Katz. To my friend Byron Saxton, your creativity is limitless.

Thank you to Natalya Neidhart for showing me the way and giving me my career. I wouldn't be here without you, Nattie.

Endless gratitude to Sara Amato for believing in me since day one. To Norman Smiley for always lending a helping hand and showing me the ropes. To Terry Taylor, thank you for being a great teacher.

Enormous thanks to the incomparable Michael "P.S." Hayes for always pushing me to be better, and for reminding me to "make love to the camera." Only you, Michael . . .

To Dean Malenko: I never thought when I was a kid walking backstage in WCW, and you were a Horseman, that one day you'd help me in my career as a WWE Superstar. Thank you for always checking on me in and out of the ring.

Thank you to the incredible Fit Finlay. Fit, you prepared me for every show, tour, pay-per-view, and *Monday Night Raw.*

Eternal appreciation to Lita for instilling confidence in me, and making sure I was ready for WrestleMania in Dallas, Texas. Your work and dedication to this business paved the way for me. Thank you.

Thank you to the McMahon family. Thank you to Triple H and Stephanie McMahon for being there for my family through all the ups and downs.

To everyone backstage and in the office from FCW, NXT, and WWE: management, production, producers, makeup artists, and set designers. It's amazing to see all of the work that goes into making WWE what it is.

WWE is my family and where I feel most alive. A great big thank-you to all!

FOREWORD

THE TRUTH MAY SURPRISE YOU

Any Saturday morning in 1985, my excitement would revolve around one thing: watching professional wrestling. One man captivated my imagination: the NWA World Heavyweight Champion, "Nature Boy" Ric Flair.

Ric looked like a tycoon as he stepped out of his limo or private jet, wearing alligator shoes, a diamond ring on his finger, and a gold Rolex on his wrist. In the squared circle, he was the sixty-minute man who was always in peak physical condition. On the microphone, when he spoke, he was mesmerizing. To many, including my dad, Ric epitomized evil and the opulence of the 1980s. To me, he was "Slick Ric," the coolest cat on the planet. Whether you loved him or hated him, he was the biggest star in the industry and one of the most recognizable people alive.

Ric's brilliant career has spanned generations, and he has inspired hundreds of today's performers, including me, to chase our dreams. Like Ric, I wanted to be "the man," the main event. I wanted to be the World Champion. Just like him.

As my career evolved and progressed, it would eventually lead me to working side by side with my hero. Our working relationship turned into a strong friendship, and eventually we became best friends. I was even the best man at one of Ric's many weddings, and he was a groomsman at my one and only wedding. I was in a group of very few people who got to see the real Ric. I learned that in front of the camera, Ric was the definition of confidence; but behind closed doors, he was self-doubting and unsure of himself. But no matter Ric's struggles, he was completely devoted to his family.

Ric called his children seemingly every hour to tell them that he loved them; he asked about their days, how they did on exams, and if they made it to practice on time. He was extremely into their athletic ventures. I would hear Ric ask them the same questions over and over . . . my particular favorite was, "Did you drink your milk today, Wink?" (Sorry, Charlotte!) Of course she drank her milk—she was seventeen years old and you asked her thirty times. Nevertheless, his love and pride for his kids was inspiring.

While at home with his kids, Ric was immersed in their lives. He spent every moment he could with them. Imagine working at a school and seeing the man known as "the limousine-ridin', jet-flyin', kiss-stealin', wheelin', dealin' son of a gun" walk into the building to personally deliver his children's lunches.

By the time Charlotte was a teenager, she was competing in cheerleading and volleyball. And while growing up in North Carolina, in the heart of Flair country, being the daughter of the Nature Boy came with big perks, like custom Land Rovers and Louis Vuitton bags; it also came with drawbacks. There was media scrutiny, high-profile divorces, and tumultuous relationships. Not to mention standing in the shadow of a legend. Not only did Charlotte have the pressure to be the best at everything, but she had to live up to the reputation, an infamous reputation, to always be the life of the party. I've seen her struggle . . . with all of it.

When Charlotte first called me to say that she wanted to get into the business and asked for a shot at the WWE Performance Center, I was shocked, as she had never shown an interest before and I questioned her motivation. I was also very clear about the challenges she would face, seemingly insurmountable challenges. If Charlotte thought standing in her dad's shadow or being expected to follow in his footsteps was hard before, she hadn't seen anything yet.

Charlotte would be starting from the bottom in trying to learn something incredibly difficult, at best. Professional wrestling is something very few ever master. She would never be given a fair shake. On top of that, any kind of success would be attributed to her father. It would be nearly impossible to overcome these obstacles and earn everyone's respect. But she still wanted the shot, and it wasn't easy. Because of her incredible work ethic, she succeeded and earned the respect of coaches, peers, producers—everyone across the board. Her success had nothing to do with her father; it had to do with raw passion and immense drive. She climbed the ranks of NXT and became a driving force in the WWE Women's Evolution. Charlotte not only stepped out of her father's shadow, she's currently creating her own legacy as one of the greatest female performers the industry has ever seen.

In these pages, you will share the journey that speaks to the true heart of Ric and Charlotte Flair. You'll experience their joys, their pain, the triumphs and tragedies, unspeakable loss, and the indestructible bond that brought them back together. It took a great deal of courage for

them to step out of the ring, away from what the world has seen of them on TV, and share the details of their true, personal lives.

I've been with Ric and Charlotte during euphoric highs and devastating lows. The best is yet to come—for both of them.

Diamonds are forever, and so are the Flairs.

—Paul "Triple H" Levesque

PART I

LIFE AS THE NATURE BOY

INTRODUCTION

HELLO, DALLAS, MY DEAR FRIEND

March 29, 2016—Dallas/Fort Worth International Airport

The greatest in-ring performer I ever saw in my life, Ray Stevens, once said to me, "Ric, the day you walk through that curtain and you don't have goose bumps, that's the day you never need to walk through it again." After almost forty-five years in the business that I describe as the greatest sport in the world, that statement's never been truer than it is right now. It's WrestleMania weekend—and I'm back. But as a sixteen-time World Champion, I never imagined I'd be a part of it like I will be on Sunday, in my daughter Ashley's corner.

I first came to Dallas, Texas, as the NWA World Heavyweight Champion in 1982. Whenever I'm in the "Big D," incredible images from World Class Championship Wrestling come to mind: battling the beloved Von Erichs, running wild with the Freebirds, and staying out until dawn with my close friend David Manning. I'm proud that during my career I headlined stadium shows in the United States and Asia. The Texas Stadium events, just outside Dallas, were special, but they happened before the world heard the name WrestleMania.

In our business, WrestleMania is the greatest time of year—like what the Super Bowl is to football, the World Series is to baseball, and the

Oscars is to film—all combined into one amazing spectacle. In 1992, I had the privilege of performing in my first WrestleMania. I entered the Indianapolis Hoosier Dome as the WWE Champion and faced my good friend Randy "Macho Man" Savage.

Tears cloud my eyes when I think of the call I received from Vince McMahon in 2007, telling me that after thirty-six years of doing the only thing I ever wanted to do with my life, my in-ring career with WWE would end at WrestleMania XXIV. I'm honored to say that the experience leading up to that moment is what I consider to be the greatest retirement in the history of professional sports.

At fifty-nine years old, I suddenly had no idea of what I was going to do with the rest of my life. Professional wrestling was all I knew. It's all I ever wanted. I should've been excited about a planned vacation in paradise with my wife; instead, I woke up the next day in St. Croix with what felt like a hole in my chest the size of a bowling ball. I began to panic.

As I make my way through the airport, sometimes I still can't believe my journey. When I look at my right hand, I see one of two WWE Hall of Fame rings on my finger. It's difficult to put into words what it meant to be the only WWE Superstar to be inducted into the Hall of Fame while still an active member of the roster . . . and the only individual to be enshrined on two occasions. I will always cherish how the McMahon family, Triple H, and WWE as an organization continue to honor my legacy. There's nothing like the respect of your peers.

I'm fortunate that for four decades I've had the honor of being part of an industry that captured my imagination from the time I was six years old. Every Saturday at 6:30 p.m. I was captivated by the mythical figures of Verne Gagne's AWA promotion: the Crusher, Dick the Bruiser, and Mad Dog Vachon. Once a year, on my birthday, my dad took me to the matches. What I had seen on television, in my living room, exploded into living color before my very eyes. There was nowhere else I wanted to be than inside that ring.

In 1972, I stepped through the ropes as a professional for the first time. After a ten-minute draw with George "Scrap Iron" Gadaski, I learned that nothing is more addictive than performing before a live audience. The thrill of the chase—the anticipation of experiencing that feeling every night—drove me as a performer. It helped me recover from a plane crash in 1975. The T10, T11, and T12 vertebrae in my back were crushed. I was told I'd never walk again, let alone wrestle—but never tell me the odds. Instead, it propelled me to unimaginable heights. But there's always a flip side. There were times it consumed me and I lost my grip on what was important.

Appearance was an essential aspect to my character—the "Nature Boy." I did whatever I could to make the people believe what they saw was the real deal: from buying a limousine from the governor of North Carolina and hiring a gas station attendant to be my driver . . . to appearing in handmade suits with alligator shoes and a Rolex President that shone like the sun . . . to filling my closets with diamond-studded robes that cost $10,000 a pop. To make them today would cost around $30,000 each. I thrived on the attention to detail that enhanced my character. That mentality served me well in my career; sometimes a little too well.

By the time I realized that I was unable to distinguish between the man Richard Morgan Fliehr, from Minneapolis, Minnesota, and the character "Nature Boy" Ric Flair, the custom-made man with the ten pounds of gold around his waist, who's left women around the world breathless, I had already been far down paths of excess. A part of me didn't care. I was having too much fun. My goals were to be the greatest wrestler in the world, and to have the "Flair" name synonymous with the world championship. The parties night after night would make the Rolling Stones blush. "Ladies, you don't have to wait in line at Disney World to ride Space Mountain" was much more than a way to keep the camera on me during a television interview. It was a way of life. And life was good. But the price I paid for that when the party was over exceeded any dollar amount.

As years went by, admiration from my peers and adulation from fans continued to soar. But outside the ring, I left a trail of collateral damage behind, including four marriages that ended in divorce.

Riding to my hotel in Dallas, I don't think of my greatest opponents— legends like Wahoo McDaniel, Blackjack Mulligan, Harley Race, Ricky

Steamboat, Dusty Rhodes, Barry Windham, and Sting—or riding high with groups the Four Horsemen and Evolution. I think of my children: Megan, David, Ashley, and Reid.

I don't know if I'll be known as the greatest wrestler of all time. What I do know is that I won't go down in history as the greatest father—not because I didn't care or didn't try—because for so long I was so focused on myself.

Earlier in my career, Megan and David only saw me seven to ten days a year. That was tough. I missed out on so much, and I know it hurt them. It hurt me too. I wrestled seven days a week—twice on Saturday and twice on Sunday—in an industry without an off-season. The business was different back then. If you didn't work, you didn't get paid. I was also a different person. I was so consumed with being the "Nature Boy" that nothing else mattered.

In some ways, it must've been hard for Megan and David when they saw Ashley and Reid spend more time with me years later. I didn't love them more. I just wasn't on the road as much. A benefit to working in WCW was that the travel schedule was much lighter than it was in the '70s, '80s, and early '90s. At times my professional and personal decisions made things painful for them. I'm so proud of the people Megan and David have become and the beautiful families they have today.

Now, as I'm thinking of my daughter Ashley, I see the stunning image of her draped across the façade of AT&T Stadium in Dallas. I'm brought to tears. Professionally, she's known around the world as Charlotte. This Sunday at WrestleMania, she'll be defending the WWE Divas Championship in one of the most anticipated matches on the card. She and I have had our share of ups and downs, but her accomplishments continue to amaze me.

To be back representing WWE by her side has been the greatest time of my life. I know of only a select few parents and children in sports or entertainment who have had the opportunity to perform together in such a prominent way, like we've had. I'm filled with pride when I think of everything Ashley has achieved. She's been in the sports-entertainment industry just four years, and as an athlete in the ring, she's already better than I ever was.

There are a lot of questions surrounding the outcome of her match on Sunday. I know she can handle any situation, but as a parent, you always worry about your child. I just want her to trust me when I say everything will work out for the best no matter what creative decision is made. Yes, this business is entertainment, and the Superstars collaborate to create an incredible show. When you walk through that curtain, the performance is more real than you can ever imagine. Everyone wants to be a champion.

Every day I think about my son Reid, who tragically passed away at twenty-five years old. The heartbreak feels like it was yesterday. The grief that overwhelms a parent who has to bury his or her child is unimaginable. It will cling to me, his mother, and his siblings for the rest of our lives. Thanks to the love and support of so many, we've been able to carry on, but we will never be the same.

In our own way, we all tried to help him. I take a great deal of responsibility for his death. During Reid's troubled times, I was not in a good place emotionally and made some poor decisions. I knew how much he looked up to me, but I didn't always lead by example. We were best friends, and I feel like I failed him. I'd give anything to hold my son in my arms again and tell him how much I love him, how much we all love him.

During the last few years, I've realized that life doesn't stop because you're no longer in the main event or the world champion. You have to make adjustments. I'm still making adjustments. But that's the gift of redemption. If you're willing, it's never too late to make things right, to turn things around, and that's one of the reasons I wanted to write this book.

For too long, being the World Heavyweight Champion was all that mattered to me. Now, I see what's really important in life: to be the best I've ever been as a person and a father. That's all that matters to me.

I

HISTORY, FATE, AND DESTINY

I'll never retire . . .

November 2007

Almost six years to the day, I stood backstage at *Monday Night Raw* in Charlotte, North Carolina. I waited for my cue at Gorilla—the position that's right before you walk through the curtain, named after Gorilla Monsoon. During an interview segment, to the "surprise" of Vince McMahon and Kurt Angle, and with my family in the crowd, I entered the arena. I was back in WWE.

On this night, after a three-month hiatus, I returned to *Raw* to give an interview about the future of my career. When you're on television every week, being away for three months is a long time. I shared with the audience what I had been doing: I considered entering politics in my home state of North Carolina; I opened my own company; and I pursued investment opportunities. All those things were true. I didn't just say them for the camera's benefit.

As my children Megan, David, and Ashley, and my wife, Tiffany, sat at ringside, there was one time during that interview where my emotions almost got the best of me. When I said, "My wrestling career can't go on forever," that thought was almost too much to bear. But my bravado returned, and I exclaimed, "I have to announce to you . . . that I will never retire! I will only retire when I'm dead in this ring—over my dead body. I've got too much juice left. I'm still the Nature Boy."

By the way the crowd responded, it sounded like I'd made the right decision.

What I was really saying was, in my mind and in my heart, I wasn't ready to say goodbye to the business that represents the only thing I ever wanted to do with my life. As the hometown Charlotte crowd roared, Vince McMahon did what I did to him six years earlier—he made a perfectly timed entrance.

In the middle of the crowds' always-colorful chants describing their feeling toward the Mr. McMahon character, Vince informed me, and the world, that the next time I lost a match, my career would be over. When the sound of boos dissipated and Vince was leaving the ring, another surprise was waiting for me: WWE Champion Randy Orton.

Randy is a third-generation Superstar. I have great history working with Randy's family: his grandfather was the legendary "Big O," and his dad, the great "Cowboy" Bob Orton. If you would've told me in 1983

when I was working with Bobby in Jim Crockett Promotions as part of the National Wrestling Alliance (NWA) that almost twenty-five years later I'd be a WWE Superstar, and Bob's son would be in a ring as WWE Champion with me and Vince McMahon, I would've said, "Are you kidding me?"

Several years earlier, Randy and I were members of the group Evolution. He began his part of the segment by thanking me: for being a mentor to him early in his career, for

being there for him when he had personal problems, and for my contributions to sports entertainment. As the perfect villain, Randy ended by
saying, "I want to thank you in advance, Ric Flair. I want to thank you
for the honor. I want to thank you for the pleasure, tonight, of ending
your career."

It was one of the aspects of our business that's often taken for granted.
In those few minutes on live television, my new story line was established,
the parameters were set, and I was about to face an incredible opponent
in Randy.

Over the course of my career, there were few story lines that were difficult for me and even fewer where I didn't have full command of my
emotions. For this story, the tone of my voice, my facial expressions, and
my feelings were the easiest they've ever been to channel for one reason:
they were real. No one—not Tiffany, my children, my friends, or Vince
McMahon—knew just how real.

What many people also didn't know was that I got a call from Vince
that summer. He told me that there was a retirement story line concept
we were going with where the next match I'd lose would force me to retire from in-ring competition. At first, I thought this was like other story
lines I had been in where I'd lose a match, "retire," and then it would be
announced to the audience that—thanks to a loophole in a contract, or
executive decision by a fictitious board of directors, or something happening to someone the audience knew I was close to—I'd be "reinstated."
Not on a full-time basis but semiregularly as a special attraction.

As Vince went into further detail, I realized that there would be no
loophole and no "emergency meeting." Vince told me, "We're going to
put you in the Hall of Fame. The next day, you'll work with someone at
WrestleMania, and after that we're going to say goodbye." He also said
that after I had some time off, I'd return to work for the company as an
ambassador. I'd make special appearances to support the different business units across the company: live events, television partnerships, consumer products, community outreach, and the occasional cameo on WWE
programming. Everything Vince said made sense and, in the context of
our conversation, sounded good. We'd talk about a new contract when

my performer agreement was coming up. Everyone, including me, knew that it was time to think about winding down my in-ring career. Accepting it was another matter.

After thirty-five years of walking down that aisle, I thought, *I survived a plane crash that broke my back; I was struck by lightning; and I spent years performing seven days a week—twice on Saturday and twice on Sunday—in an industry that does not have an off-season.* I looked back on the countless number of performers who were forced to retire due to injury, because they couldn't take the rigors of the business anymore, or because they just lost their connection with the audience. I was thankful none of those circumstances applied to me—until then. In that moment, I realized, *This is it. My career's ending . . . over the phone.* I wasn't sure which scenario was worse.

After my segment on *Raw* with Vince and Randy, I went into the locker room and traded my $10,000 suit for my $10,000 robe. I don't know if that was what the night signified or that I was in the main event in Charlotte, but when I saw *Nature Boy* stitched on the back of my robe, I thought of Olivia Walker. Olivia was the wife of the famous Mr. Wrestling II and a master seamstress. She made custom robes and jackets for everyone from George Jones and Porter Wagoner to Liberace. Everything Olivia created was stunning: hand-stitched sequin patterns with a menagerie of precious gems intertwined with elaborate designs. One of my favorite robes she made had real peacock feathers. Naturally, that was the one we ended up shredding on TV during my story line with Blackjack Mulligan in the '70s. Olivia said to me, "Ric, why would you pick that one? It took me a year to make. I'm not making you another robe like that." At one point, I had thirty-five robes.

Olivia's robes inspired my entrance: raising my arms and slowly turning in a complete circle so everyone could see the majesty of her work—and, of course, notice me. When she measured me for the first time, she took extra measurements, because she knew how certain material and fabrics would fit and how they'd look when I walked. Olivia was an incredible artist and a wonderful person. That night, I walked into the ring wearing one of my favorite robes from the '80s. I brought it with me to WWE in 1991.

For years, I've said that Randy Orton is one of the top two or three performers in our industry. Considering that I was fifty-nine years old and where I was in my career, I defeated Randy in a way that made sense. I had a little help from my friend Chris Jericho—who distracted the referee and Randy. Given my on-air reputation as the Dirtiest Player in the Game, after a low blow and yank of the trunks for leverage, the referee counted one, two, three, and we were off and running. The crowd loved it. It looked great on television and was a tremendous way to launch our story line. I appreciated that Randy set things off in such a high-profile fashion.

As my physical skills diminished with age, I could still do everything I did in the ring, just not quite as well. I learned how to become more entertaining as a performer, to strengthen other aspects of my performance and appear to do more while physically doing less.

Over the next four months, I did something that I always prided myself on: I worked with opponents of all different shapes, sizes, and skill sets, whether it was the four-hundred-pound US Olympic power-lifter and World's Strongest Man Mark Henry, the classic English grappler William Regal, the wild Samoan bulldozer Umaga, brash rising Superstars like Mr. Kennedy and MVP, or the man I believe is the best in the business when he's performing in the ring, Triple H.

Paul "Triple H" Levesque was one of the first people who befriended me when I returned to WWE in 2001. It was Paul's idea to form the group Evolution—a group that featured Paul, Randy, Dave Bautista (better known as Batista), and me. The group paid tribute to the Four Horsemen. Its main goal was to create two new stars for the future: Randy and Dave. During our travels, we formed a special bond. Even after Evolution imploded in classic wrestling fashion, I remained Paul's adviser on television until in greater fashion, his character, nicknamed the Cerebral Assassin, launched a vicious assault against me, thus ending our partnership on WWE programming. Of course, our characters came back together at different times on television.

When I look at Paul in the ring, I see myself twenty years earlier. I wish I could've worked with him when I was in my prime. From Charlotte to Norfolk to Chicago to Los Angeles, Honolulu, Tokyo, Moscow, and Germany, we would've torn the house down every night.

It was an incredible experience to close out the year performing with Paul in Greensboro, North Carolina, in the same building where I won the NWA World Championship from Harley Race at Starrcade '83. It was so much fun to work with him. Paul has such a deep admiration for me and the history of our business. His love of our craft allowed us to do things in the ring—like certain moves at specific times—that are often not used today. To give our match an added layer of suspense, the Mr. McMahon character stipulated that if Paul's character lost to me, he'd be out of the Royal Rumble match.*

In the ebb and flow of a compelling performance, the question remained: "How will this end?" That night, my career lived on after William Regal attacked me with brass knuckles, getting Triple H disqualified. The way the *Raw* broadcast ended, with the two of us embracing in the ring, symbolized more than our television personas showing admiration for one another. Since I came back to WWE, Paul has been one of my biggest advocates and closest friends. He was the best man at my wedding when I married Tiffany in 2006. My family, especially my sons, couldn't love him more.

Some of my critics have said that I have the same match and do the same moves. Based on my opponent and the specific story line and match, I always made sure to add nuances to keep it interesting. But I still made sure I performed my trademark offensive maneuvers and some of my classic moves, like the flip over the turnbuckle, which I learned from Ray Stevens, or when my opponent slammed me off the top rope, which I

---

*Paul Levesque: "I grew up in New Hampshire, about an hour outside of Boston. The northeastern United States was always WWE territory. We had cable television in our house, so I watched NWA, AWA, the Von Erichs in Texas, anything I could get my hands on. As a kid, Saturday mornings consisted of me watching wrestling from all over the country. From the moment I saw it, all I wanted to do was be in that ring. Ric was an enormous part of that."

borrowed from Harley Race. Good Lord, Vince always hated when I performed that one.

I think of something Joe DiMaggio once said—he played his hardest every game because there might be someone in the stands seeing him play for the first time. I felt that way about wrestlers and their trademark moves in a match as long as everything made sense, especially when you're a top star with a championship. When I was a kid and went to AWA shows, I was so disappointed if I didn't see Verne Gagne's sleeper hold, the Crusher's bolo punch, Baron von Raschke's claw, or Dick the Bruiser's knee drop from the top rope. It's part of what the fans pay to see, similar to the Rolling Stones and the Who, who still play their hits from the '60s and '70s at concerts today.

We were doing this story line over a four-month period on live television. For the program to maintain the level of excitement that it needed to be successful, each match had to have a different feel and create a special level of anticipation. In the age of the digital revolution and the internet, with people leaking spoilers about what's going to happen on a show before it occurs, well, it's even more challenging.

This concept was a superb combination of two classic sports-entertainment story lines: one, the career-threatening match—when you lose the match, your career is over; and two, the anticipation that comes from a "bounty." While no one in our story put up $50,000 to send me into retirement, the drama of what was going to happen to me week to week was similar. Who was my opponent going to be? Was someone going to look to bring me down so he could say he retired Ric Flair? Or would someone who was considered my friend be put in an unenviable position of having to face me? What consequences would a Superstar face from the ruthless Mr. McMahon character for losing the match? Everything revolved around the premise of "Will Ric Flair's career live to see another day?"

There was a finality and an emotion that fans could easily invest in—either I'd win and survive another week, or that night would be the last time the world saw Ric Flair as a WWE Superstar.

I found it fitting that an exciting event like the Royal Rumble was the first pay-per-view of the new year that put WWE as a company, and the audience, on the road to WrestleMania.

The Royal Rumble is a battle royal with thirty participants. Depending on the stipulation, every ninety seconds or two minutes, a new Superstar enters the match. Once you're thrown over the top rope and your feet touch the floor, you're eliminated. Pat Patterson created the concept in the '80s when Vince McMahon and NBC executive Dick Ebersol were brainstorming ideas for a TV special. The show was so well received that it became a pay-per-view event.

My first Royal Rumble match was in 1992. Some say that was the greatest one because of the array of talent: Hulk Hogan, Randy Savage, Undertaker, Roddy Piper, Bret Hart, Shawn Michaels, Sgt. Slaughter, Jimmy Snuka, Ted DiBiase, Kerry Von Erich, Jake Roberts, the British Bulldog. It was a who's who. I was proud to be a part of it.

That night, I was the third Superstar to enter the match, and the plan was for me to last the entire match: just over an hour. It will always be special because it showed that Vince had enough confidence in me to make me his champion. That night I became the second person—the original "Nature Boy," Buddy Rogers, was the first—to win the NWA World Championship and the WWE Championship during his career.

I considered it special to have a match at this year's Rumble because of what we were doing for WrestleMania and because the event was at Madison Square Garden.

The first time I performed in WWE was at the Garden in 1976. I don't consider that my WWE debut, because it was one match. But Vince McMahon Sr. put together a stacked card that night: Ernie Ladd, Bobo Brazil, Ivan Koloff, the Fabulous Moolah, and Ivan Putski performed. Bruno Sammartino defended the WWE Championship against "Superstar" Billy Graham. A couple of years prior to that, Billy's wife, Bunny, was the first person who bleached my hair.

I have incredible respect for the history of Madison Square Garden and for the legacy of WWE and the McMahon family in that building— both Vince and his father, Vince Sr., are in the Madison Square Garden Hall of Fame.

While I can do without the traffic, I've always enjoyed the energy of New York City and the passion of the New York fans. I don't feel the same about the Garden itself, because I never got to enjoy being the main attraction there on a consistent basis. In the '70s and '80s, my strongest fan bases were primarily in the southeastern and midwestern United States. That changed with the expansion of cable television and two tenures with WWE, but there are other venues like the Omni in Atlanta, Kiel Auditorium in St. Louis, and the Charlotte and Greensboro Coliseums that are sentimental favorites, considering where I was in my career at the time. I'm sure I'd feel the same way about the Garden if it were one of the homes of Space Mountain.

The fan reaction made this a farewell tour like I had never seen before. Each city I performed in was transformed into "Flair Country." I even had the opportunity to return to the sacred ground of Japan's Budokan and perform for the wonderful fans in Honolulu, Hawaii. I'll always cherish the way WWE presented my matches during this time. Being able to perform around the world in so many cities and venues that I performed in throughout my career was something that will always stay with me. I'd call Tiffany from the road and talk to her about the favorite matches I had in different buildings and memories from each city. Then I'd go to wherever the party was that evening. Sometimes I'd start the party, but at least I called my wife.

This type of recognition prepared me to publicly acknowledge another honor. We were preparing to roll out the last two components of this story line: that I was going to be inducted into the WWE Hall of Fame, and who my opponent would be at WrestleMania.

For the former, I knew from my original call with Vince that I was definitely going to be inducted into the WWE Hall of Fame. To be the only person to be inducted into the Hall while still an active member of the WWE roster was something that I knew was an enormous accolade, but it was something that didn't seem real during this epic journey to WrestleMania.

For the latter, I replayed in my mind what Vince told me during that call: "You'll work with someone . . ." One possible way my opponent

could've been decided was by selecting a young Superstar. That person would enter an intense story line with me and end up being the one to "retire" me at the largest show of the year. The hope was my opponent would get to build on that recognition and take his career to another level. Over the past year, Ricky Steamboat and I talked about pitching the idea of having a final match. I didn't say anything about that, but maybe he did. I didn't know. It was a mystery that I tried to figure out. Week after week, it became more difficult dealing with the anticipation . . . until I got a call from a close friend.

Michael Hayes has been my friend for thirty years. On television, his persona was Michael "PS" Hayes, the founder of the Fabulous Freebirds, a group who helped revolutionize our business. If there's a definition for *hell-raisers* in the dictionary, there should be a picture of the Freebirds next to it.

Since 1995, Michael's been a driving creative force behind the scenes at WWE. Any time there was a story line I was going to be involved in, a tour I was booked on, or reviewing the finer points of my match, I worked with Michael.

I picked up the phone and said, "Michael, how are you?" Right away, I could tell there was something different in his voice.

He said, "It's Shawn. It's going to be Shawn." I froze. Michael added, "He asked for it, but we haven't told him it's a go. Ric, please don't tell Shawn. Please don't tell Shawn. We're not telling Shawn for another week."

I said, "Okay, I won't tell anyone."

He ended by saying, "Don't tell anyone. Goodbye,"

It was the quickest conversation we had in thirty years.

I was hoping it would be either Paul or Shawn. It's always easy to pitch ideas to yourself. I didn't know what to do. I kept pacing back and forth, trying to relax, but I kept thinking of all the things we could do together, on the microphone and in the ring, to make this match what I knew it could be. I started thinking about the way WWE would take things to a higher level in presentation and promotion. I tried to breathe and stay calm. So I did what any other person in my position would do—I called Shawn.*

I first met Shawn at a bar in 1985 after a show. He was about nineteen years old and working in Kansas City. I came into the area to work with Bruiser Brody. I despised working in Kansas City and couldn't stand the Central States promoter, Bob Geigel. He never wanted to pay for security at the buildings. One time, a kid snuck into our locker room and took one of my robes. When I rushed out through the back of the building, the kid was in the street wearing it. He gave me the middle finger and ran away. When Kansas City came up on my schedule, I used to tell people, "I'll be in Moscow that week."

I heard of the team Shawn formed with Marty Jannetty, the Midnight Rockers, and saw him again when I went to WWE in 1991. He was still teaming with Marty but looking to start a career as a singles performer.

Shawn and I had a match in Houston, Texas, that was meant to help prepare him for a singles program with Randy "Macho Man" Savage. Shawn would be better at his craft after being in the ring with me and other established singles performers so that he'd be comfortable in a high-profile, one-on-one series with Randy. Performing in a tag team is different; you always have someone else to rely on, and you're not in the ring every second of the match. You can tag out and catch your breath.

---

*Shawn Michaels: "For me, everything goes back to being a child in Texas and seeing Ric on TV during Southwest Championship Wrestling. From the second I saw him, I wanted to be just like him. Now I had the chance to show him how much he's meant to me. I knew exactly what we needed to do."

I wanted Shawn to be better prepared for a career as a singles Superstar, which is how it's supposed to be in our line of work—helping younger talent come up. I knew it was only a matter of time before Shawn would break out as a megastar.

We worked together a second time in a tag team match where Shawn and I were partners against Randy and Bret "Hit Man" Hart. We got to work together more when Shawn returned to the company in 2002. We had a great match that lasted thirty minutes in Japan in 2005. For my final match as a WWE Superstar, I knew we could turn it on and tear it down in the ring.

The way Shawn was introduced to the story line was that he would be the one who made the announcement on *Raw* that I'd be inducted into the WWE Hall of Fame.

Since WWE resumed Hall of Fame inductions in 2004, it's one of my favorite nights of the year. That year, I inducted Harley Race. In 2005, I inducted "Rowdy" Roddy Piper. The following year in Chicago, I saw close friends Blackjack Mulligan and "Mean" Gene Okerlund take their rightful place in the Hall along with my mentor, the legendary Verne Gagne. The previous year in Detroit was extra special when Dusty closed out the show. He asked if he and Harley could join Arn Anderson and me as part of the Four Horsemen. I still fight back tears thinking of Dusty saying that during his induction speech and what it means to me.

The way things would unfold with Shawn over the next five weeks was that I would first ask him to be my opponent at WrestleMania. He'd accept but then become conflicted over the coming weeks. Because of the admiration he had for me, he couldn't be the one who would go down in history as the man who retired me. I'd come back the next week and tell him I didn't need his sympathy and that if I couldn't hang with the top guys, I didn't want to be part of the show. This was another example of something being said for the cameras but the feeling behind those words was true—the closer WrestleMania came, the more this became the realest story line I was ever a part of. As the crowds cheered louder, I struggled with whether it was the right decision.

The important part was creating enough tension between us as

WrestleMania inched closer, so that the audience felt like they were seeing a battle between two participants who would fight until they had nothing left. There would be a winner and a loser. If I lost, I'd never compete in a match again. I had just the thing, and so did Shawn.

One of my final matches before WrestleMania in Orlando was with someone who became known as one of my fiercest on-camera rivals and who has always been a confidant away from the ring: Vince McMahon.

Vince and I were getting ready for our match that day in Lafayette, Louisiana, when he stopped speaking. I saw tears in his eyes, and he said to me, "I want to make sure this is so special for you." From the moment I met Vince in 1976, he's treated me like gold. Since I returned to WWE in 2001, we've had a lot of fun working together. I know sometimes I've made things challenging for him in front of the cameras and away from them, but Vince has always been there for me.

The match I had with Vince on *Raw* was a "Street Fight." In our business, that's another way of saying things are going to get crazy—anything goes. Our first "Street Fight" was at the 2002 Royal Rumble. Paul would always joke that Vince took himself for the legendary NWA Champion Lou Thesz in the ring, but he didn't. Vince knew that in the end, the fans wanted to see the Mr. McMahon character suffer the consequences for his dastardly deeds. If Vince feels the audience wants to see something, he makes it happen, even if it means that he steps through the ropes. Vince has fallen off cages, jumped off ladders, and been put through the announcers' table. He doesn't ask anyone to do something he hasn't done or wouldn't do himself. You have to admire that in the leader of a global, publicly traded organization. Just watch the video of Vince taking the zip line from the rafters of the Pond in Anaheim, California, down to the arena floor to make sure it was safe. Then see Shawn do it later that day during his entrance in the main event of WrestleMania XII.

For this match, the mind-set was different from the others in this story line. Even though Vince can squat seven hundred pounds in the weight room, the idea *should* be that he's at a disadvantage because he hasn't been a WWE Superstar. But the Mr. McMahon character always stacks the deck and has a trick up his sleeve. From the moment the bell rang, we didn't hold anything back. Vince drilled me in the face with a television monitor, nailed me with a garbage can, flogged me with a Singapore cane, and blasted me with a chair. He said he wanted to make it special, right? Just when it looked like the sun was setting on my career in the sky of Columbia, South Carolina, Shawn came to ringside to interrupt the referee's count.

This is the turning point in the story that night. In what other line of work can you hit your boss twice below the belt, put him on a table, and dive from ten feet in the air, putting him through that table? How many people would love to do that? That's how I won the match. It was a great night at the office. That's what Vince meant when he said he wanted it to be special. He gave himself to the performance, to further the story line, where his character lost to me in spectacular fashion. It was just another example of how he's been there for me.

Incorporating Shawn into the end of the match with Vince served as a great way to keep the tension rising between us and put us on course to a standoff the next week on TV—another exciting aspect of our business that I wish more people appreciated—leaving the story at a certain point where the audience is compelled to tune in next week. There's an art to doing that, especially fifty-two weeks a year.

The following week on *Raw*, I began my interview segment by saying that I lost respect for Shawn for interfering in my match with Mr. McMahon, and I asked him to come to the ring. I brought a black velvet bag with me. The NWA World Heavyweight Championship was in it. The same title worn by people like Harley Race, Jack Brisco, Dory and Terry Funk, Dusty Rhodes, and me.

It was one of the few times that the NWA World Heavyweight Championship appeared on WWE television. There were times in the 1970s when Harley Race was NWA Champion and appeared on WWE cards to promote his "Champion versus Champion" matches against WWE Champions "Superstar" Billy Graham and Bob Backlund. Dusty and Harley met for the title at Madison Square Garden too. Vince's father, Vince Sr., was such a respected individual in our industry that he sat on the

NWA board of directors (WWE was not part of the NWA). Vince Sr. was one of the deciding votes that helped me win the NWA title from Dusty in 1981. You can ask anyone in our business, and Vince McMahon will tell you himself, in those days, if you were the NWA Champion, you were "the Man."

Some people thought Vince didn't want me to incorporate the title because it represented a onetime competition to WWE—it was the exact opposite. Vince loved the idea of adding a sense of history to the story line, considering the connection I have to that championship and the fact that Shawn grew up a fan of mine. There's even a childhood picture of Shawn, in a suit, dressed just like me.

It made for a nice addition. I wasn't sure where Shawn wanted to take things on the microphone. All I knew was that he wanted to shake things up as we headed into the final week before our match.

No one knew how true every word was that came out of both our mouths during that last segment. It took everything I had to keep my composure, because I knew the words I was saying would be my final moments on TV as a WWE Superstar.

For the audience, Shawn apologized for interfering in my match and
reiterated what the "Nature Boy" meant to him—"You'll always be the
Naitch to me—"

I cut him off before he could utter another word and fired back, "I
don't need anybody, anymore, to tell me who I am." I remember saying,
"I want you to bring out the best in me. I need that . . . I need that to
make it the rest of the way in my life. I need one more night. I need to be
the Naitch."

Shawn replied that he was going to give me everything I needed. That
he had no choice . . . but to give me the Showstopper. "Come Sunday,
Naitch . . . you're going to step inside the ring with Mr. WrestleMania."
We shook hands, signifying mutual respect and that the deal was for

both of us to be our very best. What appeared to be the end of the segment continued when Shawn turned it up on the microphone like only the Heartbreak Kid can and said, "I want to remind you of a little story. Remember the story of Old Yeller? They had to take that dog out back and finish him. Come Sunday, the Showstopper's going to take you, Old Yeller, out to the woodshed and put you out of your misery." Shawn put his finger to my temple and repeated, "And put you out of your misery."*

The crowd gasped and booed in disgust. I said to myself, "We got 'em." I threw down the NWA Championship and unbuttoned my shirt to let everybody know that we weren't going to wait for WrestleMania ... that this was going to happen right now. I slapped Shawn in the face twice and dared him to do it right there. Shawn ended the segment by reiterating, "I'm gonna put you out of your misery." Then he dropped the microphone. You could feel the tension fill the arena. You could feel the anger from the crowd as Shawn walked back up the ramp. It was perfect.

I mean no disrespect to anyone else, but looking back, no one could bring the emotion out of that story line and bring us to WrestleMania the way Shawn did.

The moment we got backstage, we knew we hit the segment out of the park. It was time to leave my last *Monday Night Raw* as a WWE Superstar and go home. I had to prepare for the final match of my career.

---

*Shawn Michaels: "Some people thought the *Old Yeller* reference during our interview segment was me taking a shot at Ric's age. I wasn't exactly a spring chicken either. *Old Yeller* is about loving something so much that you had to kill it, like a mercy killing, to put it out of its misery. Someone was in a position to do something that was so hard to do, but they knew it was the right thing to do."

2

ENTERING IMMORTALITY

*Everything I am today, everything I have today, everything
I will be, is because of the sport of professional wrestling.*

March 2008

I looked out the plane window and saw the "Welcome to WrestleMania" logo on the grass. We were touching down on the runway in Orlando. What a difference a year makes . . .

I had some ups and downs with Vince McMahon in the first half of 2007. I was supposed to be in a program with Mr. Kennedy that would've taken us through WrestleMania 23. One night during *Raw*, Vince and I got into an argument backstage about something in a match. Later that night, WWE executive Bruce Prichard said Vince wanted me to lay into WWE Superstar Carlito during an interview segment. I was supposed to emasculate his on-air character for not having passion for the business and for leaving the arena before the main event was over. That's one of the unwritten rules in our business: you never leave a show after your match. It's disrespectful to the people who are performing after you. I spoke to Carlito beforehand to make sure he was okay with the general idea of what I was going to say.

When I got my cue and we crossed paths backstage, the thrashing began. "Have you ever stopped to think why guys like you are not in the main event? Maybe you're a lazy, underachieving, son of a bitch lucky to be walking the halls of this building, lucky to be on the *Raw* roster, lucky to be here at all." I continued, "Guys like you have no passion, no guts . . . you want all the money, you want all the glory, you want to fly first class. You don't deserve it, because you haven't worked for it. You haven't paid the price." And I continued my barrage of insults.

The segment was so well received by the audience that my creative plans were changed. I was now working with Carlito. We were supposed to be tag team partners in a match at WrestleMania 23. The day of Wrestle-Mania, I found out our match was taken off the main show and put on the preshow. That was hard for me to take. Why would I be removed from the main show if what I did was so well received that my plans changed? Was I not good enough to be on the main card for Wrestle-Mania? Was I being punished for something? I didn't think either was the case. Vince told me he needed me to be a team player and lead by example. Of course, I did. But when you're the one who's taken off the WrestleMania card—the biggest WWE show of the year and one of the largest events in sports and entertainment—it's difficult not to be disappointed.

I grew more frustrated with my role in the company. I thought there were times when I didn't have a clear direction. I felt like something would do well, and then it just went away. I was drafted to *SmackDown* that June. *SmackDown* had a great roster of talent. The show also had more in-ring wrestling than *Raw*, so I thought I'd get to perform more. Batista and I teamed up. We had great matches with Edge and MVP. I thought my singles matches with Edge and MVP were also very good. Both of them are tremendous talents and great guys outside the ring. After those weeks, I was told they were figuring out a bigger picture for me. It never came.

A couple of months later, on my day off, I went to Columbia, South Carolina, to promote an upcoming *SmackDown* event. I found out I wasn't scheduled to be on the show. I asked someone with the company, "How can I be doing media for an event that I'm not booked to appear on?"

I shouldn't have voiced my frustration to the WWE employee. It had nothing to do with her. I got a text around 1:00 the next morning stating that I was "probably" going to be on the show. I thought I could do more for the company, and I wanted to do more. I didn't have to compete in the ring every week even though I physically could. Plus, I continued to receive strong reactions from the audience. I know nothing was done deliberately, but I was frustrated, and that made matters worse. "Reports" circulated online that I gave my notice to the company. That never happened.

During that period, I asked for a meeting in Stamford, Connecticut, with Vince, Stephanie McMahon, and an in-house WWE attorney. I brought two attorneys with me. I wanted to talk about where else I could use my name outside of WWE and other opportunities I could pursue with the company. That was a big mistake. Vince McMahon detests attorneys. Vince gave me a hug, we sat down, and then he tore into me for ruining our relationship by bringing attorneys into his office. He said that I had his phone number and I should've just called him. I only brought them because I thought we were having a business discussion. Now that seems so long ago.

One of the first things I did when I arrived in Orlando was to meet with Shawn and Michael Hayes about our match on Sunday.

Shawn started the meeting by saying, "Listen, you're going to do something you've never done in your life." He continued by expressing what every woman who I was ever with probably wanted to say to me. "You're just going to keep your mouth shut and listen to this. This is what we're doing." I guess it was fitting that someone said it to me for my last match.

Shawn showed me a piece of paper and described what was written down.* It was difficult for both of us not to get tangled in the emotion of what was going to happen the next day. After our meeting, it was time to prepare for my commitments for the week.

When I returned to WrestleMania in 2002, I realized how much the event had grown since I performed at WrestleMania VIII in 1992. Vince's

---

*Shawn Michaels: "I woke up one night at 2:00 in the morning. I just started writing everything down that came to me about the match. I started crying literally on the paper. I knew if we did it this way it was going to be epic. I also knew how hard it was for Ric to let someone else call the match, and it's one of the reasons that match means so much to me."

vision of a global entertainment company with an annual, live destination event went from dream to reality. WrestleMania evolved into a packed week of media events, personal appearances, and everyone doing something at Axxess. Picture a convention hall filled with everything WWE: exhibits, video game tournaments, matches, and meet-and-greet sessions. Fans can even walk down the *Raw* ramp like they're having an entrance on TV. The autograph signings at Axxess are favorites of mine. You get such a sense of how fans of our industry pass it on to their children. People show me and ask me things from every era of my career. It's another aspect of what we do that's so special.

I'm so proud that when I became the Nature Boy, I was one of the few performers who didn't need to reinvent himself and come back under a different persona during his career. There were times I was a "bad guy" and times I was a "good guy," but I was always the Nature Boy. In our profession, if you're very good at being bad long enough, the fans fall in love with you. From the day George Scott talked me into picking up where the original Nature Boy, Buddy Rogers, left off, including using Buddy's figure-four leg lock as my finishing move, I've enjoyed a wonderful journey . . . mostly.

I wrestled Buddy a couple of times in the 1970s. They weren't great matches, but it was awesome to see him in the ring with his trademark strut. One night in Greensboro, North Carolina, Buddy called me over in the locker room. He shook my hand, looked me dead in the eye, and said, "Kid, there's only one diamond in this business, and you're looking at it." I was a few days away from joining Buddy, who was inducted into the WWE Hall of Fame in 1994, along with many others I deeply admire.

Since 2004, the Hall of Fame ceremonies were held in intimate, amphitheater-type settings. They were beautiful, sold-out events. They were not full-size arenas. Amway Arena was the original site for Wrestle-Mania XXIV. After WrestleMania 22 outside of Chicago in 2006, Vince decided that every WrestleMania going forward would be held in a stadium. That meant WrestleMania on Sunday was moved to the Citrus Bowl and the Hall of Fame induction ceremony was moving to the Amway Arena. That's when I became a little nervous . . .

The Amway Arena was home to the NBA's Orlando Magic. It's where WWE events take place when the company is in Orlando. I enjoyed performing in Orlando during my career, but I never considered it one of "my towns." I was confident that people would come to the induction ceremony. When you're headlining, you never want to see empty seats.

I love what WWE has done with the Hall of Fame. I remember the WCW Hall of Fame ceremonies in the early '90s during the Slamboree pay-per-view. They were nice events. I heard about WWE's first Hall of Fame inductions in the mid-'90s. To see how the company has developed, the Hall of Fame far exceeds what I've seen in person in Cooperstown, New York, for baseball; Canton, Ohio, for football; and what I've watched on television in Springfield, Massachusetts, for basketball.

A montage of images kept whirling in front of me. I kept thinking about everything that happened during my career. I began to think about what I'd say at the podium. I kept putting my hand inside my tuxedo jacket pocket to make sure I still had my speech. I wanted to do right by this moment in my life.

That's when I thought of Ray Stevens and Wahoo McDaniel. I hope they are called to the Hall of Fame. I hope I have the honor of inducting them, because they've meant so much to me. And Mad Dog Vachon. Mad Dog was the first person I told that I wanted to become a professional wrestler. Mad Dog was on the 1948 Canadian Olympic wrestling team. He's one of the all-time greats as a professional and one of the toughest men I ever knew. Mad Dog was the real deal.

What WWE has done in celebrating its history over the last four years has been incredible. Legends and Hall of Famers having their own action figures, books, and DVDs and being in video games are such special ways to honor their—well, *our*—legacy. It's also an excellent way to be introduced to younger fans. When you reach a certain age, you start to become more aware of how you and your work will be remembered.

I'm also happy to see people like Verne Gagne and Nick Bockwinkel, who did not have WWE in-ring careers, enjoy the recognition of being in the Hall of Fame. We saw that in 2008 with Gordon Solie. I hope that continues.

My one concern with the Hall of Fame is that the stature of those who are inducted remains at a certain level. I know there's an expectation to produce a class each year for a live event that's broadcast on television. Words like *great* and *legend* are overused today. Someone who had had a long career is not automatically a legend. I don't say that to disrespect anyone. I love what the Hall of Fame is and where it's headed; I just want the essence of the Hall to be maintained because I love this profession so much.

Some fans don't like the idea of a celebrity wing to our Hall of Fame. I think it's great if the celebrity came to work with us and was successful in what he or she did. Why would the opportunity for more people to see what we're doing be a negative, as long as it's done properly? What disappoints me is when a celebrity inductor has a faint connection to an inductee. I felt an enormous sense of pride when I got to induct Harley Race and Roddy Piper. I want everything to be heartfelt. Was it cool to have Sylvester Stallone induct Hulk Hogan into the WWE Hall of Fame in 2005? Of course. But did you get the sense from Stallone's speech that it was heartfelt? That he really knew Hulk? That he cared about Hulk's career and our business?

I felt that way when William Shatner inducted Jerry Lawler. Jerry's been an enormous star in our profession for more than thirty years. I understand he did something with William Shatner once and it's a headline that he's inducting him. Did it translate to an emotional induction speech for someone like Jerry? That's what "the King" deserved.

For my induction, I had a difficult time choosing who should induct me. Dusty Rhodes had his sons, Dustin and Cody, usher him into the Hall. I didn't think my kids would like that—except for Reid. He'd probably take the microphone and go into an interview segment right there onstage. The whole place would go nuts. I thought of Arn Anderson because he's been so close to me since the Horsemen, and our children grew up together. But I selected Paul. We'd formed such a special bond over the previous seven years. When I took an extra moment to think about it, it felt like the right thing to do.

So many faces came to mind on my way to the building that day. You'd think I was making the more than three-and-a-half-hour drive to Orlando from Miami. Though if I were driving with Ray Stevens or Harley, we'd make it there in less than three. Whenever those two got behind anything with a steering wheel and an engine, you were riding lightning!

The feeling backstage at the Amway Arena was unbelievable. I've been there so many times for WWE events. It was where Hulk Hogan and I worked with each other on pay-per-view for the first time: WCW's Bash at the Beach in 1994. I imagined what it would be like when Vince put that beautiful ring on my finger. I was getting closer.

While I watched the inductees from backstage, I thought about each of them during their inductions:

I could write another book on what the Brisco Brothers mean to this business and how important they've been to me. Jack and Gerry Brisco were top performers wherever they went: Australia, Japan, Championship Wrestling from Florida, Georgia Championship Wrestling, and WWE.

When Jack Brisco was a junior on the Oklahoma State University wrestling team, he was not taken down once during the entire season. As a professional, Jack was a two-time NWA World Heavyweight Champion.

Gerry was also a standout in wrestling for Oklahoma State. He was a machine in the ring and was the NWA World Junior Heavyweight Champion. After he retired from the ring, he became a confidant to the McMahon family and an executive behind the scenes. Fans of the Attitude Era know Jerry as one of Mr. McMahon's "stooges" who helped in the fight against "Stone Cold" Steve Austin.

As a team, the Briscos held more than twenty tag team championships. They had tremendous matches with so many teams. Look at the matches they had against Ricky Steamboat and Jay Youngblood. Like Ray Stevens, by the time Jack and Gerry arrived in WWE, they were still very good. I wish WWE fans could've seen them in their prime.

The Briscos' most powerful double-team maneuver took place behind the scenes. Gerry and Jack held controlling interest in Georgia Championship Wrestling. They sold their majority stake in the territory and its

coveted Saturday timeslot on Superstation WTBS to Vince McMahon. This put the territory out of business. Fans who tuned in to WTBS that Saturday saw WWE for the first time. Vince sold everything to Jimmy Crockett within the year, but it was a step toward Vince taking WWE programming into markets across the country.

The pundits always said that what Walter Cronkite was to news, Gordon Solie was to professional wrestling.

Gordon announced stock car racing and was a news broadcaster. He loved wrestling and started out as a ring announcer. Fans heard Gordon in Georgia Championship Wrestling, Championship Wrestling from Florida, and WCW on WTBS, among other promotions. "The Dean," as Gordon was known, had an incredible work ethic. At one point, he was the voice of three NWA territories at the same time. Gordon did not want to know what was going to happen in the match. He wanted the audience to feel exactly what he felt at that moment. Gordon had such a commitment to his craft and a respect for the audience.

I remember seeing video packages after my "I Quit" match against Terry Funk at New York Knockout. Each one featured Gordon's famous

call, "Five letters, two words . . . *I quit.*" That night, Gordon called the action with Jim Ross—talk about a dream team.

As a broadcaster, Gordon was trusted and made everything sound so important. He was the voice of our business and ahead of his time.

Gordon loved his Benson & Hedges menthol cigarettes and good Russian vodka. He was also a dear friend.

One night in 1994, I was in the locker room at *WCW Saturday Night*. I couldn't believe that WCW had Gordon Solie, "Mean" Gene Oker-lund, and Bobby "the Brain" Heenan on the same broadcast team with my good friend Tony Schiavone.

In 2000, I knew Gordon was not in good health. I called him one night to see how he was doing. We had one of our great conversations. We talked about our great times working together, the state of the busi-ness, and all the fun we had. I told Gordon I loved him. He told me that he loved me. Gordon passed away the next day.

As I watched Gordon's family induct their dad, I thought of another of his unforgettable lines, his send-off each week closing out the Florida program: "So long from the Sunshine State."

For decades, Mae Young was one of the toughest wrestlers, male or female, in the business. Mae was a major star from the 1940s into the 1970s and held different championships in the NWA. Mae was one of the trailblazers in the business for women when it came to places that hosted women's matches and females having competitive matches.

Mae enjoyed a second part to her career when she debuted in WWE in 1999. I wasn't with the company when this happened, but I heard Mae was ecstatic at the idea of the Dudley Boyz putting her through a table. Mae loved being with everyone backstage. She always tried to find ways to do more during her segments on the show. I could relate to that.

Eddie Graham was one of the famous Graham "brothers." Eddie was an all-time great in the ring. Eddie and Dr. Jerry Graham were Vince McMahon's favorite tag team growing up as a kid. The team was so successful that the "family" grew to include other "brothers"—"Crazy" Luke and "Superstar" Billy, the latter of whom was inducted into the WWE Hall of Fame in 2004. Eddie became one of the top promoters for the NWA in Florida and was a close business associate and friend of Vince McMahon Sr. Eddie was elected as NWA president in 1976. Eddie helped promote the first ever NWA versus WWE Championship unification match that saw Harley against "Superstar" Graham.

Eddie always liked to throw something into my match when I was NWA Champion. When you were the champion, it was understood that you were going to be in the main event and wrestle for sixty minutes. One night, Eddie put me in a steel cage match against Butch Reed. Right before I went out, Eddie told me I couldn't use the cage at all, that I couldn't throw Butch into it. That certainly kept me on my toes.

You want to talk about someone who had it all—an incredible physique, amazing athleticism, and a boatload of charisma? It was Rocky Johnson. And his son hit the nail right on the head during the induction speech when he talked about his dad's dropkick, in my opinion, probably only rivaled by Jim Brunzell's. Don't forget about the heroic comeback. The arena would be shaking when Rocky Johnson made his comeback. Man, Rocky knew how to get the crowd going!

I remember seeing Rocky's son Dwayne in the locker room when he was a child. It's been incredible to see what Dwayne, known around the world as The Rock, has accomplished in his career. I had a blast working with him at WrestleMania XX.

When it came to Peter Maivia, I can listen to Pat Patterson tell stories all night about working with Peter in San Francisco. The Polynesian fans in that area would rush the ring and defend the honor of their hero the High Chief. It was dangerous to be a villain in those days. Peter was a champion in different NWA territories and was a legend in the South Pacific, the West Coast of the United States, and WWE.

Peter promoted shows in Hawaii for NWA. The fans came out in droves for those events. After Peter's passing, his wife, Lia, continued to run the business. The memorial shows honoring Peter were exciting events. Anyone who was anyone during those years appeared for Lia Maivia: Andre the Giant, Antonio Inoki, Bruiser Brody, the Von Erichs, Michael Hayes, Dusty Rhodes, Magnum TA, Jerry Lawler, me, and of course Rocky Johnson. It was rare in those days to have a Super Card with stars from WWE, NWA, AWA, Japan, and other competing companies. Everyone was happy to come together to honor Peter. The Maivia and Anoa'i families had that much respect in the business. They still do today, because they deserve it.

Backstage, after Vince put the Hall of Fame ring on my finger, Paul brought me a box. When I opened it, it was something I had never seen before—cuff links of the NWA World Heavyweight Championship's main plate. Watching my induction video put together by the production department was like an out-of-body experience. Hearing Paul's words was something I never imagined. To see all of this for me was almost too much to absorb all at once.*

Naturally, after all he's done for me, I wanted to include something

---

*Paul Levesque: "There were times along the way where Ric was the only guy in the room who didn't know he was Ric Flair. He did things that he thought were the best things to help business, because he cared, but they weren't the best things for himself. You go through our locker room and so many guys, myself included, were there because they wanted to be just like Ric. I wanted him to know how much he means to all of us. I said it at the Hall of Fame, and I meant it: Ric Flair was, is, and always will be the man."

about Vince in my induction speech. I thought of one specific example. A few years ago, I got into financial trouble as a result of my costly divorce (from Beth), paying around $20,000 per month in alimony, investment opportunities not panning out, and maintaining a high-profile lifestyle. Vince lent me the money I needed. He said to me, "I wouldn't let my kids borrow this amount of money from me." It wasn't the first time Vince helped me out financially.

All he wanted to hear me say was that I'd pay him back. I definitely wanted to talk about that in my speech. I wanted the world to know how Vince had been there for me over the years. When I let him know what I was planning, Vince's eyes widened. He said, "Absolutely not. If you do that, I'm going to come out there and lay you out with a chair." A few moments later, Kevin Dunn said to me, "Have fun out there." I thought that was a nice way to balance things out before taking the stage.

My music hit, and I was ready. I walked out with beauties Kelly Kelly and Eve Torres. I saw so many of my peers I could feel myself being overcome with gratitude. It reaffirmed the direction I wanted to go with my speech.

After this storybook journey, the last four months, and knowing what was happening the next day, I wanted to leave the Nature Boy in the hotel room and introduce the world to Richard Fliehr. Lord, think of how much easier my life would be if I had done that more often. It's so humbling to hear from fans, the WWE talent, and crew about how much I've meant to them. Sometimes I don't know if I deserve that level of recognition. I wanted to let people know how much they'd meant to me.

In this profession, since you spend most of your time away from your family at home, the people you work with become your family. If you leave this business with ten true friends, you're very fortunate. Standing at that podium with my children, Tiffany, and so many whom I admired and called friends in the audience, I felt like the luckiest man on earth.

It was so important to acknowledge Kevin Dunn and the incredible production team that makes WWE what it is every week. Kerwin Silfies and his team, the camera crew, the lighting crew, the makeup artists, producers, announcers, ring crew, talent relations, everyone who works at the TV studio, the departments at headquarters in Stamford . . . there's nothing like WWE. It's an amazing operation.

When I think of the incredible work done by the agents, Fit Finlay, Arn Anderson, Dean Malenko, Mike Rotunda, Barry Windham, Jamie Noble, Ricky Steamboat, Sgt. Slaughter, Jerry Brisco, and Pat Patterson—who wanted me to come out in my robe for the induction speech—I'm so grateful for the wisdom they impart on the locker room.

The Hall of Fame was another instance when I thought of the wonderful Olivia Walker and what her artistry did for my career. Clifford Macias was the man who made my wrestling boots. Based out of Houston, Texas, Clifford made everything by hand. Bruce Prichard helped me figure out that I must've worn around 580 pairs of boots during my career. I always wanted my attire to look brand new—every night I performed. If we did live television every week and pay-per-views back then, I'd have to work another two decades just to pay for my robes and boots.

I needed to mention Chris Jericho, someone I've known for a long time and have tremendous respect for. Whenever I see Big Show in the ring, I'm amazed at what he can do. I was so disappointed when he was brought into WCW as "the Giant" and billed as Andre the Giant's son. Going to WWE was the best thing he ever did. When Big Show is focused like he's been since his return to the company, he's the best big man in our business. Period. I broke in with Andre the Giant. I drove Andre around when he'd come to Minneapolis for Verne Gagne. He didn't speak English, so I'd talk for the both of us. I know Andre did dropkicks and came off the top rope earlier in his career. I think Andre got tired at a certain point. Tired of the travel and keeping himself in the type of physical condition to be able to perform those types of moves. Big Show can do it all: work with cruiserweights, heavyweights, other big men. Look at how he moves in the ring and his footwork. Big Show played NCAA basketball. He can do anything in that ring and is a hell of an interview on the microphone.

I knew Edge was going to be in attendance. I needed to make sure I mentioned him in my speech. He's another member of the locker room who befriended me. I was stunned when Michael Hayes called me on a Thursday night. Michael told me that I'd be in a Ladder Match against

Edge that coming Monday on *Raw*. Up until that point in 2006, I think I had every type of match except a ladder match. Edge made that match one of the best experiences of my career. He made it possible for me to show I could do what no one thought I could do.

Edge will be remembered as one of the greats. I'm proud of him as a friend and as a colleague. I think he did a tremendous job as World Heavyweight Champion. The championship he wore traces back to the NWA. The Rated R Superstar, as Edge is known, would've been really something in those days. The design of the championship itself is based on the title I brought out for the first time on WTBS in February of 1986, which is the same one I brought with me when I came to WWE in 1991.

I wanted people to know how much the previous seven years with WWE had meant to me. Over a thirty-five-year career, almost ten of those years were with WWE. They were some of the best of my life.

Writing my speech made me think back to Ken Patera, whom I first met in a bar in Minneapolis in 1972. Ken could bench-press 500 pounds six times, incline press 505 pounds eight times, and behind-the-neck press 440 pounds seated on a bench.

I was twenty-one years old and loved weight lifting. Ken was the first person in the world to press 500 pounds over his head. Ken was on the cover of every weight lifting magazine. I was the bouncer at a bar in Minnesota called George's in the Park. I was leaning on the cigarette machine, and all of a sudden, I saw this guy walk in the bar. He took out a Salem cigarette and ordered a beer and a shot of vodka. I thought, *There's no way that's Ken Patera. He can't have any of that stuff.* As I got closer, I realized it was.

I said, "You're not Ken Patera, are you?"

He said, "Yeah. How are you?"

I was shocked. This was someone who won a gold medal at the 1971 Pan Am Games. He was training for the 1972 Olympic Games. I had just seen him on ABC's *Wide World of Sports*. Ken said his life wasn't going to change because he had to train. I just couldn't believe it. We ended up drinking together that night. Two weeks later, we were roommates in south Minneapolis. Every Thursday, Friday, and Saturday night, we had parties. It was like the movie *Animal House*. The rest . . . well, the rest is history. It was through Ken that I met Verne Gagne.

I'll always be indebted to Verne Gagne for giving me my break. I remember being in his office and convincing him to let me come to his camp. Verne told me that if I was going to his training camp that I'd better not quit on him like I quit college. I assured him that would never happen.

I reported to his farm where there was a ring inside a barn. In the frigid Minnesota winter, we started with five hundred free squats, two hundred push-ups, two hundred sit-ups, and a two-mile run in his cornfield. I quit after the second day. I thought wrestling was like watching the Crusher and Dick the Bruiser. You'd talk on the microphone, go in the ring, beat some guy up, and then have a beer after the match. I had no idea of the hard work and conditioning that went into it. The next day, Verne came to my home and threw me on my front lawn. Verne said to me, "I gave you an opportunity. I expect you to make it every step of the way." I was back the next day. One week later, I quit again. The next time, thankfully, Verne just called me. "You'd better be here in the next hour." I drove back to camp right away. Two months later, I was in the business.

Every year, Verne had Christmas parties at his home. Once midnight rolled around and we enjoyed some cocktails, Verne wanted to wrestle all the guests. Talk about an invitation! Those were wonderful days. Thank you, Verne, for believing in me and not allowing me to give up. I wouldn't be here without you.

Wahoo McDaniel changed my life. Wahoo was an outstanding athlete. He played professional football for the Houston Oilers, Denver Broncos, New York Jets, and Miami Dolphins. Wahoo was a special performer in the ring and one of the toughest men I've ever known. I can't count how many times he'd be in the locker room and a doctor would sew up a huge gash without giving Wahoo Novocain. He'd just say, "Okay, Doc, let's go." I always knew Wahoo was tough. I had no idea how tough until years later. He had a vasectomy at 4:00 and wrestled me the same night at 8:00. I did not appreciate what that meant until I had my own vasectomy years later. Wahoo was on the waiting list to receive a kidney when he passed away in Houston, Texas, in 2002. It was about a month after WrestleMania X8. I carry the memories I have of Wahoo with me every day.

I couldn't wait to talk to the audience about Blackjack Mulligan. Blackjack was a US Marine and played football for the New York Jets. For eight years, I traveled three thousand miles a week with Blackjack Mulligan. We bought houses on opposite sides of some guy in Charlotte, and we drove him nuts with our parties and going back and forth. Jack and I owned the Knoxville territory for a little while. I learned so much from him. There are few men in the history of our great sport who were as respected and feared as Blackjack Mulligan. That was for good reason. If Jack didn't like something, he would let it be known. If someone disrespected him, he'd feel the wrath of someone who stood six foot eight and weighed more than three hundred pounds. Along with Jack Lanza, Mulligan formed the Blackjacks tag team. Bobby Heenan was their manager. The trio represented the most feared villains in the business for a long time. I worked closely with Jack's son Barry. He also had another son, Kendall, and his son-in-law, Mike Rotunda, was Irwin R. Schyster in WWE. Mike was broken into the business by the legendary Destroyer, who helped my son Reid many years later in amateur wrestling. I know Jack has grandchildren who have entered the business. If they have his genes, they'll be custom-made for the ring.

When I think of another person who personified our business, I look to Harley Race. Harley is someone I owe an incredible amount of gratitude to for the wisdom he instilled in me, how he took me under his wing, and for what he did for me at Starrcade '83. Dusty created Starrcade and dubbed the inaugural event a "Flair for the Gold." There was a lot going on leading up to that match. There was one of the worst snowstorms in the history of the Carolinas that night, flights were canceled, and what many didn't know was that Harley met with Vince McMahon before that event and had the choice not to show up. Harley made it to the Greensboro Coliseum.

I was standing in the locker room with Dusty and Jimmy Crockett. Harley came in and said, "I want to talk to you." Everyone left. Harley and I stood face-to-face. I didn't know what was going to happen. Our business was different back then. Let's just say it wasn't as controlled and civilized. Harley looked me in the eye and said, "I'm here for you tonight, kid." With Gordon Solie calling the action and Gene Kiniski as the special guest referee, I won my second NWA World Championship from Harley inside a steel cage. That night made me. "Thank you" is not enough, but it's all I can say to Harley for what he did for me.

I couldn't have a Hall of Fame induction speech without describing my greatest opponent and someone who's been a great friend: Ricky Steamboat. I must've competed against Ricky in the ring more than two thousand times. Throughout my career, there was nothing better than going to the arena and knowing I was working with Ricky. I'm honored to think how much fans and people in the business feel about the trilogy of matches we had in 1989. I wish more people had seen the matches we had in the late '70s. There were no cameras rolling then. I remember how much fun we had when Andre the Giant was the special guest referee for our match in the Mid-Atlantic territory for the United States Championship.

Whenever I entered the squared circle, I wanted to make sure no one went home feeling bad about spending their hard-earned money to see me perform. I'm honored to say I had incredible opponents to work with. I'm speechless to have had the good fortune to work with Ricky Steamboat throughout my career. My work with Rick is timeless.

That point in my speech brought me to the great Sam Muchnick. Sam was a key figure in the formation of the National Wrestling Alliance and served as president of the NWA on more than one occasion. From the 1950s until the mid-'80s, if you were a wrestler, there were two places you wanted to work: New York for Vince McMahon Sr. and later Vince McMahon, and St. Louis to work for Sam. St. Louis was the place to be if you were in the NWA. If you wore the NWA World Heavyweight Championship, like the one I'd brought out recently on *Monday Night Raw* in my interview segment with Shawn Michaels, you were regarded as a sports icon in that city. Performing in St. Louis for Sam was on the same level as performing in Madison Square Garden. It was an honor working for Sam Muchnick. Thank you, Sam.

It was important to speak about the Crockett family. The Crocketts had a vision for their business. They worked so hard to make their Mid-Atlantic territory, professionally known as Jim Crockett Promotions, the most successful territory in the NWA. Jimmy Crockett pushed for me with everything he had to make me the NWA Champion, his champion, and someone that the people of the southeast felt was their champion . . . whether the fans were supposed to be cheering for me or booing me. The Crockett family will always be special to me.

I could never talk about my career without speaking about the Four Horsemen. The original group with me, Arn Anderson, Tully Blanchard, Ole Anderson, and J. J. Dillon as our manager was magic.

We each wanted to have the best match of the night. We pushed each other and supported each other every step of the way. The group was so successful because, one, we backed up everything we said and did on television, and two, it was real. We traveled together, trained together, ate together, and partied together. That was a special moment in time.

My favorite iteration of the Horsemen was me, Arn, Tully, and Blackjack Mulligan's son Barry Windham. I also had a phenomenal time in

the '90s when the Horsemen included Arn, Dean Malenko, Mongo McMichael, and me.

No matter what iteration of the Horsemen there was at a given time, the backbone of the Four Horsemen was Arn Anderson.

Arn Anderson is the brother I never had. Arn's one of the greatest people I've had the honor to know and someone who made me better as a person and as a professional every step of the way throughout my life. Arn and his family have been there for my family so many times over the years. I'm so touched when fans and colleagues talk about my ability in the ring and how much they enjoyed my work on the microphone. In every way it pertains to this business, and as a person, Arn Anderson is in a class by himself.

When I spoke about close friends, it was easy for me to speak about the incomparable Jim Ross. Jim and I have been friends for more than thirty years. Along with Gordon Solie, Jim's responsible for creating an unforgettable sound track to my career. I believe Jim Ross is the greatest announcer in the history of our business. I thank him each day for his friendship, support, and making my work sound so special.

Speaking of broadcasters, I couldn't leave out one of my best friends, Bobby "the Brain" Heenan. Bobby started out as a manager. He got under people's skin so much that he could start riots just by speaking to the crowd or trying to interfere in a match. Bobby's one of the top-ten people to ever work in our industry and the greatest manager of all time. Bobby could do it all and make it look easy. Bobby was an amazing influence on me. Thank you, Brain.

In 1972, I received an invitation to a party at "Mean" Gene Okerlund's home. That was the first time I got to speak with Gene outside of work and the first time we had a drink together. Gene was the announcer for my first match. We've been friends ever since. I loved reuniting with Gene when I came to WWE in 1991. I would not have made it through my darkest days in WCW without meeting Gene at the hotel bar and enjoying martinis. "Mean" Gene is synonymous with our industry and did his job like nobody else.

Since my return to WWE in 2001, one of the highlights for me has been working with Michael Hayes. As the leader of the Freebirds, PS was a star everywhere he worked. Michael was essential as part of the support system that kept me going when I was working through self-confidence issues. Michael has always been there for me. His friendship and counsel have meant the world to me. When people talk about how cool it is that Superstars have entrance music, they need to look at Michael. He made entrance music in our industry famous. Michael is another individual who was far ahead of his time.

I couldn't be speaking the night before WrestleMania and not mention Undertaker. He's another person that doesn't like public praise. I got to work with him during my first run with WWE. I'll never forget how special our match was at WrestleMania X8. When I returned to the company, I wasn't supposed to perform in the ring. Within months, I was lacing up my boots. I'll always remember when Paul told me that Undertaker requested to work with me at WrestleMania. I thought we had a very good match. I'll always remember what Undertaker did for me that night and how important that match was for restoring my confidence as an in-ring performer.

I knew this was going to get me in trouble, but I did it anyway—and that's not the first time! You're not supposed to talk about Vince McMahon during your Hall of Fame speech. But when you discuss the success of WWE, you have to talk about Vince and his wife, Linda. It's almost indescribable to think about what they did throughout the years to elevate the status of this industry—and what WWE has become. I just wanted them to know how much their work and how they've treated me over the years have meant to me.

It was important to me to recognize John Cena. John is a great ambassador for our business and is the franchise Superstar for WWE. I consider John a friend, and he's someone who's part of a select group of Superstars. If my record of sixteen World Championships is broken, I'd smile if he was the one to do it. I didn't take aim at anyone when I said John won't leave WWE for Hollywood. I wanted the audience to know how dedicated John is to the business. I wish people could see the heart and work ethic John puts forth every day. John Cena will go down as an all-time great.

There's been so much talk about who's the greatest WWE Superstar of all time. I wanted to take a few moments during my speech to give my opinion on the matter. Stone Cold Steve Austin is without a shadow of a doubt the greatest WWE Superstar ever. Period. Some people thought that remark was a shot at Hulk Hogan. It wasn't. It was based on business records that Steve set as a performer when he was on top for the company. I knew Steve in WCW, and I admire what he did with his career. Steve loves the history of our business and cares so much about every detail. I've been in the ring to witness almost everyone's entrance over the last thirty-five years. There's nothing like what happens in an arena when the sound of that glass breaks and Austin walks to the ring.*

While I looked out in the crowd, I saw two people I needed to talk about: Randy Orton and Batista. When I see everything they've accomplished on their own, it proves that our group Evolution was a success. Randy is one of the top performers in our business and a tremendous champion. Dave was an incredible talent who could do so much in the ring. I felt his match with Undertaker at WrestleMania 23 was a glimpse of the greatness that's in him.

I also wanted to say something special to Paul. I needed everyone to know how much his friendship and support have meant to me, and how much I think of him professionally. There were times during my speech where I tried to see how the cuff links he gave me looked.

I decided that I was going to go into character and say something to Shawn Michaels about our match the following day. It didn't feel right. I said what came naturally to me. I wanted Shawn to know how special he is as a performer and how much my sons looked up to him as a person. I had to let Shawn know that "to be the man, you gotta beat the man."

At this point, my attention was directed to the front row of the audience: to my family.

I thought of my parents, Kay and Dick Fliehr, who are no longer with us. When writing this part of my speech, I remembered when I watched

---

*Stone Cold Steve Austin: "You say professional wrestling to me, the first name that comes to my mind is the 'Nature Boy' Ric Flair. He's given his entire life to this business and paved the way for so many people, including myself. He's the greatest world champion in the history of the business."

the AWA in their home as a child, when my dad took me to AWA shows on my birthday. To think that all these years later I went from cheering on the Crusher to standing at that podium. It was something that was difficult to put into perspective. I was still amazed that I was the only inductee going into the Hall while still an active WWE Superstar. I wish my parents could've been in the front row with the kids, whom they loved so much. I know they'd have been proud. When I look at my children Megan and David, I can't help but think of their mother, Leslie. Leslie and I met at the University of Minnesota. We were married for twelve years. Leslie is the greatest woman I've ever known. She had to be to tolerate me the way she did for so long.

A big part of being accepted into the business in the early '70s was going out with the guys after the shows. Dusty Rhodes and Dick Murdoch were two wrestlers who were in a tag team called the Texas Outlaws. I was enamored of Dusty. He was one of the idols I had in my life. His presence in the ring, captivating cadence on the microphone, and the way he held the audience in the palm of his hand every night inspired me. Dusty went on to become "the American Dream," one of the greatest heroes in our business, but even then, before his heroic stardom, Dusty was larger than life. I just wanted to be a part of what he was doing.

I drove Dusty and Dick around, carried their bags, and went out with them. They gave me a good share of rookie-type hazing, playing jokes on me like shaving my head in Japan, throwing my clothes off a hotel balcony, or calling me and telling me they needed me to drive them to the airport because they were going on *The Tonight Show*. I loved it. I loved it so much that I'd tell Leslie I had to go on the road with Dusty to appear at shows in different towns, but I wasn't booked to work on those shows. After two weeks, I'd come home with no money. It didn't take her long to figure out I was going out just to be with Dusty.

There was a point when I wanted to be his "brother" and call myself Ramblin' Ricky Rhodes. I even curled my hair like his. When I asked him for his blessing, he said, "Be the first Ric Flair." Amid the rookie hazing, Dusty always watched out for me.

I've never seen someone with a stronger connection with our audience than Dusty. He's the most charismatic person I've ever been around. Someone showed me an interview where he was quoted as saying, "There's one Babe Ruth, one Muhammad Ali, and one 'Nature Boy' Ric Flair." I can't articulate, even in my own book, what Dusty saying that means to me. All I wanted was to be like the Dream.

Though Dusty and I would go our separate ways, I loved going out after shows, going on tours, and being part of the camaraderie with the other guys in the locker room. Leslie and I moved to Charlotte in 1974, and I continued doing the same thing. After years of this, Leslie had enough. I came home one night and she kicked me out. By the tone of her voice, I knew this was it. Our marriage was over. I went to the one place I knew I could stay until I got back on my feet.*

I wanted to make sure I mentioned Leslie in my Hall of Fame speech,

---

*Ricky Steamboat: "Around 1:00 a.m., there's a knock on my door. I looked out my window and saw Ric standing there in the rain. I opened the door and saw him holding four or five of his robes in one hand and a gym bag in the other. Right then, I knew this argument was different. Leslie was done for good."

because she deserved it. Megan and David needed to hear from me, in front of the whole world, how amazing their mother was, how much I knew that then, how much I knew at that moment, and how much I will know that for the rest of my life. What I didn't know when I was married to Leslie was that I had an angel. I was so engrossed with my own life and establishing myself professionally that I didn't do what I needed to keep her. You only get one chance with a woman like that. Leslie gave me countless chances. Each time, I discovered new and inventive ways to mess things up. But you'd never know that by speaking to Leslie or seeing what wonderful people Megan and David grew up to become.

My second wife, Beth, stayed with me for twenty-three years. She traveled around the world with me during my hectic schedule as NWA Champion. Sometimes I'd be on the road for eight to twelve weeks at a time. She helped me get through the bad times in WCW in the late '80s, encouraged me to sign with WWE in '91, and was there with me when things happened in WCW again in the late '90s. She always held on to her dream of being a mother. No matter how many times the doctors told her that her chances of carrying a pregnancy to full term were dwindling, she never gave up. It's because of her determination and strength during those years that I have the honor of being Ashley and Reid's father.

In 2006, I decided to leave Beth, and we got divorced. Things became acrimonious between us. Our split damaged Ashley and Reid worse than I ever imagined. Things had been slowly repaired to the point where my wife Tiffany, the kids, Beth, and I could spend holidays together. I'm very thankful for that. It was important to acknowledge Beth in my speech for her years of dedication to the children. There were times when Beth was close to Megan and David too. I loved Beth very much. I just felt it was time to leave.

Seeing my four children sitting in the front row reminded me of the time we spent together as a family. It was difficult not to look at them for my entire speech.

I worried that I wasn't there enough for my children, and I was concerned about the long-term effects on them. I'll cherish the image of the four of them sitting together at the Hall of Fame for the rest of my life. My children are my greatest gifts.

At times, I agonized over the fact that professional wrestling gave me so much but that it also took so many things away. It gave me the opportunity to make a living and provide for my family, but to do that, I had to be away from them. I still struggle with accepting that today. I always loved my children, but I didn't realize until I spent time with Ashley and Reid what a special gift it is to be a parent and be home with your kids.

And to my wife Tiffany: being close friends before we dated gave us the opportunity to know one another on a different level. We entered our relationship with a mutual respect. Tiffany's been a calming presence in my life and has communicated with me in a way that no woman has before. The past two years had been up and down for me professionally, and Tiffany was there for me. She's helped me begin to understand that my career is not over; it's just continuing on a different path. That's been difficult for me to make peace with, but I'm getting there. Tiffany's also helped me become comfortable with the idea that it's okay to show the public who Richard Fliehr is. She's inspired me in so many different ways and helped me understand that the next phase of life is not a step down or a death sentence. During my speech, I mentioned that I tested her—no more "Naitchin'"—no more going out until the sun comes up and dropping $1,100 at dinner and another $3,000 at the bar.

Tiffany's relationship with my children developed to a point where everyone was comfortable being together. We started to do a lot of fun things as a group: going to dinner, spending holidays together, and visiting each other's homes.

After the induction ceremony, we all went to a reception. I was anxious, nervous, worrying about the next day, thinking about putting on my trunks, lacing up my boots, and putting my arms through the sleeves of my robe for the final time. I stood at the reception like a statue. I sipped a glass of red wine. Michael Hayes said to me, like only he can, "What the hell are you doing? You're wrestling Shawn Michaels tomorrow. You've done this more than ten thousand times. Have a few drinks. Have you ever not had a drink the night before a match? Why would you change now? Are you crazy?" Michael was right. I needed to loosen up a bit. So I got bombed. That's right, I went old school. I drank all night and had a blast. The only thing missing was J. J. Dillon making arrangements with the limo driver about where we were going next. The Horsemen used to go out until four in the morning and be at the gym two hours later. Then we'd shower, get something to eat, go to the building for the show, and repeat that . . . every night. That was the closest I came to duplicating those days in a long time, and it felt wonderful.

I got back to my suite and looked out the window to a new horizon. In a few short hours, the sun would come up. The day I'd been so conflicted about, the day that led me to one of the greatest periods of my life, also represented the end.

3

TO BE THE MAN, YOU GOTTA BEAT THE MAN

Time waits for no one.

March 30, 2008 . . . My final match . . .

In the hysteria of WrestleMania week, there are few quiet moments. I found one. We were getting ready to make our way to the Citrus Bowl. Tiffany was in the other room getting dressed. I looked at myself in the mirror. I didn't say anything. I just looked at myself. Thirty-five years doing everything I ever dreamed of: from headlining events all over the world to being recognized as a World Champion to doing my best as an ambassador for this great sport. I was now hours away from all of it coming to an end on the greatest stage our business has ever known: WrestleMania.

I never spent a lot of time watching my matches, because I was so focused on what I was doing. When one program with someone was over, I just started another with somebody else. That became my main concern. This can be an all-consuming business. At least that's how it was with me. I knew if something was good. I didn't have to ask anyone. Today, it bothers me that a lot of younger talent go on the internet as soon as their matches or interview segments are done to see what people say about their work. The week before, for the first time, I watched my trilogy of matches from 1989 in WCW against Ricky Steamboat in their entirety: Chi-Town Rumble, Clash of the Champions VI: Ragin' Cajun, and WrestleWar: Music City Showdown.

I had to say they were really good. I was forty years old. Steamboat was about thirty-five. We were still in our prime. Looking at myself that day, I knew I could be that man one more time. The company had put so much into this. Shawn had dedicated the last three months of his life to this and would be giving his all today. He asked to work with me. I had to be that man one more time. That day must be today.

There have been periods during my career when I had anxiety and self-confidence issues. There were moments I got into my own head and couldn't escape. I doubted that I could still perform at a high level. There were times I didn't know who I was. I worked so hard for my entire career so that everyone in the world would know who I was. It's difficult to describe what anxiety and self-esteem challenges can do to a human being.

Even though this is a wonderful industry, it's tough to be a success. It can be cruel and unforgiving. When you're done, you're done. The road can be your best friend or your worst enemy. My love of partying after the matches was not recommended. I don't either—now. It was my way of dealing with being away from my family and avoiding boredom and loneliness. When the show's over, you're dealing with your own reality. There's no off-season. The professional sports leagues have seasons: the NFL has 16 games; the NBA and NHL have 82; Major League Baseball has 162. An actor could be on set for a film for a few months or do a limited engagement, also a few months, on Broadway. For a television show, it could be a number of different episodes per season, but there is time off. In our line of work, there's no off-season. No intermission.

There's a harsh irony to this business: people see us on television, and they see us at live events and personal appearances. They grow up with us. They feel they know who we are. You're in a new town every night. You make acquaintances and you move on. You can be at the center of an arena with thousands of people, under bright lights. Those people are chanting your name. For the time you're in front of that crowd, it's the most amazing rush of adrenaline you could ever imagine. You're in total control of yourself and the audience. You can evoke emotions from that capacity crowd by saying one word, and you can trigger another emotion by saying something else. You can take them to another level with a single movement.

That's the kind of power a top performer in our industry has; it's a special connection with the crowd. In other forms of sport and entertainment, players can tune out the crowd in order to focus. In this business, you feed off the crowd. But when you step through the other side of the curtain and the show's over, your "real life" begins. You shower, change into your clothes, and you're off to the hotel or the next town. There's seclusion in that cycle. It's like a spinning wheel you can't get off from, and I didn't want to. There's a loneliness that people can't fully realize until they experience it themselves. It's why I'll always cherish the camaraderie between the performers and production crew in this business.

During the '70s, '80s, and '90s, we didn't have the time off performers have today. It was almost impossible to have a life outside the business. It's still tough now, don't get me wrong, but back then, it felt like we were all we had. I loved the nightlife. I loved to travel, and I quickly realized that the more I was seen in public in true story-line persona, the more success I enjoyed.

There was a time when it backfired, like when famous wrestler and promoter Carlos Colón booked me to perform in Trinidad. To help promote the match, Carlos told me to tape an interview segment where I said something bad about Trinidad. When the camera was rolling, I said how I was the Nature Boy and Trinidad had nothing for me. I was the World Champion, and the people of Trinidad should consider themselves lucky that I was going to their country.

A few weeks later, I got off the plane in Trinidad, and the police arrested me because I said bad things about Trinidad on television. I tried to explain to them that I had never been there before and that it was just "for the show." They kept me in a jail cell for two hours until Carlos came to get me.

Everyone dealt with the road schedule differently. We make choices. There are some of our brothers and sisters who went into their hotel rooms and never came out. Seeing so many friendly faces and feeling this overwhelming sense of adulation from the fans this week made me think of how lucky I've been. Shawn dedicated every waking moment of the last three months to me. This was his idea: he asked to work with me; he came up with building the story line and creating the flow. I hounded Shawn every week backstage at TV. I'd say to him, "It's me, you're paired with me, WrestleMania . . . how are you doing?"

Shawn would look at me and say, "Not good." Then we'd laugh. We were so happy to be sharing this moment.

During the months leading up to WrestleMania, WWE devoted so much time to making my final match a special part of that historic night. I couldn't let the company down. I couldn't let Shawn down, or my family, or my fans. Most of all, I couldn't let myself down. That match was bigger than any main event title defense I ever made. It was greater than any match when I helped establish a new star in a territory or fought to maintain the prestige of the NWA World Championship, or show WWE the man they had in the Nature Boy. This was defending my career and my legacy in an industry that held my life's work. It is the guardian of everything I ever dreamed about doing and everything I ever accomplished. When I think of our business, I think of performing every night. You're only as good as your last performance.

I needed to summon all my self-confidence one final time to be the performer, even at fifty-nine years of age, I knew I could be. I gave one last look in that mirror and said, "Damn it, one more time. Let's go."

Going through the talent entrance at the Citrus Bowl was like moving in slow motion. People were so kind, stopping to wish me well and let me know that they were looking forward to my match. I knew I'd be back doing things with the company, but the realization that today would be my last day in the business as a WWE Superstar loomed over me like an albatross around my neck.

I caught up with my kids backstage. It was wonderful being with the four of them. It was the first time in a while that all of us were together in the same place, especially for more than one day. The kids were looking forward to my match. I couldn't wait to see them onstage, greeting the crowd with the Hall of Fame inductees.

Before I went into the locker room, we ran into Snoop Dogg. Snoop is one of my favorite people and someone who's very respectful when he comes to our shows. He loves WWE and always wants to do more when he's scheduled to appear on WWE programming. Snoop was with us today at WrestleMania to serve as the master of ceremonies for the *Playboy* BunnyMania Lumberjill Match.

Snoop and I were talking about what he was going to do on the show when he said, "Nature Boy, you were bling before bling was bling. Please join us. We're having a party in here." He motioned to his trailer.

I said, "Sorry, but I can't have a Kettle One and soda right now."

Of course, my son Reid, who loved everything about the business and was training to become a wrestler, asked, "Dad, can I stay?"

I put my arm around him and said, "Hell no. Let's go. Now."

If I were his age and saw the girls around that trailer, I wouldn't want to leave either. Earlier that day, Reid was hanging out with Snoop, Floyd Mayweather, and Kim Kardashian. There wasn't a friendlier person who was the life of the party than my son Reid.

I gave Tiffany and the kids a final goodbye. They would be sitting at ringside during the show. It was time to get ready for my match. When you do something for so long, it becomes second nature. I do things like putting my trunks on, lacing up my boots, and putting on my robe—all without thinking about it. I was aware of the significance of what I was doing, but the emotion of it didn't really hit me until I was waiting by the Gorilla Position to make my entrance. I'd just put my ring gear on and walked to the curtain as a WWE Superstar for the last time. I remembered my friend George Scott. Thinking of it now, it's apropos that my final match would be at WrestleMania because of the part that George played in encouraging me to carry on the Nature Boy persona and the part he played in helping launch WrestleMania in 1985.

From the late 1940s through the early 1970s, George, alongside his brother Sandy, were the famous tag team known as the Flying Scotts. They wowed audiences from the territories of the NWA to Verne Gagne's AWA, Australia, and across Canada, including Stu Hart's Stampede Wrestling. When George's in-ring career was over, he became revered within the business for his work behind the scenes, most notably, creating matches—or, as the position was known at the time, the booker. George arrived in WWE's front office in 1983. He became a part of Vince McMahon's inner circle and a crucial member of the team that made the concept of WrestleMania a reality.

During a WWE live event several years earlier, Vince McMahon publicly acknowledged George's pivotal role in presenting WrestleMania to the world. He was so important to WWE during those years that the McMahons wrote him a letter stating that should anything happen to them during that time, the company would be his to run.

George knew what it was like to come back from a career-threatening injury. After a match with Buddy Rogers in the '50s, George was paralyzed for six months. In the early '70s, he suffered a broken neck. When I broke my back after the plane crash in 1975, he was one of the few people who could truly empathize with the uncertainty of a career being over and the possibility of never being able to walk again. But he didn't exactly show it. When I walked into Jim Crockett's office with my back brace on, George yelled at me, "Take that damn thing off! All your other muscles are going to atrophy." So much for, "Hi, Ric, how are you feeling?"

Bringing myself back to WrestleMania and the more than seventy-four thousand people who were in attendance, Shawn reminded me to keep quiet during the match and listen to him. In our business, you work together to create an incredible performance. Almost always, one of the performers leads the match by "calling" certain things to be done at certain times. When I came up in the business, we called it in the ring, so we knew where our story was going and how it would end. But the points in between, in terms of *how*, were left to the performers' abilities to tell a story based on the audience's reaction.

Today, a lot of younger talent preplan too many things. Certain moves are set to take place at a specific time with certain things happening before and after. I understand that to call it in the ring, you need a certain level of experience, but part of developing that experience is doing it that way from the beginning; otherwise, you never learn. As a performer, you want to be prepared and know where you're going, but you also need to give yourself the creative freedom and flexibility to decide how you and the person you're working with will arrive at the end point of the story. The crowd is such an important part of what we do. It's performance art in its highest form. This was Shawn's match. I knew I was up for the ride.

Shawn concluded by saying, "Let's do it."* Then he made his way to the ring. Waiting behind that curtain during Shawn's entrance felt like an eternity. It reminded me of what Ray Stevens said: "The day you walk through that curtain and you don't have goose bumps, that's the day you never need to walk through it again." I had goose bumps.

The sounds of my entrance music, "Sunrise" by Richard Strauss, played, and like I had thousands of times before, I walked that aisle. I hit my mark and raised my arms like I had so many times before, and I began my slow, 360-degree rotation. I wanted the world to see the magnificent diamond-studded blue regalia that seamstress and designer extraordinaire Terry Anderson created.

Seeing fireworks brighten the Orlando night sky was amazing. Each step closer to the ring made it more difficult to control my emotions. My close friend and WWE referee for the match, Charles Robinson, lifted the rope so I could enter the ring.

Of all the times my family had been ringside, this was a moment like no other.

The first act had me settling into the match and doing some of my signature mannerisms like my strut across the ring, and when my opponent thinks I will lock up with him, but instead, I pulled away, ran my hands over my hair, and sounded off with my "WOOOOO!" catchphrase. We followed that with different moves and takedowns that the audience would associate with two "good guys" competing in a good, clean match. When I backed Shawn into the corner, we wanted people to think nothing was going to happen. That's when he slapped me in the face. The

---

*Shawn Michaels: "The one demand I had made on him before the match was, 'You don't say anything! I know you've been a ring general your whole life, but not tonight. You don't speak. Not one word. Let's do it.' That was a big pill for him to swallow, and he did it for me. When the stage was the largest and the lights were shining their brightest. It's one of the reasons that match will always mean so much to me."

tension began to rise as we locked in a stare. Shawn said, "You can leave now." The roller-coaster ride began.

We traded holds and body blows in a more aggressive manner, with a heated exchange of reverse knife-edge chops. Something I wanted to make sure I established was, do I have some tricks up my sleeve? Like when I landed a flying cross body on Shawn from the top rope. It wasn't something you'd see from Steamboat, but if I was going for it, this was the match for it.

I knew there'd be a turning point, but I didn't know when or to what degree. We battled on the floor, and I ended up on the announcers' table. You could feel the ebb and flow of the audience. Shawn climbed to the outside middle rope and launched himself like a missile to perform a flip, what we call a moonsault—and crashed right through the announcers' table. That was something he wanted to do for me, to heighten the drama in the match. That's the type of dedication top-tier performers have in our industry. They sacrifice their own bodies to make the match even more exciting. I didn't know if Shawn had broken his ribs, if something was severely bruised, or if he was okay. The crowd fell into a chilling silence. Shawn said I was going to get his Mr. WrestleMania persona, and he wasn't kidding.

Shawn continued to lead the match. Out of habit, I opened my mouth, but he quickly told me, "Shut up." We wanted to make sure I performed some of my classic maneuvers: the knee drop, where I roll forward afterward, my chops, which are some of the only offense I had so they were consistent throughout, and my standing vertical suplex, which I loved performing. It was important for me to begin executing moves that "hurt" Shawn's knee so that I could put him in my figure-four leg lock. The audience invoked the response we were hoping for.

Just when the audience thought I was on a roll and would assume full control of the match, we did a classic sequence from early in my career. Shawn sent me over the top rope with a backdrop, and I landed on the floor. I don't think anyone expected to see that. What some people didn't know was that I used to take that and land on a concrete floor. Even at fifty-nine, I felt good afterward, though this time I appreciated the padding!

Shawn continued to lead the match. Shawn is a once-in-a-lifetime performer, but I couldn't believe that after going through the announcers' table, he could climb to the top rope and performed another moonsault—this time out to the floor. This was a perfect segue to teasing a double count-out, because that meant we would both lose and I'd still have to retire.

This was where the second act of our story began. We established the competitive fire of both our characters and showed that we were willing to pull out all the stops. This was where we really turned it up.

We wanted to emphasize Shawn's conflict. Here he was trying to end the career of the man he tried to emulate his entire professional life. When it came down to it, could the Heartbreak Kid put an end to his idol? For the Nature Boy, it was about whether or not I had one more trick up my sleeve. If I had one more figure four to keep my career alive. It was inner conflict clashing with desperate determination. It was also another example that many times the best performances in our business are rooted in reality. Shawn was conflicted about my retirement, and I didn't want to retire. Shawn was leading the audience on an emotional roller-coaster ride that they had never been on before. He was leading me to a beautiful performance and certainly the most emotional one of my career. I fed off every ounce of adulation and support from the crowd, knowing how much they wanted to see my career live another day.

I was on the canvas. Shawn prepared to deliver his "Sweet Chin Music" Superkick. His hesitation in midmotion resulted in my taking him down and locking in the Figure Four. The crowd erupted, and the conflict within HBK was established.

Our epic tale looked like it was coming to its glorious conclusion. But Shawn reversed the hold, crushing the hopes of the seventy-four-thousand-plus crowd on hand—not to mention fans tuning in around the world—that my career would continue. We kept the intensity up with heated exchanges of offense. Shawn threw in some classic ways to quickly pin an opponent, including some that led to my losing the World Championship a few times: the back slide and the inside cradle. I was fighting for my career. Shawn was in the Figure Four for a second time before using his strength to break the hold.

As for the tricks up my sleeve, I showed that I remained the Dirtiest Player in the Game with two: taking the turnbuckle pad off the bottom rope, teasing that I'd use that to my advantage later, and sticking Shawn with the good ol' thumb to the eye.

Shawn knew just the thing to send a shock wave through the audience— he drilled me with Sweet Chin Music when no one expected it.

Like I said before, in this business, if you're bad long enough, the crowd loves you. When you distract the referee and kick your opponent with a low blow, the audience normally doesn't cheer. At this moment, it was happening to the Heartbreak Kid at the hands of the Nature Boy. And right now, it made sense. The audience understood that I was doing everything I could to avoid closing the door on my career, even if it meant breaking the rules. I felt like they didn't want to see me go.

Shawn did a great job of adding a show of disrespect to prove he was overcoming his character's inner conflict: he locked me in my own finishing move, the Figure Four.

I continued to pull the rabbit out of the hat and pulled his tights on a roll-up. During the months leading up to this match, it had worked really well. But it didn't work that night. It wasn't supposed to. And so we entered the third and final act.

Moments later, Shawn, also known as the Showstopper throughout much of his career, dropped me with an encore performance of his Sweet Chin Music kick. The story continued. Each move we made was like paintbrushes moving with different colors on a canvas. Shawn's facial expressions betrayed his physical and emotional pain from the match and from his conflict about sending the only wrestler he ever idolized into retirement.

I stayed on the mat. The emotion of the last four months, the Hall of Fame the night before, and the fear of the unknown . . . that after this sequence my life would never be the same, it all caught up to me. I could hear the crowd, but it sounded like they were far in the distance. I knew the fate that awaited me. I now clutched the canvas and the final moments of my career. I was gasping for air. I knew what I had to do. As someone who had spent most of his career as a villain, I had to stand up, clench my fists, and show that I wasn't going down without a fight.

Torn between what he wanted to do and what he knew was the right thing, Shawn stood in his familiar position. He said, "I'm sorry. I love you,"* and delivered a third Superkick. I fell on the mat. Referee Charles Robinson's hand touched the canvas for the third consecutive time signifying a three-count.† Shawn kissed my forehead and left the ring. After thirty-five years, the dream was over.

I went to the front row to see my family. I hugged David, I kissed my wife, Tiffany, hugged Reid and Ashley and then Megan. I wanted each of them to know how much I loved them. It meant so much that they were with me for this entire journey. We'd had ups and downs like any family, but the feeling I had being with my children that week was the greatest of my life. It felt like whatever happened was forgiven and we were able to move on together, as a family.

As I walked up the aisle, the ring became smaller each time I turned around. The emotion from the crowd lifted me up. I wanted them to know how much I loved them. Once I walked back through Gorilla, it was gone. There was something else in front of me.

The roster and production crew filled the backstage area to give Shawn and me a standing ovation. I was overwhelmed by their response. Shawn deserves all the credit for the match. He had a vision for what

---

*Shawn Michaels: "There's a part of you that thinks back to your childhood. Ric was such a big part of that. Then, fast-forward twenty-five years, and we're very close friends. This was so important to him. It was so important to me. During my career, sometimes I'd get obsessed with the details of my WrestleMania matches to the point it became unhealthy. The emotions between us for those three months and the match at WrestleMania were real. They were some of the most real emotions I've felt in my life. I kissed Ric at the end of the match. I told him I loved him and that I hoped the match was everything he wanted it to be."

†Charles Robinson: "To be chosen to be the referee for this match was the biggest honor of my career. When we went into the finish sequence, before Shawn landed the Super Kick, I was already in tears. I counted three and covered my face. I rolled out of the ring and walked back to the locker room. It was an amazing match and an incredible moment in history."

this story line needed to be, and we stuck with it every step of the way. I'm so grateful to Shawn for his work, to Michael Hayes for working with us, and to Vince for the support and for making this so special. If everyone felt that way about the match, it must've worked. Right before we parted ways to be with our families, Shawn asked if he could speak to me. We sat down and he took out a box.

Shawn got me a Rolex. It was engraved with the day and the date, and it said, "To be the man, you gotta beat the man." There was a *24* on it in gold and diamonds. He bought himself the same one.* I couldn't believe what I was holding in my hand. It's wasn't the price of the gift; it was the thought behind it. Shawn bought this watch for me and the same exact one for himself. It reminded me of the NWA Championship cuff links Paul gave me. You put those two things together, and it symbolizes the bond you develop with people in our industry. That's what means the most.

After I met with Shawn, there was one other person who asked to see me. It was Vince McMahon. Vince put his arms around me and handed me my WrestleMania check. I couldn't believe what I was seeing. It was the largest amount of money I'd ever received. "Thank you. I can't take this," I told Vince, grabbing a pen and signing it back over to him.

"Are you sure?" he asked me. "I can write off the loss, and I'd never hold it against you."

"Absolutely, I'm sure," I said. "I told you I'd pay you back."

There was a reception that evening after WrestleMania, and then we went to dinner. There was no wild partying like the night before. Tiffany and I were flying to St. Croix the next day, and the kids were going home. Or so I thought.

I got a phone call about 10:00 the next morning. I was told that I needed to be at the arena for *Monday Night Raw* and that my family had

---

*Shawn Michaels: "I wanted Ric to know how much he means to me and that he has a friend for life in me. I asked jewelers I know if they could do this for me with the date and his famous catchphrase. The only thing they couldn't get on there was the *24* in roman numerals. The watch is only so big. When I gave it to him, I didn't think everyone would be waiting for us in the back."

to come too. When we got to the building, I saw people backstage I never expected to see: J. J. Dillon and Tully Blanchard. I knew then that something was up. I just didn't know what.

I was told to say farewell during the final segment of the show. I wanted to let them know how much their support meant to me over the years. And how much I've loved them.

I started by saying, "Last night, I wrestled my last match at Wrestle-Mania. I'll never, ever wrestle in this ring again." The more I spoke, the harder it was because this time, unlike that night in Charlotte, there were no surprise stipulations and no surprise opponents. This was it. I continued, "I'm not sad about not wrestling . . . you should rejoice in the fact that I wrestled in front of more fans, raised more hell, had more fun, and loved all of you every day of my life."

Hearing the audience chant, "Thank you, Ric," and seeing so many people hold up their hands in the symbol of the Four Horsemen is something I'll always remember. Before I left, I wanted to say one last thank-you to the fans for their support and for making me who I am today. We are nothing without the fans, who choose to spend their hard-earned money to attend shows. It's a special bond. Just when I thought the segment was over, in classic WWE fashion, it had only just begun . . .

Paul's music hit. He made his way to the ring. People may have a difficult time believing this, but I didn't know what was going to happen next.

Paul said, "If you think the people here in Orlando are the only ones who want to say, 'Thank you,' if you think the millions of people watching on TV are the only ones who want to say, 'Thank you,' well, my friend, you've got another thing coming." He gave me a hug, and in front of the whole world, he told me he loved me. He went so far as to praise me on his knees. The floodgates opened. I'm glad I didn't make a bet with anyone backstage that I wouldn't cry during the segment. Paul continued and said there were more people who wanted to say thank you. Then he made the sign of the Four Horsemen—which, for the record, if he was in the NWA when we were riding, Paul would've been a Horseman. No doubt about it.

Before I knew it, I was hugging Tully Blanchard, J. J. Dillon, Arn Anderson, and Barry Windham in the center of the ring.

The company truly revered the Horsemen even though we never rode one day on WWE television. It was the first time the five of us had been together since 1988. Barry and Arn worked for the company, but we were never acknowledged as the Horsemen on TV. This was Tully's first time on WWE TV since 1989. J. J. worked behind the scenes for years in WWE, but to my knowledge, he had never appeared on television as J. J. Dillon. Being back in a ring with that group was amazing. It was another moment where if you would've told me in 1988 that one day I'd have my final match at WrestleMania and the next night I'd be with the Horsemen in a WWE ring, I wouldn't have believed you.

Paul served as a master of ceremonies and introduced people from my career who were special to me: my brother from Evolution, Batista; Ricky Steamboat; Harley Race; Greg Valentine, who was my tag team partner in the '70s; and one of my favorite Horsemen from the '90s, Dean Malenko. I was thrilled when Chris Jericho made his way to the ring. Since I returned to WWE, we had formed an awesome friendship. And then there was John Cena, another person who became a great friend. I returned to WWE in 2001; John debuted on *SmackDown* in 2002. I didn't know that the best part was about to come.

Then Paul introduced my family. I never thought, in my wildest dreams, my family would walk the aisle and meet me in the ring like this. It was so special to be able to share all of this with them. I know how much being there meant to them. It was extra special for Reid because of the journey he wanted to take into the business. He knew it was going to be tough, but he was ready.

Shawn was the final person to come to the ring. I knew how much the last three months had meant to him.

Paul had another surprise for me: the entire WWE locker room came out to celebrate my career. The greatest thing as a professional is the respect of your peers. The show was going off the air, and I thought we were calling it a night. But Paul wasn't done yet.

The bells tolled, and the Undertaker's harrowing chords filled the arena. The most respected member of the WWE roster, the man who's just as responsible as anyone else for WWE's success, parted the roster and came into the ring. Undertaker shook my hand and saluted me in the greatest way possible: with thunder and lightning in the arena. He broke character and hugged me. Then he raised my arm to the crowd. It's rare that Undertaker allows the public to see how great a man he is. That memory is one of my most vivid.

I thought the evening was finally over. Then Vince McMahon came to the ring. We hugged like I've worked for him my entire career. He took me to each side of the ring and raised my arm to the fans in the building. That's the type of person Vince is. It was rare that Vince would show his personal side while the show in the arena was still going on. It was another special moment from a man who's always been there for me.

It was time to wind down. I couldn't leave WWE's beautiful canvas without doing one more thing. I laid my jacket on the mat, bounced off the ropes, and dropped an elbow. And then for good measure, I bounced off the ropes at the other end of the ring and landed my knee drop. Now I was ready to exit the squared circle.

It was time to go back to the hotel. I was looking forward to going on vacation with Tiffany and then settling into my new role as an ambassador with WWE. Tomorrow would be the first day of the rest of my life.

4

I WAS IN PARADISE—IT WAS ALL A MIRAGE

I started to panic.

Three days removed from my final match . . .

Sheer terror is the only way I can describe it. I woke up in St. Croix in a luxury hotel suite with a beautiful view of the ocean. It's not like I was waking up in traction in a hospital. But out of nowhere, I felt my heart pounding. I couldn't breathe. It was like the oxygen was being sucked out of the room and the bed was getting smaller. I tried to sit up, but I felt dizzy. My thoughts were racing faster than my heart. I was out of control.

I've had panic attacks before. Sure, there were times in my life when I had self-confidence issues or when I felt anxious before a match, but this was different. All of a sudden, I realized that the world as I knew it had slipped away; my career was behind me, and I let it happen. Wrestling was my life. It was all I'd ever known. Now it was gone. My God, what had I done? What was I going to do?

Tiffany tried to talk me through it. Okay, I was the new WWE ambassador. I'd be making appearances for the company, I'd be on TV every now and then . . . that kind of thing. There were opportunities with large corporate partners outside my work with WWE that I'd be pursuing. And Tiffany and I were exploring some ventures together. But all I kept thinking about was, *What about Ric Flair? What will happen to the Nature Boy? What will happen to me?*

Like many of my contemporaries, I entered the wrestling business so early in life that this was all I really knew how to do. You try to diversify as you progress in your career: make investments, pursue business opportunities, and try new things, which I always did and enjoyed. Wrestling was always where I felt the most comfortable and where I enjoyed the most success. You have to accept that there will be a time when you can no longer perform in the ring on a full-time basis—or at all.

You have to realize that as a person and as a professional, it's time to succeed at something else. It's difficult, because you still have this measuring stick for yourself—an expectation that your level of success outside the industry should be the same as your accomplishments inside it. When people see you, they immediately identify you as the person you used to be. You try to evolve from that persona, but it's a real challenge for people to look at you in an objective way. In one sense, it's a testament to your success. In another, it's like being typecast. I was always comfortable trying new things. At one point, I owned and operated eleven Gold's Gyms. When I sold them, half the money went to my second wife. That's divorce, American-style.

I looked forward to the challenge of finding something new while still being involved with WWE because I loved the company and business so much. At least I thought I looked forward to that challenge—until now.

The person who had the most difficult time seeing me other than the Nature Boy was me. When I think about it, the difference between the name "Nature Boy" Ric Flair and my legal name of Richard Morgan Fliehr is purely semantics.

The essence of this individual, the spirit, and what drives him all come from me.

Ever since high school, I've appreciated nice things. I always liked the idea of being well dressed, having a beautiful watch on my wrist and a shine on my leather shoes. In Minnesota, I was raised in an upper-middle-class neighborhood.

My father served in the US Navy. After he was honorably discharged in 1945, he returned to Minnesota to practice obstetrics and gynecology. He also obtained a master's degree in theater and arts at the University of Minnesota. He was affiliated with the Theatre in the Round Players and directed and performed in several productions while he practiced medicine. In addition, my dad was the president of the Theatre in the Round Players and was the president of the American Association of Community Theatre.

My mother was a writer. She wrote newspaper and magazine articles and coauthored a book about the famous Guthrie Theater in Minneapolis. She was a marketing executive at the Guthrie. I was adopted as a baby, allegedly stolen, in a Tennessee black market baby scandal that received national media attention. When my parents told me that I was adopted, I didn't care. I never had an interest in finding my biological parents. To me, Kay and Dick Fliehr were my parents. They took care of me. They loved me. I loved them. I look back and laugh when I think that they didn't really get a true sense of what they had on their hands until I was a teenager.

I got into a lot of trouble when I was a kid. It was never malicious or violent toward others, but it was mischievous. I drove my motorcycle to the lake when my parents weren't home. When I was fourteen, my mom and dad caught me driving my friends around town in their car. When, as an underaged teen, I was caught trying to buy alcohol, well, that was the last straw.

My parents felt that I needed a more disciplined environment. They sent me to Wayland Academy, an all-boys boarding school in Wisconsin. I was around kids from all over the country who were there for the same reason I was. The main difference between me and them was that they were from very affluent families. They were part of a world that seemed like an elite society to me. I was at the school a few days when someone handed me an ID that said I was eighteen so I could go into bars. I went on spring break with my friends and their families. It was amazing.

During the spring of 1966, I hitchhiked all the way from Minneapolis to Fort Lauderdale, Florida. It was thirty degrees below zero the day I started. I remember stepping off a truck in Macon, Georgia. I had never seen anything like Macon in my life. From there, I hitched a ride down the Florida Turnpike and cruised right into Fort Lauderdale where I met my friend Bruce McArthur.

One year we rented an apartment above a beauty salon. The next year, we rented a place directly over the Elbow Room, which was *the* hot spot in Fort Lauderdale. The year after that, we stayed at Bruce's mom's house. Those were three phenomenal years. Going to Fort Lauderdale as a teenager back then was unbelievable—the weather, the women, the partying—and the atmosphere was something out of a movie; it was anything goes. That was when I really developed a taste for the finer things in life. I liked it.

When I was wrestling for Verne, at the suggestion of Wahoo McDaniel, I moved to Charlotte in April of 1974 to work for Jim Crockett's Mid-Atlantic Championship Wrestling territory. My first wife, Leslie, was still in Minnesota, and I left our car with her. I lived in a bad part of Charlotte where I rented a room for nine dollars a night. I hitchhiked wherever I needed to go. I had to find a place to live and a way to get around—fast.

I went into Jimmy Crockett's office the day after my first match at the Charlotte Coliseum. Jimmy told me he was impressed with my match the night before and asked if there was anything he could do to help me out. I told him I needed to get on my feet and find a place to live and a way to get around. After I told him I wanted to move my family to Charlotte, he gave me a check for $2,000. Within a month from that day, I was making $1,000 a week working for the Crockett family. I paid Jimmy back, and the first thing I did to celebrate my new job and income: I bought a black, four-door Cadillac Fleetwood.

This beauty had power windows, power locks, power seats, cruise control, and an AM/FM radio with an eight-track cassette player. There was nothing like a Cadillac in those days. When it came time to become the Nature Boy, it was like putting my hand in a glove. I liked a certain lifestyle, but I wanted to work for it. Nothing was handed to me.

Looking back to the previous seventy-two hours, I couldn't believe that WWE had taken so much time from *Raw* to pay tribute to me. The goal at the end of the TV show was to make sure that people tuned in the following week, but I wasn't returning the following week. I wasn't coming back as part of a new story line with a new opponent in a few weeks. As an in-ring performer, I was gone. Forever. I was still really touched that the company had given me that moment with my family and my peers, but I also knew that the company and the fans were saying goodbye to the era I represented.

It was there in my hotel room that I realized I was not emotionally prepared to walk away from wrestling. I didn't know how I could make it through a vacation with Tiffany in St. Croix. The rest of the week, I was preoccupied. My mind was elsewhere. I was also trying to prevent another panic attack.

I'd never felt like this before. Not even after a never-ending series of standoffs with WCW executive Jim Herd in the late 1980s.

Jim Herd came into WCW sometime in 1988 or 1989. He was a friend of Jack Petrik, a top executive at Turner Broadcasting. At one point, Jim was the channel manager at the KPLR television station in St. Louis that broadcast the *Wrestling at the Chase* program. When Jack hired him to run WCW he was an executive for Pizza Hut. I'm not saying that someone can't come into our industry from another profession and be a success, but it's important to become familiar with the product, the audience, and your talent roster before making major decisions. So here was a guy who was a station manager at a big TV station that produced a very popular wrestling program, who basically knew nothing about wrestling when he arrived at WCW. Except that his station produced this great show. Not him, the station. That's like someone who worked in the finance department at Nike telling people he worked with the team who created the Air Jordan sneaker.

It seemed everything Jim touched during his tenure with WCW was destined for failure. One of his "big" ideas was to create a tag team who performed under masks; they had a bell in their corner, and they'd ring it when one of them performed an impressive move. He called them the Ding Dongs. They had bells around their wrists and ankles so the audience could hear bells chiming every time Ding or Dong moved. They debuted at Clash of the Champions VII: Guts and Glory and were booed for most of their match. Jim Herd was recruited to Turner Broadcasting to run a major company that was trying to compete with Vince McMahon and the WWE.

Another idea Jim had was to create a tag team called the Humpbacks. The premise—and I don't know if I've ever used a term so loosely—was that since these guys had humpbacks, they couldn't be pinned on the mat. The only way to pin them was to dig a hole outside the ring, and put one of them on his back in the hole.

I remember thinking about the NWA's incredible history and its unbelievable tradition in tag team wrestling: Ole and Gene Anderson, the Briscos, Slaughter and Kernodle, Steamboat and Youngblood, Arn and Ole, the Rock 'n' Roll Express, the Midnight Express, Ivan and Nikita Koloff, Arn and Tully, the Road Warriors, the Freebirds, the Steiner Brothers, Doom . . . and this guy wants to enter a new decade with innovative concepts like the Ding Dongs and Humpbacks? This is what WCW was going to do with Ted Turner's money to compete with Vince?

Jim wanted me to change my name, cut my hair, and put in a diamond earring—all to appeal to a younger demographic. I wanted to make an effort, so I agreed to cut my hair—what a mistake! I remember flying out of the Charlotte airport the following week and no one knowing who I was. I almost lost it right there in the terminal. I couldn't wait for my hair to grow back!

Even if you didn't know anything about our industry, if you're evaluating your talent and looking at my body of work from the first Starrcade to the Four Horsemen to the Great American Bash and War Games events to my matches with Steamboat in '89—why would you tell me I needed to be repackaged as a different character? Jim's idea was to get rid of the name *Ric Flair* and call me Spartacus. I remember Kevin Sullivan saying, "Why don't we take the number seven off Mickey Mantle's uniform while we're at it?"

To make matters worse, I was second-guessed and undermined at every turn. They tried to manipulate me when it came to signing a new contract. I didn't understand why. I was sitting in Daytona, Florida, with Arn

Anderson, Terry Taylor, and Kevin Sullivan, and Jim called and told me that he wanted me to fly to a show and drop the title to Lex Luger.

I said, "We're right in the middle of a contract negotiation. Let's get this worked out."

He said, "No."

His usual demeanor was hollering and screaming, very demanding. I went back and talked to Beth, my wife at the time, and meanwhile, he called me back and said, "You know what? Just come to Columbus, Georgia, and drop it to Barry Windham. We don't want you at the [Great American] Bash."

I made up my mind then and there that it was not worth this. I flew back to Charlotte and left Beth and the kids in Daytona. While I was packing my bags, Herd called me at the house. He said, "Don't worry about it. We don't want you." So between me leaving Florida and flying back home, they had a meeting and said, "Let's just strip him of the championship." I said, "Okay, that's fine." Then he told me he was sending Doug Dillinger over to pick up the belt. I said to make sure he had a check for $25,000 plus interest, because I still had my deposit down from my initial NWA championship run. The NWA was still its own entity. After Crockett sold to Ted Turner, Ted tried to buy the NWA. There were legal reasons that prevented Ted from doing that. The name of Crockett's Saturday program on WTBS, *World Championship Wrestling*, was used as the company name. That's how the company got the letters *WCW*.

When I said, "Send the twenty-five grand plus interest," he said, "Stick it up your ass. Keep the belt." While I didn't listen to the former part of that statement, I was more than happy to oblige with the latter. So I did. The next thing I did was call Vince McMahon.

I asked him if he still wanted me to come. He said yes, and when I told him I had the belt, he said, "Bring that too." I flew to New York, and we made the deal. I was going to be a WWE Superstar. In the meantime, the executives in WCW realized they screwed up. Now everybody was on top of Herd, from Jack Petrik on down. I went home and talked to Beth. WCW decided to fly me to Atlanta. They offered me three times what I'd ever made in my life to stay. But I made my decision based on the fact that, one, I gave Vince my word, and two, my wife, my lawyer, and a bunch of my trusted friends said that once WCW had me locked into a contract, they would never let me go. I might get paid, but I'd be miserable. No, thanks.

So I left. I sent the NWA World Heavyweight Championship to Vince. In July of 1991, the championship appeared on WWE programming in the arms of Bobby "the Brain" Heenan. On the September 9 episode of *Prime Time Wrestling*, I made my WWE debut alongside my great friend the Brain.

When I came home from St. Croix, I met with my agent about our planned projects and appearances. WWE allowed me to do outside work as long as it wasn't televised or recorded for an independent wrestling company and it didn't conflict with WWE bookings. I was not going to do anything that tarnished my legacy. I received offers from promoters all over the world to have "one last match." This included a friend in Japan who offered me a huge six-figure salary for a ten-day tour of Japan. And I knew we could have great matches together. I turned it down. I turned them all down. Nothing was going to take away from the prestige and splendor of that WrestleMania XXIV weekend. Nothing.

I so appreciated that WWE would even have the conversation with me about balancing outside opportunities with contracted work for the company. I felt an enormous outpouring of goodwill from the public and different companies after my match with Shawn in Orlando. It gave me an enormous sense of pride. I was even honored on the floor of the US House of Representatives by Sue Myrick of Charlotte. Within a couple of weeks of being home, I made my first appearance as a WWE ambassador in Washington, D.C. WWE won an award at the GI Film Festival, an event that celebrates the lives of veterans in films, for its annual Tribute to the Troops.

Something else I looked forward to was continuing my son Reid's training for a career in the business. From an early age, Reid, more than any of my other kids, loved wrestling. Reid, whom I called Champ, jumped

at the opportunity to come to shows with me. He moved even faster at the possibility of being on TV as part of a story line, along with being seen getting out of a limo with me or being at ringside.

Reid was a superb athlete. The sport he excelled in more than the others was amateur wrestling. He won the AAU National Tournament when he was a child. He wore that medal around his neck when he appeared in the ring beside Arn Anderson on *Monday Nitro*. When Reid was twelve, he was invited to Japan for the Japan Nationals by the legendary professional wrestler and great amateur competitor Dick "the Destroyer" Beyer. Reid did a homestay in Japan for ten days and was part of Team Destroyer. He won a silver medal. Throughout high school, my son was one of the top-four amateur wrestlers in the country in his weight class.

Reid graduated from Blair Academy, one of the preeminent private schools in the United States, which also boasted one of the best amateur wrestling programs anywhere.

After his freshman year of college, he wanted to pursue a full-time career in the business. I was hesitant because I wanted him to finish school.

But if he applied himself like he had to amateur wrestling, he would make it.

In my career, there have only been a few truly great amateur wrestlers. Two who come to mind are Jack Brisco and Kurt Angle, who were able to make the transition from being great amateur champions and standout performers to World Champion professionals.

Reid understood that he needed to combine the discipline, conditioning, and athleticism from his amateur background with charisma, speaking ability on the microphone, and the ability to tell a story. Reid was so quick-witted that I knew it was only a matter of time before he was, as we like to say in our line of work, "talking them [the fans] into the building." And his athletic gifts and work ethic could back it up.

Given the experience my son David had in WCW in the late '90s, I wanted to make sure Reid was introduced to the industry correctly and had proper training so that when the time came, he would have the best opportunity to showcase his skills to be considered for a WWE contract.

David was a great athlete growing up. He liked wrestling but did not express a strong desire to enter the business, which was fine. He didn't have to. While I was in WCW, Eric Bischoff asked me if he could invite David to be part of something on TV. David said yes. It was supposed to be a onetime thing.

David did such a good job, and it was so well received by the audience, that he was asked to do something else. He also received a nice check, which attracted him to the business. I was happy that he was paid a nice amount of money and that he wanted to pursue wrestling, but he never had the chance to properly train. David had a crash course, and when you're on TV every week, your life becomes a whirlwind, especially on live TV. He wasn't able to hone the skills that are needed to reach a certain level. I wish he had an opportunity to learn the business first. Instead, he came in on the fly and was more of a TV character who played his part very well. After WCW, David trained in WWE's OVW development system, traveled to Japan, and lived in Puerto Rico for two years while wrestling.

I was proud of David and the job he did working with Undertaker to help set the stage for our match at WrestleMania X8. I think by the time he got to OVW, there was so much talent there, and so much talent on WWE's main roster between WWE Superstars and performers who came to the company from WCW and ECW, the company was already loaded with talent who were under multiyear contracts.

Contrary to what people think, just because someone is the child of a former wrestler or promoter, that doesn't mean he or she gets a contract. That may help get him or her a chance to submit footage or receive a try-out, but when it comes time for WWE to sign someone to a contract, none of that matters. You either perform or you don't. And the generational kids have it harder because, one, they need to prove right away that they belong and aren't getting preferential treatment and that they don't expect any, and two, if a family member achieved any type of success in the business, he or she would constantly be compared to that person. Like any other form of sport or entertainment, it's very difficult for children with famous parents to get a fair shot, and succeed, in the same industry.

I think of the incredible paths blazed by second-generation stars who broke their families' molds in the business: Nick Bockwinkel, Dory Funk Jr. and Terry Funk, the Guerreros, the Von Erichs, Curt Hennig, Ted DiBiase, Randy Savage, Barry Windham, and Bret Hart. Then you have third-generation Superstars like The Rock and Randy Orton. All these performers walked a tough road to reach success.

I could spend days listing all the kids who tried to enter the business who either failed or couldn't step out of their parents' shadow. I think of Dusty's son Dustin, a great talent. For years, Dustin couldn't reach that next level because people saw his persona as the Natural, as a good performer, but a younger version of his dad. Dustin was stuck. That wasn't his fault or his dad's. Dusty's one of the greatest of all time. It wasn't until Dustin came to WWE for a second time, donned a gold-and-black spandex outfit, and became Goldust that all his range of talents as a performer were fully appreciated.

I brought Reid to someone I trusted, close to home, who would train him the right way and help him develop a strong base in the fundamentals. That was George South.

For years, George was a staple of Crockett television and an enhancement talent (a wrestler whose primary role is to lose matches) to the stars of the NWA. He worked for WWE too. In the ring, George could do anything and do it very well. He didn't have lots of charisma, so the interview and showmanship skills were not there for him to make his way up the card. But if you needed someone to look great on television, someone to get experience in the ring, or just to show a great match on television, George was the guy you wanted standing on the other side of the ring. He was the best.

It was toward the end of 1988 on the WTBS Saturday morning World Championship Wrestling show—the classic 9:05 a.m. EST time slot. Around that period, I didn't wrestle full matches on that show very often, but I did interview segments. Dusty and I got into an argument before we went on the air. I told him that if I was having a match, I wanted someone who could go in the ring with me. I wanted George. Before we went out there, I told him, "Buddy, today you're Ricky Steamboat."

From the opening bell, we were off to the races. We exchanged holds and chopped each other like lumberjacks cutting down redwoods. I did the flip over the turnbuckle, and George even slammed me off the top rope. We went almost fifteen minutes. Dusty yelled at me, "What are you doing?" I told him I wasn't going to wrestle on the program and beat a guy with George's skill in one or two minutes. No way. Sorry.

Reid spent a lot of time training with George at his facility in Charlotte. George also trained Steamboat's son, Richie. I also sent Reid to Missouri to train with Harley Race. I wanted to make sure he was learning different techniques and styles to make him more of a complete performer in the ring. I wanted to make sure Reid was ready for this and knew, up front, how hard it would be. Not like when I walked into Verne Gagne's barn in Minnesota and thought I was going to toss some guys around and that would be it.

The next stop for Reid was Tampa, Florida. WWE moved their developmental system to the Sunshine State to a place called FCW. Reid was there for a full workout: conditioning drills, work in the ring, and to meet with the training staff. As expected, they threw everything at him—free squats, push-ups, sit-ups, running the ropes, drop-down drills, you name it, and Reid did it all that day. And he was awesome. We flew back to Charlotte and were told we'd get a call soon with the news. Either Reid would get a developmental contract, or he needed to continue his training elsewhere and come back.

I think all this was hard for my son David. This was another instance of my being able to spend more time with Reid than I had with him. I regret that. David deserved better.

A week or so after our trip to Tampa, I got a call from Stephanie McMahon. Stephanie told me that Reid's workout was, from a physical standpoint, viewed as a success. Stephanie added how impressed everyone was with him physically and how well he carried himself personally. I knew this, but it felt great hearing someone else say those things about my son. Especially from someone like Stephanie, who's a fourth-generation member of the McMahon family. What she said next was something I never expected to hear in a million years.

"Ric, Reid failed the drug test."

I stood there. Silent. I replied, "What? There must be a mistake." I didn't know all the things that could come up as a positive or a false positive. All I knew was how hard Reid worked to get to that point. We scheduled a second test to rule out the possibility of a false positive.

The next time my phone rang from a WWE number, I thought it was going to be regarding my next ambassador appearance. Instead, it was an invitation to appear on *Raw* during the story line between Shawn and Chris Jericho. Even with the work I was doing, being away from everyone at TV for three months felt like an eternity.

Following our career-threatening match in Orlando, Shawn entered into story lines with new opponents based on him being the one who retired me. Batista confronted Shawn and said he took Shawn retiring me and calling me Old Yeller personally, and that Shawn was selfish. Batista continued and said he should've talked me out of doing the match at WrestleMania and that he'd trusted Shawn to do the right thing, and that he'd never trust Shawn again. WWE let fans text their vote if they felt Shawn did the right thing in retiring me, which was a fun way to incorporate the fans in the story line. Batista and Shawn had their match at Backlash. Chris Jericho was the special guest referee.

The story, as it is known to do, took an interesting twist when, during the match, Shawn faked an injury to help secure a victory. Since Chris was the referee, this gave Chris a superb entry point into the story and a way to be at odds with Shawn. On Jericho's talk show segment, "The Highlight Reel," he berated Shawn with insults and said he was a poor excuse for a human being. The final wave of the attack came in the physical form when Chris attacked Shawn. The parting shot was when he threw Shawn into the flat-screen TV and shattered the screen into pieces. Chris did a tremendous job of assuming the role of ruthless villain.

The next week, Chris told the fans he was punishing Shawn for their sins and what he was going to do to Shawn was their fault. It was such a well-delivered interview. Chris continued to taunt Shawn. He continued to insult the crowd. And that's where I came in.

I was back at Gorilla Position, waiting to make my entrance. I had that familiar feeling: goose bumps. I waited for my cue, and when my music hit, it was like I never left. Walking down that aisle to the ring, feeding off the energy from the crowd, it felt tremendous. I had to remain composed during the fans' standing ovation. Chris and I had to go to work. In this instance, since I couldn't have a match with him in the ring, I did the next best thing—I challenged him to a fight in the parking lot. I dropped my famous elbow on my jacket, rolled out of the ring, and walked up the ramp, through the backstage area, and outside. Chris followed me, and right before he walked through the doors of the arena, he crossed paths with Paul. It was a great stare-down between the two. This set them up to have a match later that night, and in the story line, Vince kicked me out of the building, since I was retired. I was just getting my engine running when my part came to an end, but it felt good to be back. Through my performance, I wanted to do my part to further what Chris and Shawn were doing and to let the fans know how much that ovation meant to me.

The match Chris and Shawn had at WrestleMania XIX was phenomenal. Two of the very best had what many consider to be the match of the night that year. Their work together now would be some of the best of the year.

I returned to *Raw* the next week to be onstage with Vince. This was during his "McMahon's Million Dollar Mania." Each week, Vince awarded a lucky caller his own money, right there on live television. At the end of the segment, Vince would give away a total of $1 million. Fans had to register through WWE's website and then watch *Raw*. While the audience and everyone at WWE were happy to see me on television two weeks in a row, there was one person who wasn't.

Things became tense with Tiffany at home. At first, the company flew her first class with me to the different ambassador appearances. Some of the guys asked why they couldn't have the travel for their wives paid for by the company and I could. Vince did that for me as a favor. I understood that gesture couldn't cause unrest with anyone else and that I had to go on these appearances by myself or pay for her to come with me. She didn't like being left home. When you bring your significant other on the road with you, or during special times of the year, they think it's like that all the time, that there are parties, receptions, and huge dinners like at WrestleMania weekend, or when I made ambassador appearances.

The "When does Ric Flair end and Richard Fliehr begin?" conversation continued to come up. Even when it wasn't brought up verbally, I could feel her frustration. It became a constant struggle. Tiffany felt the time had come for me to be comfortable in public as Richard Fliehr. I understood what she meant. I didn't feel she understood the complete meaning, the gravity, of letting the Nature Boy go. To me, without Ric Flair, there was no success for me as a person. If I couldn't be Ric Flair, then who would people want to see at appearances, who would walk out in front of a capacity crowd on WWE programming when my music hit?

Tiffany expected me to retire, do some appearances, go on WWE TV once in a while, and the rest of the time I'd be home with her. I think she also felt like that was going to happen immediately. I have to be able to be me. Whether I'm working or have a day off, I'm up at 6:00 in the morning, ready to go. That's who I am. The thought of sitting home sounded more like a prison sentence than a luxury that I earned thanks to years of hard work. One night we got into an argument, and I told her, "I'll be Richard Fliehr when I'm dead. How's that?"

There was something else I was dealing with in my marriage. This was far beneath the surface, something that very few people knew about.

When Tiffany and I began dating, I moved her from San Diego back to Charlotte. Since this was a major sign of a commitment from me to her, I asked Tiffany if she'd had any relationships or close ties with anyone in Charlotte, before our marriage, who I'd know. We weren't high school kids. Obviously, she had other relationships. At that point, I had lived in Charlotte about thirty years. I wanted to know if there were people I knew in the city: people I did business with, professional associates, organizations I supported, and even on a personal level. I wasn't asking so I could criticize or judge; I wanted to know ahead of time so that there wouldn't be any uncomfortable situations. She told me, "Oh, no, I would've told you that. I wasn't with anyone in Charlotte. After you ended things the first time, I was heartbroken, and I moved out here [to California]."

I moved her back to Charlotte, and we got married in 2006. One night we went to Morton's Steakhouse for dinner. We saw a friend of mine, and right away I could sense something wasn't right. Something was just off. I didn't say anything.

Contrary to what people may think who've seen me on TV, away from the cameras, I'm not a confrontational person. For better or worse, my biggest thing was that I always wanted to have fun in whatever I was doing. I had no problem over the course of my life leading the charge to the bar, having too much fun, like one time I was having dinner at the Palm in Charlotte with "Mean" Gene and the drinks were flowing. For laughs, I took my jacket off, took of my shirt, and really turned things up—and off came the pants, right there in the restaurant. I did that a few other times when I was out with Gene. He ended up coining the phrase, "Uh-oh, there goes the laundry." That's a different type of scene—of having too much fun. But I wouldn't cause a scene, like getting into an argument, in a restaurant over something personal.

The next day, I was flying to Europe for a WWE tour. Tiffany was flying there the next day to meet me. Before I left, I called my friend we'd seen at Morton's. I said, "I know this sounds crazy, but were you with Tiffany at any point?"

He answered, "Do you want to know the truth?"

I said, "Yes. What the hell's the matter with you? Of course I want to know the truth."

He told me that while Tiffany lived in San Diego, he flew out there once and spent a few days with her. This was someone who I thought was a good friend of mine. I said okay, got on the plane, and let it go. I thought that it wasn't necessary to start an argument, and again, we weren't kids.

Over time, when we attended different functions or went out to dinner, there was an awkward feeling whenever we saw certain people. That continued to intensify. It reached a point where it felt like the floodgates had opened. Each time it happened, I asked Tiffany about it. Her answer was always the same. There was nothing for me to be concerned about. I didn't understand why she wasn't being truthful. We were friends before we entered into a relationship. We told each other we were going to be together and that we wanted to get married. We went to see a minister. We went to counseling. I thought that would make things better. It didn't.

As months went by, I learned about relationships Tiffany had before we decided to see each other. The more time went on, the more of these relationships I discovered. I was not told about them and learned about them in the moment. These embarrassing run-ins with former "friends" kept happening. For instance, I found out that she had a relationship with one of Ashley's friends' fathers. I know I had my own faults, but that was something I just couldn't get past. Two years after we said, "I do," in what I thought was the perfect wedding ceremony to the perfect person, we separated. This was not what I had in mind for our wedding anniversary.

Two anniversaries were approaching that brought me great sadness. Because of the camaraderie in our profession, whenever someone passes away, it's like losing a family member. Even if you're not necessarily close with the person who passed, you feel for them and their families a little bit more, because you know the time away they've spent from them. In these instances, I was close with the people who passed away a year earlier.

I met Sherri Martel in the '80s. Sherri was trained by Fabulous Moolah and became a star in Verne's AWA. In the ring, Sherri was another per-former who was so tough and so talented that she was as successful in Japan as she was in North America. She was the WWE Women's Cham-pion in the late '80s before becoming a valet—and man, did Sherri rule the outside part of the ring.

As a manager, Sherri was a wildcat on camera. She was so good as a manager that I think some people forget how good she was in the ring as a performer. She'd jump off the top rope, leap off cages, dive off the ring apron. She'd do anything to make the match more exciting and make the audience believe that the hero was about to face the ultimate destruction. Sherri was the perfect villainess and added so much to the character and presentation of so many great performers: Randy "Macho Man" Savage, "Million Dollar Man" Ted DiBiase, Shawn Michaels, Harlem Heat, and, luckily for me, me.

Whether she was in the ring as a competitor or on the outside as some-one's manager, as a performer, Sherri was way ahead of her time. On a personal level, Sherri was a wonderful woman who was kind, loyal, and tough as nails. Sherri could be the belle of the ball in an evening gown at a black-tie event or run the pool table at a bar and raise hell with the rest of the boys.

I was so happy when she was inducted into the 2006 WWE Hall of Fame. I thought her speech that night in Chicago was one of the best the Hall of Fame has ever heard. Like so many others we've lost, I wish I could tell Sherri one more time how much she meant to me over the course of my career. I always think of her around this time of year, just a few months from the WWE Hall of Fame ceremony. Sherri was a wonderful friend.

There are certain things I'll never be able to understand. The Benoit family tragedy is one that will stay with me for the rest of my life. It still doesn't seem real.

I met Nancy Benoit in 1979. She worked in Florida Championship Wrestling. She married my close friend Kevin Sullivan, who was a top villain for the Florida territory. Kevin was also a great mind behind the scenes when it came to story lines and developing characters, especially villains.

Nancy was Kevin's valet in those days. After she appeared as "fan" Robin Green in WCW, Nancy became Woman and managed the tag team called Doom—Ron Simmons and Butch Reed. Shortly after that, Nancy and I worked together. She was part of ECW before returning to WCW, where we worked together again.

Nancy met Chris Benoit while they worked together in a story line in WCW. There was speculation about the timing of her relationship with Chris and her separation from Kevin. I never interjected myself into that. I certainly wasn't the person to stand on a pedestal and pontificate about relationships. Early in my career, I learned how harmful rumors could be to someone's career and personal life. Nancy eventually left the business.

I first met Chris in the early '90s when he made appearances for WCW. Chris trained in the famous Hart Dungeon in Calgary, Alberta, Canada, and in the New Japan Dojo. During those years, the dojos in Japan endured some of the most physically rigorous training anyone in our profession could imagine. Chris loved the business. When he started out, he wanted to emulate wrestler Dynamite Kid. Chris's star shone brightly in Japan. His work there got him noticed by executives in WWE and WCW. Paul Heyman brought him to ECW, where many of the fans followed the international wrestling scene. I thought it was a great move by WCW to sign Chris to an exclusive contract in 1995.

At that time, WCW also had a working relationship with New Japan Pro Wrestling. Chris was a gentleman, had incredible dedication to perfecting his craft, and was very easy to work with, behind the scenes and in front of the cameras. Arn and I thought so much of him that we made him a member of the Four Horsemen. He was one of the younger talents—along with the Giant (Big Show in WWE), Chris Jericho, and Eddie Guerrero—I hoped could work for WWE and benefit his career.

Nancy and Chris got married, and Chris went to WWE. I was happy to work with him again when I returned to the company. The match between Chris, Shawn, and Paul at WrestleMania XX was phenomenal. It was everything I thought it would be and more.

I loved Nancy and Chris, and so did my family. I can't count how many times Nancy and Chris watched all four of my children at different times over the years. The Chris Benoit I knew always talked about his family. Chris was always so proud to show pictures of Nancy and their son Daniel, and his children from a previous marriage, David and Megan. I never thought Chris could take Nancy's and Daniel's lives. And then end his own. The Fayette County Sheriff's office in Georgia ruled the case a double homicide-suicide. I'll never be able to understand what happened in their home over that three-day period.

What upset me a great deal was the motley crew of random people from our business who commented on what they thought happened to Nancy, Chris, their son, Daniel, and their tragic deaths. When there is heartbreak involving people in our profession, the media seeks anyone who may have had a cup of coffee in it to comment on people and situations he or she knows very little about. A few people did an excellent job in speaking about their lives. I wish there could've been a group of us designated to speak to the press so that people could learn about Nancy and Chris from those who knew them best professionally rather than from irresponsible sources who wanted to get themselves back on television.

Each time I added an appearance date to my work calendar, I thought of the words spoken by my close friend Jim Ross: "Business is about to pick up." Endorsement deals were signed with Coca-Cola, Walmart, and the North Carolina Education Lottery. Talks began with NASCAR too. I also enjoyed working with independent wrestling promotions to do autograph signings and Q&A events around the United States, Canada, and Europe. It was exciting and something I was grateful for. Things began to go a little too well. I'd give them as much advance notice as I could when something was brought to me. I tried to be extra selective in what I did because I knew how big of a deal it was that WWE was allowing me to work when it went outside the scope of our agreement.

The company believed that my work with so many independent wrestling companies was indirectly endorsing them, which I understood.

I didn't interpret it that way because I'd do one appearance and then the next day or week I'd do another. I wasn't working for just one promotion; I looked at it as an income opportunity: I would earn a minimum of $20,000 to sign autographs and take picture for two hours. It's one of the reasons why the ambassador role worked so well. I loved being around people and meeting fans. This allowed me to do both, but it seemed that something would have to give.

There was discussion of a reality TV show. I wanted to explore the idea to see how it could be different from other shows in the reality genre. It became more challenging to balance my contractual obligations to WWE and do outside appearances and projects without conflict.

But if this was the caliber of work being offered at the beginning of my retirement, what could I accomplish once I got into a groove and showed what I could really do? Professional sports teams also contacted me about motivational speaking to their players. Fortune 500 companies made the same inquiry, inviting me to speak to their sales and marketing divisions.

I was still so torn about my retirement from WWE and missing the day to day of being in the business. Now I was faced with another type of conflict. I worked with my Legacy Talent agent, Melinda, to create a portfolio of high-profile opportunities that were great for me, and I maintained WWE's standard as a publicly traded global entertainment company. My appearances with independent wrestling promotions were with reputable companies and were so much fun. They were great opportunities to meet the most dedicated wrestling fans in local markets. I would never have had these exciting opportunities if not for WWE, Shawn, and this storybook retirement.

But I needed to make sure that the work I was doing was rewarding and that I could maintain a certain income level. Especially for someone like me who has been an independent contractor for his entire adult and professional life. Even with a contract, that is a mind-set I never lost—if you don't work, you don't get paid. After several conversations with WWE and trying to reach a happy medium, we realized that my being under contract to WWE was not in our mutual interest. On August 3, we agreed to end our contract. WWE would still call me for TV-related opportunities, but everything going forward would be on a pay-per-appearance basis.

For the first time since November of 2001, I was no longer under contract to WWE. I wasn't completely sure if this was the right thing to do, but I knew that if there was a time to gamble on myself—on Ric Flair—this was it.

5

WHAT A YEAR

There's no way I could've anticipated what happened.

December 2008

D ating back to the early years of the business and wrestling territories, the holiday season always meant huge shows. Some were called Holiday Spectaculars, especially on Thanksgiving and Christmas Nights.

One of the most special is 1983's Starrcade. It emanated from the Greensboro Coliseum on Thanksgiving Night and was broadcast on closed-circuit television. Starrcade's card was loaded with top talent from all over the United States and featured several classic matches: Ricky Steamboat and Jay Youngblood versus the Brisco Brothers, Abdullah the Butcher against Carlos Colón, the Dog Collar Match between "Rowdy" Roddy Piper and Greg Valentine, and in the main event, it was me versus Harley Race inside a steel cage for the NWA World Heavyweight Championship. Advertised as a "Flare for the Gold," the legendary "Big Thunder" Gene Kiniski was the special guest referee.

The event's overwhelming success ensured my status as the long-term NWA Champion and cemented Crockett's Mid-Atlantic Championship Wrestling as the premiere NWA territory. Superstation WTBS and Starrcade later served as a catalyst for Crockett's foray into turning Mid-Atlantic into a nationally touring wrestling company under the NWA banner. It was our precursor to WrestleMania. It didn't last, but we had a lot of fun in the early days of the Starrcade events.

The holidays continue to provide memorable moments for me. I returned to WWE in November of 2001, and we'd launched the retirement story line the previous November. This year held a special significance because of my career change. I was still coming to terms with that. I was extremely pleased with my company endorsements and motivational speaking events, but I missed being in the business every day. I missed the camaraderie. I missed the feeling that you can only experience when you're performing in front of a live audience.

Looking back on how the year began, I didn't think I'd be where I was. Looking at how it was ending, there were things that were professionally exciting, but things that personally concerned me. I was trying to make sense of what happened with Tiffany. There were two people I needed to tend to right away: my youngest children, Ashley and Reid.

From the moment I held Ashley in my arms, she was my princess, and I spoiled her. I spoiled all my kids. I wanted them to have the best of everything and not worry about ever needing anything. Ashley and I are probably more alike in some ways than me and my other kids. I don't love one more than the other, but Ashley and I have always had a special connection.

Since her mother and I divorced, our relationship has experienced some bumps in the road. I know Ashley felt conflicted about Beth, her mother, being alone after I left and if she should be upset with me for that. It was also difficult for her to see me with another woman and the thought of having a stepmom. It took a long time for things to be comfortable around Tiffany, and now that relationship was ending. I never expected that to happen either.

Ashley began dating a guy she met when she was home in Charlotte on break from school. Within months of meeting him, she left school, quit the volleyball scholarship she worked so hard for, and left everything behind just to be with him. They moved in together and lived in Chapel Hill, North Carolina. That's when I realized how wrong things really were. Everything happened so fast. There was no talking to her about it or talking her out of it. All attempts to reason with her fell on deaf ears.

There's a point where your kids reach a certain age and you can speak to them, but if they're over eighteen, they're adults. Was I going to ground her? I had to accept that this was what she wanted to do. This was the person she wanted to be with, regardless if I approved or not, kind of like the way she and her siblings had to understand and respect my choices whether they agreed with them or not. I was not going to disown my daughter because she made a couple of decisions I didn't approve of.

One weekend, I visited them in Chapel Hill. Ashley, her boyfriend, and his sister were my guests for dinner at Top of the Hill Restaurant. We all had a great time and looked forward to spending the next day with each other.

About 2:00 a.m., there was a commotion in the living room. Ashley and her boyfriend were raising their voices at each other. I didn't want to interfere. The shouting escalated. I went into the living room to see if I could help calm things down.

"Guys, what's going on?" I asked.

He yelled, "Your daughter—!" and that's all I had to hear. My daughter did everything for this guy. He could barely hold a job. I got up and said, "Do you think you're a man behaving this way? You're not a man." Ashley's boyfriend exploded in a fury and started throwing punches at me. I just stood there. I knew her boyfriend had emotional troubles. He lost his father suddenly about two years earlier. And that night, we all had a great time and had some drinks at the restaurant. Ashley became very upset and tried to defuse the situation. When I thought things were starting to calm down, the police arrived, and all hell broke loose.

Ashley was trying to stop the altercation and calm her boyfriend down. She became more upset. This was not the type of setting she was used to. When one of the police officers entered her space and asked her to put her hands behind her back, I heard her say, "Don't touch me. I said don't touch me." The next thing I knew, the officer used a Taser to subdue her. She was brought to the floor and taken into police custody in handcuffs. Her boyfriend assaulted me, I had bruises on my face, and somehow my daughter, who tried to be a peacekeeper, was arrested. That wasn't the worst of it.

The media got involved and selectively included details to create a story. All of a sudden, Ashley's police department mug shot was plastered across local news stations, newspapers, and online. Somehow, she became the focal point of the story. Ashley never got into trouble growing up. When she was in high school, it was a big deal if she came home past curfew. Once, she threw a party when Beth and I came home, and I took the cases of beer away from the kids who were there. That was it. This was not her element. It upset me to see my daughter in this situation.

I didn't press charges against her boyfriend. I wanted this to be resolved privately. My concern became my daughter's well-being. I knew that sometimes she and her boyfriend had arguments—every couple does—but his behavior was deeply troubling. I was very concerned for her, but she assured me that this was something that had never happened before and that I didn't have to worry. Her boyfriend and I spoke privately, and he apologized. I did the only thing I could do. I accepted his apology and prayed that what Ashley told me was true—that this was a bizarre occurrence and it would never happen again. Even though I didn't want my daughter with this person, I didn't feel like I had any control over the situation. I wasn't going to stop having a relationship with my daughter.

I continued to enjoy making appearances for independent promotions. It gave me the opportunity to meet fans and see friends I used to work with whom I hadn't seen in many years. It hurt me to see some of them going through tough times because they made certain life choices, but that never diminished what they accomplished professionally.

Over the previous ten to fifteen years, the old wrestling territory system had been romanticized, maybe even to a fault. I understand people look back fondly on a great time in their lives, but for the most part, the territories were great if you were a top guy. If you were performing in the opening match or somewhere along the bottom of the card, most of the time, you were starving. With the business model that Vince McMahon created in the '80s with licensing (action figures, video games, a home video line, lunch boxes, etc.) along with merchandising (T-shirts and jackets, to hats and foam fingers), you could be a performer in one of the early matches on the WWE card and make a nice living. That was one of the reasons WCW relied on high-priced, guaranteed contracts. They didn't have anything like that for years, and when they got around to it, it was rudimentary compared to WWE's generous offerings. I've always said that if Vince McMahon had the Four Horsemen, we'd still be riding high today.

The best part about the territory system was that performers had different places to learn their craft. They had the opportunity to work with different opponents with their own in-ring style in front of a variety of live audiences. These guys also had more than one viable place to work. Our industry, like others, has evolved. If people still wanted to pay to see what the territories offered, then Vince's move to make WWE a nationally recognized company in the '80s wouldn't have succeeded. Vince put it all on the line to go national and make WrestleMania a reality. It was the gamble of a lifetime, and it paid off a hundredfold.

As I looked ahead to the month of December, I had an exciting event to prepare for, though it came with mixed emotions: the thrill and concern of Reid's in-ring wrestling debut.

To mark the occasion, a local promoter in Charlotte had an idea that my sons, Reid and David, should work as a tag team with me as their manager. I thought it was a great idea but wanted to make sure they had opponents who were experienced, were known to fans, and were guys I could trust to be safe with my sons. I called two guys I knew were up for the task, and they couldn't have been more excited to help: Brian Knobbs and Jerry Sags, the Nasty Boys. And they weren't coming alone. Knobbs and Sags were coming to Charlotte with their manager, "The Mouth of the South" Jimmy Hart, and of course that meant Jimmy would be bringing his megaphone.

The Nasty Boys are known as one of the toughest, craziest teams to come down the pike. Knobbs and Sags worked for Verne in the AWA, Jerry Lawler in Memphis, Eddie Graham in Florida, WCW, and WWE. I've had so many laughs with the Nasty Boys in all sorts of establishments all over the world. One time, I thought I was going to kill Knobbs. That was in WCW. We're on a plane flying to Europe. I told my son David that I was going to take a nap and asked him to make sure Knobbs didn't do anything or start joking around. My son David dated Stacy Keibler at the time, so I guess I should've known his focus was going to shift rapidly. Could you blame him? Then I asked Lex Luger to watch Knobbs. After a little while, Lex went off and did his own thing.

I woke up in London, and everyone on the plane was laughing at me. I said to myself, "What the hell happened?" I felt my eyebrows. My right eyebrow was gone. Totally gone. The second I started screaming, Knobbs came out of the bathroom, and both of his eyebrows were gone. He said, "Goddamn that [Curt] Hennig. Wait until I see him." I couldn't believe it. This guy was so set on playing a joke on me and shaving off one of my eyebrows that he shaved off both of his so I'd think Curt had played a joke on both of us. In a twisted way, you have to admire someone's commitment to pulling a prank when he'd go so far as to do it to himself, though I didn't feel that way at the time.

Before I could think about this special tag team match, something weighed heavily on me. It was another matter that I hoped to resolve privately. Reid failed a second WWE drug test shortly after the first one during the summer. This time, the numbers for an illegal substance were even higher. When I received another phone call from Stephanie McMahon, I couldn't believe it. It was such troubling news. After I hung up, I tried to gather my thoughts. When I spoke to Reid, he had an answer for everything. I didn't understand it because he trained so hard. I knew he wanted to be in FCW. No one questioned his ability, potential, and positive attitude. He was so respectful to coaches and FCW staff. We needed to straighten things out with him personally before we could even consider going back and asking WWE for another chance.

I felt that if he was with me, I could see him and know what he was doing. I would know who he was with. Beginning on the independents where he could learn was not WWE, but it was the next best thing, besides going to Japan. For his event in Charlotte, it was extra special that his brother, David, was his tag team partner. After David's tenure in OVW, Puerto Rico, and Japan, he had developed into a heck of a wrestler.

I think it was a matter of timing as far as working in WWE. He left the business and is very happy in his life, which is the most important thing. He has a beautiful wife and family. I know a lot of fans looked forward to seeing him in the match. I hoped David was going to be able to have fun tonight.

The event was at Vance High School. Rock 'n' Roll Express versus the Midnight Express, and Ricky Steamboat's son, Richie, were also on the card. We made a special announcement the day of the event. I got a phone call a few weeks before from a friend who said he heard about what we were doing for Reid. He said he didn't want to be paid to appear or have his travel taken care of; he just wanted to be part of my son's first match. So we added a special guest referee to the match: Hulk Hogan.

This was a great way to end the year—in a ring, in Charlotte, with both my sons. Sitting at ringside was Reid's mom, Beth, and his sisters, Megan and Ashley. There was a special feeling inside that building, which now overflowed with 1,800–2,000 fans in the audience. It was time for the main event.

The Nasty Boys entered the ring. Knobbs grabbed the microphone and used his natural gift of gab to dump on Charlotte as a city and referred to the people in the audience as "idiots." Talk about hearing a chorus of boos. It was tremendous.

The Hulkster came out to a hero's welcome and wore the referee's striped shirt well. Standing behind the curtain with my sons as they waited to be introduced was wonderful. Of all the emotions I felt over the previous twelve months:—anticipating my backstage cues during my farewell tour, the WWE Hall of Fame, going through Gorilla the next day at WrestleMania, and now, standing behind the curtain at this event with David and Reid as a tag team . . . well, it had to be one of the most amazing nights of my life.

The match was so much fun. Knobbs and Sags were great villains. They broke the rules with the greatest of ease, taunted the crowd, and mixed it up with the "immortal" special guest referee. And you know it's going to be a fun night when Jimmy Hart's at ringside. I got involved too, as any father in his sons' corner would.

I thought David and Reid worked well together and did a nice job working with Knobbs and Sags. They were skilled in the ring and tough enough to hang with two of the best brawlers our business has ever known. In the end, the hometown boys won. They each had a Nasty Boy locked in the Figure Four. After a big boot on the Mouth of the South from the Hulkster, I came in and locked Jimmy Hart in and made it a trifecta of figure fours. The memorable night ended with me, David, Reid, and Hulk standing in the ring with our arms raised. I stepped out of the ring and saw an image I never thought I would: my sons as a tag team standing with Hulk Hogan as the referee. What a night. I hoped that the positive energy and the thrill of performing would remind Reid of all the promise he had as a wrestler and how many people loved and supported him. I felt that better things were ahead as he began to embark on his journey and follow his dream.

Two days later, fans heard my name on *Monday Night Raw*. My match with Shawn from WrestleMania won the Slammy Award for "Match of the Year." If things worked out the way I expected, fans would soon see me walk that aisle on *Raw*.

The next week, I flew to Hollywood for the premiere of a new movie starring Mickey Rourke called *The Wrestler*. At the premiere, several media outlets interviewed me about my thoughts on the film. I was reminded of something only a true industry historian would know: I was in the original film called *The Wrestler*.

In the 1970s, Verne Gagne made a movie that centered around himself as aging wrestling champion Mike Bullard. The character felt heavy pressure from his wife and promoters to retire. The movie starred Ed Asner as promoter Frank Bass and Elaine Giftos as the person who helped run his booking office.

Through Verne's connections in the business, real promoters from different territories were featured in the film along with footage from different matches and scenes shot at various events. Notable figures who appeared included Billy Robinson, Dick the Bruiser, the Crusher, Lord James Blears, Eddie Graham, Nick Bockwinkel, Ray Stevens, Dusty and Dick, Wahoo, "Superstar" Graham, and Ken Patera.

What's funny is that Ed Asner's character talked about this "Super Bowl of Wrestling" idea that revolved around putting the champions from each league in matches. In one of the scenes, Ed talked about that with a group of promoters around a table, one of whom was Vince Mc-Mahon Sr.

It was a rare glimpse into the workings of our profession. In those days, wrestling was still shrouded in secrecy in order to uphold the personalities and story lines that were portrayed on television. As directed by promoters, "good guys" and "bad guys" were forbidden to be seen together in public. They were not able to travel in the same cars or buses, they had separate locker rooms in the venues, and the ultimate rule was enforced: if a wrestler was in a public place like a restaurant or bar and a "rival" was already there or walked in, one of them would have to leave. Reason being, if you said on TV that the next time you saw said rival you were going to do X, Y, and Z and everyone in the place knows that, and you're standing there doing nothing, now everything you say on television is meaningless. We went to any lengths to protect the business back then. Promoter Bill Watts had a rule that if any of his wrestlers got into an altercation in public and came out of it looking weak, they were fired immediately.

I enjoyed a cameo in the film as one of Verne's rookies. I was in the dinner scene with Verne's character and Billy Robinson's character, talking about retirement. I was also in a training session scene. I have dark hair and sideburns, and in the credits, I'm listed as "Rick Flair."

Back on the red carpet in Tinseltown, I continued to talk about the film and what a marvelous job Mickey did as Randy "the Ram" Robinson. I was truly moved by his performance. I was proud to be in our profession when he said to me this film was the hardest—and the best—movie he ever made.

The Wrestler had the athleticism and the drama of a great sports film and the emotion that all great stories need. I would've liked to have seen just how big the Ram was in the character's prime and have gotten a stronger idea of the heartbreak Randy's relationships brought him. I've always loved movies and love our sport, so of course I left the theater wanting more!

What people didn't know was that Vince McMahon worked something out with Mickey Rourke to have a match against Chris Jericho at the twenty-fifth anniversary of WrestleMania. And there was one man who'd be in Rourke's corner: the Nature Boy.

Mickey couldn't wait to do it. Normally, when you bring celebrities into our business, having them do basic things like walking up to the ring, stepping through the ropes, and moving around the ring can be challenging. Since they're not trained, some people physically look uncomfortable in that kind of situation. Add to that the element of doing it in front of a live audience, you never know what you're going to get. And that doesn't even include the performance.

That didn't apply to Mickey. In addition to his training for the film, Mickey had been a professional boxer earlier in his career. He knew how to move around a ring. Since he was trained for *The Wrestler* by WWE Hall of Famer Afa, he maintained the required confidence level and gave a strong performance as long as things were kept within certain parameters.

Mickey was so excited about what was planned that he mentioned a little too much about the match. At the Screen Actors Guild Awards, Mickey told Nancy O'Dell, "Chris Jericho, you'd better get in shape, because I'm coming after your ass." That's when the direction for Mickey and WrestleMania changed drastically.

From what I was told, Mickey's representatives were concerned that if people had advance notice that Mickey was going to perform in a match at WrestleMania, it could hurt his chances of winning an Oscar. (He'd just been nominated for the SAG Award for Outstanding Performance by a Male Actor in a Leading Role.)

On *Raw*, Chris Jericho delivered a powerful interview segment in which he introduced *The Wrestler* and mentioned how I had given the film a glowing review. Jericho showed footage of Mickey's SAG interview along with Mickey's special message to Chris. Jericho said he was offended by the comments and left the ring.

Rumor had it that Mickey was not going to appear at WrestleMania at all. He went on *Larry King Live*. Chris also appeared on the show as a guest in the hopes of getting the match back on.* Chris was happy to flaunt his skill as an obnoxious villain. The more Mickey tried to take the high road, the more Chris continued his endless stream of condescending remarks. Mickey loved the whole idea. I don't think his people fully understood that Chris was working and that his goal was to set the stage for something that would be very entertaining, not to put Mickey in any danger. We're professionals. I think the *Larry King* segment came off so well that Mickey's handlers thought, if this was what it was like on a talk show, what would happen on the lead-in? What would the match be like?

There were reports that the movie studio executives were very nervous. They didn't want Mickey in the ring or doing anything physical with anyone in any way. Mickey was cast as the lead villain in the *Iron Man 2*. Everyone had to be comfortable. At the same time, you need enough of a commitment to build the story line on television so that something like this can be fully realized during a show with the power of Wrestle-Mania.

Chris's tirades continued on *Raw* each week. He insulted the movie, Mickey Rourke, and me. The foundation of the story was being built on Jericho's disgust for the film, my praise for it, and that the legends he once admired were feebly holding on to the past. He called out "Rowdy" Roddy Piper and Jimmy "Superfly" Snuka and referred to them as leeches on the industry. Then I made my return to *Monday Night Raw*.

A year removed from my match against William Regal at Budokan in Tokyo, Japan, I was in the center of the ring during WWE's flagship program. It was exhilarating to be back in front of that audience and

---

*Chris Jericho: "The match was supposed to be me versus Mickey Rourke at WrestleMania. Vince sent me on a mission to go on *Larry King Live* and basically be such a bad guy and say things to Mickey that were so disrespectful that he'd agree to do the match right there. Mickey wanted to do the match. His representation did not want him to do it. As the show went on, you could see Mickey get visibly annoyed at my remarks."

engage in a battle of wits with Chris Jericho. We used the real-life emotion of my retirement last year and Chris being in the ring during my
send-off as ammunition for him to launch a verbal assault against me. It
was great.

Chris said that he found *The Wrestler* offensive and that it was pathetic
that legends of the ring were still trying to hold on to their glory days.
Chris's interviews were strong. He went so far as to say the fans enabled
the legends' behavior by cheering for them. The fans became more upset
with each scathing statement that Chris made. In my opinion, Chris
jacked his performance to an even higher level for this scenario.

If there was one thing that had more emotion behind it than anything, it's when I said, "I'll never go back in that ring . . . I'll never wrestle
again . . . I have too much respect for Shawn Michaels . . . too much respect for WWE." We continued bringing the fans into this story. I continued to speak words that were straight from the heart. "Yes, I retired
from the ring. But I'll never retire from this business. I'll live my life the
way I want to because I can."

Mickey's involvement in the story line was not made public. On TV,
I laid the foundation with Chris. Face-to-face encounters were set up on
Raw. The following week's segment between Chris and "Rowdy" Roddy
Piper was one of their best. You could feel how much Roddy's career
meant to him and how being a part of the business was so close to his
heart. Piper then extended his hand to Jericho, but instead Jericho attacked Roddy and yelled at him repeatedly. The fans detested Chris more
with each passing week of WWE programming.

Roddy loved the bond and the respect between performers as much as
anyone else. He knew about being a boxer and an actor too. Roddy was a
Golden Gloves champion and left WWE at the height of his fame after
WrestleMania III to film John Carpenter's *They Live*. My friend Hot Rod
has more than one hundred credits as an actor.

The next week was followed up with the incredible announcement that
Ricky Steamboat was going into the Hall of Fame. It was the perfect opportunity to allow Chris to launch another smear campaign against a ring

legend and continue to add to the conflict for television. Since I was not coming out of retirement to face Chris, another Hall of Famer was needed before the match could be set.

When fans tuned in to the following episode of *Monday Night Raw*, Chris re-created the set of Roddy's famous "Piper's Pit" segment. There, Chris berated and attacked one of the most beloved Superstars in WWE history, Jimmy "Superfly" Snuka. This was a very intense segment. Chris re-created elements of the classic segment Roddy and Jimmy had in the '80s. Jericho whipped Snuka with a belt and stuffed a banana in his mouth. The more beloved the personality, the more of an opportunity the villain has to become more detested by the audience. As someone who did that most of his career, I can say it's much more fun being the archnemesis than the white knight.

To give Chris a reason to want to have a match with us as opposed to Mickey Rourke, I interfered in Chris's match and cost him the chance of being one of the participants in the Money in the Bank match, which, behind the scenes, was a match that was Chris's creation.

When Chris challenged me, I told him that I was retired but knew some guys who would be happy to face him. Then Superfly, Hot Rod, and the Dragon surrounded the ring. Just as Chris ran off, I clocked him with a right hand.

While we were working to build up our showdown with Chris Jericho away from the cameras, someone else made sure it was all systems go with Mickey Rourke.

Vince McMahon called the head of Marvel Studios and described the idea of how things would work. It was a great fit for WWE and Mickey to work together at WWE's largest event of the year and one of the largest live events in sports and entertainment. Any Hollywood executive would love to have the revenue generated from WrestleMania as the numbers for a summer blockbuster's opening weekend. It was all set: Mickey would be at the Hall of Fame and sit ringside the next day at WrestleMania. I know he would've been a participant in the match if he could have. I also spoke to Mickey to reassure him that everything would go according to plan and that I'd see him in Houston.

There was one more *Monday Night Raw* for me before WrestleMania. Jericho's previous week's challenge was accepted: he'd face Steamboat, Snuka, and Hot Rod in a handicap match at WrestleMania. Chris continued to turn the dial up and ranted that no one cared about us anymore and how he was going to euthanize his opponents. Chris brought it home when he attacked me, threw me over the announcers' table, threw my shoes into the crowd, tore my shirt, and nailed me with the TV camera he took from the cameraman. Then he took the watch everyone thought was Shawn's gift from last year and stomped it to pieces. Fans were really upset at what Chris did. We loved it. The more animosity Chris showed toward us, the more fans wanted to see him get what he had coming at WrestleMania.

I was so honored to be back with WWE for WrestleMania. I didn't expect to be an integral part of a story line one year removed from my retirement. I certainly wasn't complaining, but since people talked about the previous year's send-off everywhere I went, it felt like it was just yesterday.

It was like déjà vu being backstage at the Hall of Fame. This time, I watched the incredible career retrospective video for my dear friend and greatest opponent, Ricky "the Dragon" Steamboat. And to think that the next day, I'd be walking to the ring with him, to be in his corner for a match at WrestleMania.

I knew Ricky trained with Verne in Minnesota. I heard that there was a talent trade between Jimmy Crockett, who had the enormous, four-hundred-pound One Man Gang, and Jim Barnett in Atlanta, who had Steamboat. Talent trades were a part of doing business in the territory days—promoters wheeling and dealing, almost like general managers do for professional sports franchises.

When I saw Ricky walk into Crockett's office, I saw this handsome guy with an incredible body and a heck of a friendly personality. I knew we could tear it down. I asked him if he'd mind if I suggested something to George Scott for us to do together, and he said he'd love to.

I knew Steamboat could wrestle. Since he was new and I had about a year and a half more experience around a tough group of guys like Wahoo,

Johnny Valentine, Gene and Ole Anderson, and others, I was confident I could work with Ricky, and I jumped at the opportunity.

I wish people could see the thousand or so matches that we had from 1977 to 1984.* I wrestled Ricky practically every night throughout the Mid-Atlantic territory. We'd go at it for one hour, almost every time. The only people who will carry those moments with them are the live audiences we performed for, ourselves, and the referee. We also had a great one in Japan for All Japan Pro Wrestling. We must have worked together more than three thousand times in total.

I was so fortunate to have Ricky in my life. There is only one Ricky Steamboat. The only reason I can't say he's the greatest performer of all time is because he was never a villain, and he couldn't have been. Steamboat had one of the best physiques in the history of our industry. He was so handsome that the girls wanted to spend the night with him. He was such an incredible competitor in the ring that the guys wanted to work out with him in the gym. And the kids loved him too. Ricky's appeal spanned every demographic. The fans fell in love with him from the moment they laid eyes on him.

I'm proud to say that there's a time and a place for Steamboat and me in every generation. Whatever we did back then would be as good as it was then ... now ... anywhere. Ricky was that good. His level of performance was second to none. We had a great time working with each other and had unbelievable chemistry. Even though we've lived very different lifestyles, we've been great friends who will always share an abundance of mutual admiration and respect. And you'll never meet a nicer, more humbler guy than Ricky Steamboat.

Walking to the ring in Houston, it reminded me of how much history I have with each of these guys. At one point, we were all in Mid-Atlantic

---

*Ricky Steamboat: "I'm very grateful that people feel the trilogy of matches Ric and I had in the late '80s in WCW are some of the greatest of all time. I wish people could've seen the matches we had in Greensboro, Charlotte, Greenville, and places like that a decade before. I can't count how many matches we had that were better than those."

territory together. Piper and Steamboat were in my wedding party when I married Beth, and the three of us were part of the first Starrcade together. Then they went to WWE and appeared, along with Jimmy Snuka, at the first WrestleMania.

I always said that if Vince gave Hot Rod the ball for a run as WWE Champion, Roddy would've been just as successful as Hogan. Roddy, and we talked about this many times, always had his guard up, and sometimes it was tough for Vince to feel comfortable working with him and make him the WWE Champion. Roddy's appearance at WrestleMania xxv marked his thirteenth time on WWE's grand stage. And talk about taking resilience to another level, Roddy battled cancer and won. He was ready for this match.

As for Superfly, you're talking about one of the most athletic and exciting performers to step through the ropes. Jimmy had an incredible career in North America and Japan. During our days in the Mid-Atlantic territory, Snuka must've landed on me more than three hundred times in four years with his splash from the top rope.

When the bell rang, the fans saw Roddy insist that he start the match. That happened backstage too. Roddy was so fired up. I didn't realize just how fired up he was until I saw him take Chris over the top rope out to the arena floor, come off the ropes with a sunset flip over Chris, and (I don't think I ever saw Roddy do this) throw a dropkick.

Chris showed what kind of performer he was and took the offense from his legendary adversaries. The crowd roared when Superfly tagged in the Dragon.

Not even twenty-four hours from his induction into the WWE Hall of Fame, Steamboat flew from the top rope to land his signature chop on Jericho. Ricky followed that with his trademark arm drags—the best in the history of business. In front of more than seventy-two thousand fans, my friend turned back the hands of time. And lucky me, I had the best seat in the house.

The match stipulated that to win the match, Chris had to beat all three legends individually. After Snuka tapped out to Chris's Walls of Jericho submission, Roddy kept the fight going. Chris pinned Roddy, and the match's designed showdown took place. It was Chris versus one of his childhood heroes, the Dragon.

Ricky looked so good, and as usual, his cardiovascular conditioning was superb. Our challenge was which guy would make the other breathe hard first. Here, Ricky didn't even break a sweat. After Ricky's flying crossbody off the top rope, I knew the crowd was ready to see Jericho humiliated in defeat.

Chris attacked me, giving Ricky the opportunity to send Chris over the top rope. Ricky shocked everyone when he launched himself over the top rope onto Chris. This was another "good versus evil" Steamboat battle that continued to go back and forth. You could hear the gasp from the crowd after a near fall on Chris. They wanted to see their hero the Dragon leave Houston victorious. Even more so after Ricky reversed the Walls of Jericho and went into a small package pin, the move that beat Randy Savage in their incredible match at WrestleMania III. Chris's youth and endurance won out. But the story was not over yet . . .

Jericho and I mixed it up until it was time for the stand-off that had been months in the making. Chris grabbed the microphone and demanded that Mickey Rourke apologize to him. Chris continued to insult Mickey, and then it happened.

Mickey took off his jacket off and climbed in the ring. All eyes were on the ring to see what was going to happen. Mickey was more than comfortable between the ropes. He showed that he still had his quick hands and jabs. Chris took a swing at Mickey and the Oscar nominee landed a left hook.

Just like that, Jericho was on the canvas, and Mickey and I celebrated in the ring.

I know Mickey wanted to do more, but it was great having him part of WrestleMania and the Hall of Fame ceremonies the night before.

And talk about amazing performances. From our opening scene to the curtain, Chris Jericho did a phenomenal job. He is someone who dedicated his life to the business. As a performer, he can do anything well, and personally, he's a great guy. The two years Chris was gone from

WWE were a huge loss for the company. He was sorely missed. His latest incarnation of a Nick Bockwinkel–inspired, arrogant, self-righteous villain might be Chris at his best.

As for the Dragon, Ricky's work was so well received in the match that he returned to the ring for a comeback. This included a bout with Chris at the Backlash pay-per-view, Ricky's first singles match in roughly fifteen years. I also made some appearances for the company in May and June and worked with Batista and Randy Orton during their matches together.

WrestleMania weekend also marked something new for me. I started seeing a woman, Jackie, I met years ago at the grand opening of the new Morton's Steakhouse in Charlotte. She was in Houston with me for the week. After WrestleMania, there was a reception for the talent and employees. My ex-wife Beth's sister lived in Houston, so Beth went there to visit. They all came to WrestleMania. So Vince, Linda, Stephanie, and Paul were greeting people as they entered the event. They said hello to Beth, whom they knew as my ex-wife, and her sister. They knew Tiffany too. Paul was the best man at our wedding.

They met Jackie for the first time that weekend. Vince looked at me like I was crazy. The only other time he gave me that look was when I pitched a story-line concept that involved having both of us in a match together. I asked him what he thought about the story line of him discovering that his wife, Linda, and I had an affair. There was no verbal response, just that look. Sometimes I drove Vince nuts.

Knowing that my second and fourth wives were at this reception reminded me of two things from the airplane crash I survived in 1975. The EMTs pulled us out, and I heard one of them say, "Hurry up. We might lose this one." I thought, *They're talking about me.* So I said to the guy, "Go into my shaving kit. There's a letter in there. Take it out and get rid of it. I wrote a letter to a girl telling her how much I loved her." If I wasn't going to make it, I didn't want my wife Leslie to discover the letter when she was sorting through my personal effects.

That was the first time I learned that when something major is happening, you'd better not have any "open issues" that someone could find out about. The second time I learned that was shortly after I visited the pilot in the hospital.

No one knew this, but the pilot was engaged to two women at the same time. One of them was from Denver, Colorado, and the other was from Charlotte. I met both his fiancées in the span of about thirty minutes. I was speechless. Talk about a close call. Sadly, Michael passed away a year later from injuries sustained during the crash, but I always wondered what happened at the funeral. Must have been some memorial service.

When I got home, the phone rang, and I got some chilling news. Reid had been pulled over by police for driving while impaired. A month earlier, he was pulled over for a similar offense. This latest one involved something else, something I never considered or even talked about: heroin.

I realized at that moment that I had been in denial about the severity of Reid's problem. This was not a "boys will be boys" type of thing or having too much fun at a party. There was no more hoping for the best. As fine as he looked on good days or as functional as he was, this news sent shock waves through my body. After his two failed WWE drug tests, I felt something was wrong. Putting everything together—the partying at school, those failed tests, and the recent road incidents with police—I felt like a building fell on me.

This was something I never understood. Yes, I was known to party and have a few drinks. I never did drugs. I'm not saying one is better than the other, but I was never around it, so it was not something I immediately understood. I never tried hallucinogens, speed, pain pills. I never pulled a drag from a joint. But none of that mattered. The fact that I didn't understand the drug culture was irrelevant. It was immaterial that none of my other kids had a problem like this. It was time for me to speak to the right people and educate myself about my son's problem. Reid was in serious trouble that was almost impossible for me to comprehend. I needed to find a rehab facility that could help treat a severe and life-threatening illness.

As I was dealing with Reid's addiction and how to help him, my divorce from Tiffany became final.

She hired a moving company to come for her belongings. When I wasn't home, she entered the house, and what happened next, I still can't believe. Tiffany went into my memorabilia room and took four of my robes. She also left with my mother's ruby necklace that I inherited after her death. She also took smaller possessions, like pieces from my firearms collection and special edition action figures from different eras of my career. What I later learned in court was that she met someone online and allegedly sold the robes on the side of the highway for about $7,500. They were easily worth an estimated $50,000. Over the course of our relationship, Tiffany took what I believe to be seven of my original robes.

To make matters worse, I was still trying to resolve the matter of my life insurance. When we were married, I bought a new policy from Tiffany's mother. I paid $180,000 in premiums over the course of a year, and made my kids the beneficiaries. When we split, I found out Tiffany took the policies and made her sister the beneficiary.

Before I left town for a string of personal appearances, my phone rang. It was Hulk. He worked with a promoter in Australia to put together a four-city tour. The shows were scheduled for Melbourne, Perth, Brisbane, and Sydney. He gathered a collection of former WCW, WWE, and independent talent, but he needed an opponent to work with him in the main event each night. One of the first things I said to him was that since we were both divorced, this should be called the alimony tour. I won't discuss Hulk's divorce, but when I got divorced from Beth, I was fifty-nine years old. The judge awarded her $900,000 in alimony.

People will say that I came out of retirement for that, and yes, I did, but to me, these were four live events in Australia. I got to travel and work with my friends and just have some fun.

If the press conference promoting the tour was any indication, Hulk and I were going to let loose and have fun. Members of the media left that event and thought the hostility between Hulk and me was real. I hit Hulk with my belt and left him on the floor bleeding.

The matches were fun. It's so easy working with Hulk because the fans love him. He's their hero. I got to spend a week in Australia and work with guys like Hulk, the Nasty Boys, and Jimmy Hart, people I've been friends with for years.

Another positive from that tour was that I got to have the daughter of an old friend of mine in my corner. Lacey Von Erich is the daughter of Kerry Von Erich and granddaughter of Fritz. She was in my corner during the tour and was the one who got to mix it up with Jimmy Hart.

If Lacey dedicates herself to learning what we do, she can be a star. She certainly has the bloodline for it and would be a third-generation performer. Her grandfather Fritz was tough as nails, a phenomenal villain turned beloved hero in Texas, and one of the foundations of the NWA.

I knew her dad, Kerry, very well, and I have some great memories of working with him. Kerry was a wonderful guy. He had his own challenges away from the ring, but when he was on, he was as good as anyone. The difficult part was that you didn't know when that would be. Kerry had one of the best physiques in the history of our business, and to this day, I've never seen anything like the Von Erichs' popularity in Texas. As much as I enjoyed the nightlife, business hours were business hours. You can't fully understand it unless you've worked in our profession, but the trust that you put into the people you work with to keep you and them safe every night in the ring is something that is taken very seriously. Even the slightest wrong move can mean the end of a career, or worse. Professionally, I didn't look at someone the same who was careless with himself and entered the ring impaired.

The year was coming to an end when Hulk gave me a call. He wanted me to consider a new opportunity. I thanked him and told him I'd think about it.

Even after WWE and I agreed to end my contract, I didn't feel like I left WWE. The recent work for WrestleMania and that summer were great examples of how it was going to be. I wish we could've come to terms on a new agreement, but my work with corporate partners expanded to NASCAR, and there was talk of more on the way.

Hulk's new opportunity was not a four-day tour on the other side of the world that would not be broadcasted. This would be signing a contract with another organization that had a weekly television program on a national cable network. They wanted to pay me for working sixty-five dates a year. Plus, I could keep my corporate partnerships.

I didn't need much provocation to think of Vince, Paul, and Shawn. Now I needed to really think about this.

My legacy would not be what it is if it weren't for my second tenure with WWE. I'm so proud of my career and the matches that I had with so many: Wahoo, Bobo Brazil, Blackjack Mulligan, Steamboat, Dusty, Harley, Barry Windham, and Sting. But those were so long ago. You always have to evolve. The period from 2001 to 2008 was such an important time in my career not just for my legacy but for me as a performer. How would my career have gone if the last thing people saw of me was my final match against Sting on *Nitro*? How would my career have gone if I went to Vince the very first time he called me about coming to WWE?

It was late 1987, early 1988. Vince wanted me to face Randy Savage in the main event of the first SummerSlam. The more we spoke, the more serious this started to look, and the more I envisioned myself making my WWE debut. I went to Dusty, who was in charge of creative for Jim Crockett, and told him I was thinking about "going to New York," which was the way WWE was referred to in the territory days. Dusty said, "Do what you want. You can drop the title tonight in Roanoke [Virginia]."

I was so conflicted. What Vince laid out sounded so exciting. Plus,

I had helped break Randy into the business in the Carolinas in the 1970s. We were good friends. As the deal got closer to happening, I decided to pull back at the last second. I was so loyal to the NWA and the Crockett family. When you wear those colors for so long, it's hard to just take them off. The NWA World Championship was such a part of who I was. For so long, it was everything I strived to be. I also didn't want to leave the Horsemen: Arn Anderson, Tully Blanchard, Barry Windham, and J. J. Dillon. None of us could've foreseen what would happen to Jim Crockett Promotions.

Within the next year, Arn, Tully, and Dusty appeared in WWE. Arn and Tully performed at WrestleMania V. Both of them and Dusty were part of SummerSlam '89, and Dusty worked with Randy at Wrestle-Mania VI. Barry returned there, and J. J. ended up in WWE too, working behind the scenes as the head of Talent Relations. When I did eventually come to WWE in 1991, Vince was thrilled that I was part of the team. He never held it against me that I was loyal to his competition for so much of my career or that our deal didn't come to fruition. How would he feel now?

It reminded me of another time with Vince. Oddly enough, it also involved Randy. It was after our match at WrestleMania VIII. During that time, there was a strict rule in WWE about not having blood as part of our matches.

Without getting the okay from the boss, Randy and I decided to do something different. We wanted to add something extra to the match, since it was for the WWE Championship and Randy would be winning it there in Indianapolis. We had our match, and I bled from my head. I didn't expect a parade in my honor when I got backstage, but I thought we had a very good match. When I saw Vince, he was furious. He said, "Just when you're close to greatness, you do something stupid." I hoped what I was considering would not fall into that category.

Everything Vince ever told me about myself was true. Whether I wanted to hear it at the time or not, Vince was always right when it came to me. Especially when I was a little "too much Nature Boy."

I looked back on something Mickey Rourke told me when we had drinks one night. He told me that Darren Aronofsky, the director of *The Wrestler*, fought hard with the movie studio to make sure that he got the part of Randy "the Ram." Though the details are not the same, it reminded me of many different times when people went to bat for me: Jimmy Crockett pushing with everything he had to make me the NWA Champion following Starrcade '83; Vince giving me the ball to run with coming back to WWE in 2001; Paul putting it on the line for me for my match with Undertaker at WrestleMania X8; and later, to be the senior member of Evolution.

In the same breath, I thought about Shawn. I looked down at the Rolex that was on my wrist. He had a matching one. WrestleMania XXIV weekend was the biggest thing I'd ever done in my life in wrestling, which is my life. It's bigger than any Starrcade, bigger than when I wrestled Paul in Greenville, bigger than any of the times I locked up with Hogan. It was the biggest match of my career.

Shawn Michaels will go down in the history of this wonderful industry as the greatest performer of all time. To have that match with him at WrestleMania, at that level, was unquestionably the largest honor ever bestowed on me. I did not want to disrespect Shawn and the timeless story he created for my final match at WrestleMania XXIV. I did not want to diminish the meaning of our work by stepping in the ring again. I kept calling Shawn to tell him what I was feeling.

Harley, Blackjack, and Dusty reached a point in their lives where they found this peace within themselves to leave wrestling in the ring behind and move on to something else. Shawn's career was not over, but I knew he had also found that peace. While Shawn quietly laid the foundation for plans to exit the business in the next couple of years, I found myself doing everything in my power to find a way to stay in it.

Before I gave Shawn what I promised would be my final call, I needed to call Reid to find out the date of his next doctor's appointment. Then I needed to call Ashley to find out how things were going in Chapel Hill.

6

AN OFFER I COULDN'T REFUSE

Everyone was so respectful, but I had to go home.

May 2010

Medical bills from Reid's trips to the emergency room, along with his hospital stays and physician visits, mounted. At one point, the doctors were concerned that his continued drug use could result in the loss of his leg. There was a point when he relapsed and went through treatment. He completed the program and remained committed to beating this disease. I really felt for him. The intense scrutiny from the Charlotte media, while he tried to deal with a private matter, made things worse for Reid. I'll never forgive them for going out of their way to publicize my son's struggles and what he was dealing with.

As I educated myself about addiction, I learned that heroin is considered by many experts to be the most, or one of the most, addictive drugs anyone can use. I read about triggers: these are stresses, people, locations, memories . . . anything that can cause someone who's battling addiction to feel the need to start using again.

We met with experts. Something I didn't understand was the approach known as "tough love." This would be to kick my son out of the house or turn my back on him unless he stopped using drugs. I didn't understand how anyone could do that to his or her child. I felt it was easy for someone to say that Reid's mother, Beth, and I should've done that. You don't know where your child is, who he is with, or what he is doing. And you're telling him that you're shutting him out. If something happened, if he needed help, would he contact us? No matter how upset or frustrated I got, I couldn't tell my son that he was out of my life.

My belief was that if he was out with me at a restaurant having dinner or at home watching a game on TV, at least he was with me. I could see what he was doing. There were times when he lived with me until he broke one of the house rules. Then he would go to stay with his mom for a while; something would happen there, and then he'd be back with me and then back with her. We desperately tried to find something that worked, especially since he wanted to get better.

Reid came out of the treatment facility with a great attitude. In fact, he was so well liked that he became friends with the staff.

During this time, Reid was healthy and making progress in his battle with addiction. He continued to train in Charlotte for a career in wrestling with former WCW star Lodi. Reid was determined to make more appearances at independent wrestling events and gain more experience working in front of an audience. He wanted to earn another tryout with WWE.

Ashley remained dedicated to completing her studies at NC State and was graduating in May. She was also getting married. I was so proud of her for earning her college degree. I was not overjoyed about her getting married to Riki. The more time I spent with him, the less appealing he became; negative aspects of his personality and behavior became more and more obvious. But what can you do when your daughter appears happy with the person she's with, even if you're not?

While Reid was trying to pull his life together and Ashley was planning her wedding, things in my world were starting to change too.

At the end of 2009, I spoke with Shawn one last time about an opportunity that the Hulk mentioned. I wanted Shawn to know that I didn't want to do anything to disrespect him. As always, Shawn put my mind at ease.*

---

*Shawn Michaels: "I know that Ric struggled with the decision on whether or not to go to TNA. I know for two reasons: one, because I know Ric as a person; two, he called me several

Hulk had signed with a company called TNA Wrestling. Longtime promoter Jerry Jarrett and his son Jeff founded the company in 2002. TNA started by airing their program through weekly pay-per-view broadcasts. They were associated with the NWA. Over the years, TNA management changed. By this time, Dixie Carter was well established as the president of TNA. The company was far removed from being affiliated with the National Wrestling Alliance, and TNA had its own weekly cable TV program.

Hulk was going to be the on-air authority figure for their weekly television program on Spike TV. Hulk felt he needed an opponent fans knew he had a history with, and that opponent had to be viewed as an archrival. I called Hulk back, told him the news, and said, "I'm coming."

Over the years, the animosity between Hulk and me was developed for the cameras. For so long, we were the faces of two companies that competed against one another. During the '80s, the monthly wrestling magazines were an important way for fans to keep up with what was going on in our business.

Hulk and I were featured on many of the covers, appearing to clash in a match between the NWA World Heavyweight Champion and the WWE Champion—the dream match, between me, the ruthless greedmonger and definition of opulence, and Hulk, the all-American hero. Because of that, people thought we really were rivals and didn't like one another.

What many people both in and outside the business didn't know was that Hulk and I were always friends.

The first time I met Hulk was in the early '80s. I was in Atlanta, Georgia, at the WTBS TV studio. I was the World Champion. He was then known as Sterling Golden. Hulk worked in different territories

---

times to talk about it. Ric's happiness and peace revolved around being inside that ring. He wanted me to tell him that going there was okay. I wasn't going to deny him of that. I told him as his friend that I hoped at some point he could find that peace somewhere else. To me, our match in Orlando will always be his last match."

through the southeast and started to come into his own when he worked for Verne in the AWA.

Promoter Jim Barnett said to me, "This guy who's coming here today, Sterling Golden, is going to be the biggest star in the business someday."

I said, "Huh? What about me?"

When I went to WWE in '91, I learned that WWE legend turned road agent Chief Jay Strongbow's nickname for Hulk was "the Golden Goose." And that was for good reason.

In the '80s, Hulk and Vince McMahon worked together to bring WWE to pop culture status and mainstream prominence. As a professional, I'll always be proud of the schedule I kept when I performed. The *World* Champion meant you performed all over the world. There were times when I was gone twelve weeks at a time, flying and driving all over the place. Maintaining the prestige of the NWA and the championship were the focal points of my interviews. The guys who worked for WWE in those days were often on the road for seventy consecutive days. Everyone in the business ran hard.

There were a few times, before I came to WWE, that Hulk and I crossed paths while we worked for different companies. We met up in St. Louis when he worked for Verne, and we saw each other in Philadelphia when WWE was in the Spectrum and the NWA was in the Pennsylvania Convention Center. Both venues were sold out.

We were on two different teams: I was the face of the NWA, presented to audiences as legitimate sport; Hulk was the face of WWE, sports entertainment, and the greatest spectacle on earth. Our in-ring styles, characters, and philosophies were completely different. Hulk and WWE were in the big arenas with a consistently larger fan base thanks to WWE's cable TV, syndication, home video line, and incredible marketing and promotion. I went through the NWA territories and worked a variety of small, medium, and large venues all over the world.

The companies we worked for were managed in completely different ways: The NWA had a board of directors who voted on who would be the champion, where that champion would work, and how long he would be champion. For WWE, everything began and ended with Vince McMahon. Big difference.

When Crockett sold to Ted Turner and WCW was created, there were booking committees: a group of people who decided on creative direction. I was part of a committee at different times, but I was not in charge. Other executives handled business matters and ultimately reported to Turner Broadcasting. Again, a completely different system from a corporate entity being run by one person.

At Turner, most of the executives didn't want wrestling as part of their programming. They didn't know anything about it or make any attempt to educate themselves about our business. Many of them tried to transfer the business experience they had in other areas to professional wrestling. Talk about trying to put a square peg in a round hole! The NWA and WCW never knew how to market their product. I remember being in WCW, and CNN, owned by Turner, would do a story on wrestling and only feature WWE—we were part of the same organization as CNN. Are you kidding me?

At WWE, the people who work there live, breathe, eat, and sleep the sports-entertainment business.

I remember when Hulk and I learned that we had something in common: an incredible love of wrestling since childhood. I idolized the stars of the AWA in Minnesota. Hulk loved the wrestling he saw in Florida. We shared an idol in Dusty Rhodes.

After I hung up the phone with Hulk and told him I was coming to TNA, it reminded me of when I made the deal with Vince in 1991 to come to WWE. My phone rang the next day. When I picked it up, I heard, "So you're finally comin'?" It was Hulk.

A part of me will always be flattered that fans will wonder what the main event between us would've been like at WrestleMania VIII for the WWE Championship. I think we could've had a great match, but it's not something I dwell on. There are a few reasons for that: Vince never promised me that I'd work with Hulk; he never guaranteed that I'd win the

WWE Championship; he never established who else on the roster I'd work with.

The only thing Vince promised me was that he'd make me more money, and he did. The year and a half that I worked for WWE, from July of '91 to January of '93, I made $130,000 more than if I had stayed in WCW. I was having so much fun working for WWE that when the WrestleMania match with Hulk didn't happen, my focus turned to what Vince had lined up for me. Whether it was on TV, on pay-per-views, or at live events, I worked with all the top names in the company: Roddy Piper, Randy Savage, Hulk, Bret Hart, Razor Ramon, Undertaker, and Curt (Mr. Perfect). So to me, I was making more money than I had with WCW, working with the top guys, and having the time of my life. I thought it was great.

When Hulk came to WCW, the dream match that fans wanted to see on a pay-per-view level happened. Bash at the Beach did excellent business for WCW, and only a few people behind the scenes knew that I was the person who made the connection between Hulk and Eric Bischoff, who was in charge of WCW at the time. Eric asked if I knew him and if I could set up a meeting. I drove with Eric to Orlando while Hulk was there shooting the show *Thunder in Paradise*. The two spoke, and the rest was history. I arranged a similar meeting for Eric a couple of months later with Randy Savage. We were building a team. It was a lot of fun. I didn't know it would be temporary.

Every time Hulk and I did something together in WCW, it sold out or was very close to a sellout. We had twenty-minute matches, not the two- or three-minute main events that angered WCW fans. What frustrated me was despite all that, our matchup was only used when WCW needed an opponent for Hulk. Then they went in another creative direction.

For example, in 1999, Hulk said that he thought he wanted to take off the colors of the nWo and go back to the red and yellow of Hulkamania. I told Eric, "I can do it. I can turn him back." We worked together in the main event at weekend shows in the United Center in Chicago with a gate of close to $600,000; in Milwaukee it was $200,000, and the next weekend on a Sunday afternoon in Detroit, we did $400,000. I'd arrive at the building for *Nitro* on Monday, and Hulk was doing something else. I had no idea why, and no one spoke to me about it. It didn't make any sense.

What bothered me was that I felt Eric ignored the success Hulk and I had working together. At that time, Eric's style of managing talent was what I like to describe as "divide and conquer." Hulk and Randy would be in one corner, Arn and I would be in another; Scott Hall and Kevin Nash would be in one, and Sting and Luger would be in the other.

Working with Hulk was always so easy and so much fun. Were there times Hulk and I argued about things professionally? Absolutely. Were there times we agreed to disagree? Of course. That happens when you work with people. I was long past any frustrations with WCW.

Eric was going to TNA with Hulk. Eric and I had a rough start when he came to work for WWE in 2002, but by the time the opportunity with TNA came along, that was all water under the bridge.

Of course I didn't go to TNA to compete with WWE. You measure a company in this industry by TV ratings, pay-per-view buy rates, ad sales, live attendance, merchandise sales, consumer products sales, sponsorships, and licensing, among other criteria. WWE has not had direct competition in the sports-entertainment genre since 1999. When they did, it was with WCW, and that was primarily in television ratings. And if you looked at what WCW was doing then, you knew that success was going to be temporary. Since the late '90s, WWE expanded to the point that all forms of sports and entertainment were its competition.

I agreed to go to TNA because I missed the business. I love performing in front of an audience. I love entertaining people. The thought of sitting at home or going out on my boat every day drove me nuts—and I love my boat!

Every time I went back to WWE after we amicably parted ways in 2008, I pitched ideas about being a manager for a Superstar, or the General Manager/authority figure of *Raw* or *SmackDown*. It didn't happen. That was okay. I wanted to keep working, which was a good thing, because I had to support myself, my wife, and, well, pay money to two ex-wives.

I also wanted to be there for my kids. As someone with two daughters, I can tell you that weddings are expensive.

From my first conversation with TNA, everyone at the company treated me with incredible respect. And then there was the offer they made me.

My contract was a six-figure deal to work sixty-five dates a year. More dates could be added if it was mutually agreeable. It wasn't WWE money, but it was very good. The TNA contract also allowed me to continue making promotional appearances with independent wrestling companies and to further my work with the corporate partners. We were in discussion to expand the North and South Carolina lottery concept into several other states.

TNA had a national cable TV partner in the United States in Spike TV. The company also had a strong fan base in Europe. Some said the following was stronger than in the States.

TNA had a combination of established stars that included Sting, Kurt Angle, Mick Foley, Kevin Nash, Scott Hall, Sean Waltman, and the Dudley Boyz, though they couldn't use the Dudley name. They called themselves Team 3D. Then I learned about the outstanding roster of young talent who worked hard to build the company brand.

From the time the Jarretts started the company in 2002, if you removed WWE mainstays from the equation, almost every major name in our business over the last twenty-five years had appeared in TNA.

When I looked at what the company had planned in terms of building out other parts of its business with consumer products and merchandise and put all of that together, it seemed like the company had a lot of potential and was headed in the right direction, not to compete with WWE, but to carve out its own niche.

For my on-air role, the idea was that I would create a group of stars to manage. That group would cross paths with Hulk's, and from that, different matches and rivalries would be created.

My debut on the first show of 2010 was designed to give the audience a strong sense of who I would be aligned with: AJ Styles.

When I first saw AJ Styles, I thought he was outstanding. He was a handsome guy who had a great look, could physically do anything in the ring, and was recognized by the audience as one of the first stars of the company.

AJ was a tremendous athlete and the TNA World Heavyweight Champion. The idea was for me to come into the company and act as his mentor. That's one of the things I wanted to do in front of the cameras and behind the scenes: I wanted to help bring the younger talent along. I looked forward to working with them and teaching them whatever I could.

I thought the idea of working with AJ was great. Like any good mentor would do, I started walking him to the ring, being in his corner, and, of course, interfering in his matches to help him keep the championship. I became concerned when I learned that individuals within the company wanted to take my mentoring in a completely different direction.

TNA management wanted AJ to become the new Ric Flair. They wanted him to dye his hair blond, wear a robe to the ring, and use my mannerisms. I didn't want AJ to be the next Ric Flair. I wanted him to be AJ Styles. I don't want to speak for AJ, but I'm confident in saying that he felt the same way. And he should have; he had it all. AJ just needed time to put everything together. That feeling was reaffirmed for me the night I debuted with the company and saw the excellent match he had with Kurt Angle.

Kurt and I became friends when we worked together in WWE. He's the only person in the history of our business who was an Olympic gold medalist in amateur freestyle wrestling. Kurt was a pure machine in the ring. The only other person I saw come into our business from amateur wrestling who succeeded like Kurt was Jack Brisco. If someone could last in the ring with Kurt Angle, he was the real deal. AJ did.

I was settling into my new surroundings at TNA. After a little more than a month, Dixie Carter and Hulk hosted a press conference at Universal Studios in Orlando. TNA announced that it was moving the *Impact!* program to Monday nights. This was to go head-to-head with WWE and *Monday Night Raw* from 9:00 p.m. to 11:00 p.m. That made me nervous.

I understood the idea. I understood that the dedicated fans who closely follow our business wanted to elevate an organization so that there could be something similar to the "Monday Night War" in the '90s, or Jim Crockett and the NWA versus Vince and WWE in the '80s. Those were special eras that will likely not be duplicated. I thought that for TNA the time wasn't right.

At the beginning of 2010, the episodes of *Impact!* did well in the context of TNA programming. That should have been a promising sign. I didn't think TNA had the brand awareness with viewers or the advertising budget to compete with WWE. At that point, WWE had been around for close to fifty years. On the air since 1993, *Raw* had been an institution of the Monday night TV schedule. TNA had only been in existence almost eight years.

On TV, my story line was set up for the first episode of Monday night's *Impact!* I came out of retirement to perform in a tag team match with AJ as my partner. The story was set up where AJ and I teamed together to face Hulk and a monster-type character called Abyss.

By the end of the match, a friend returned to TNA TV as a surprise: it was Sting. Sting had performed in TNA since the early days of the promotion. At this stage of his career, Sting still looked great, kept his character fresh, and was giving some of the best interview segments of his career. I was so happy to work with him again. I told him the same thing I'd been telling him for years: "Get to WWE before it's too late."

I understood TNA wanted to make a run at bringing *Impact!* to Monday nights. If the show drew somewhere between 1.0 and 1.7 million viewers in the Nielsen ratings on a Thursday night, what could it do on Monday, which is considered *the* night to watch wrestling? My concern that it wasn't the right time was soon validated. Two months from the announcement at Universal Studios, *Impact!* was moved back to Thursday nights. It was good to have a goal; it was great to see people in the company excited; and I think that, in time, it may have been a good move. But not at that time. I just thought it was premature.

Despite TNA moving back to Thursdays two months after announcing the move to Mondays, the first few months working for TNA were excellent. I was able to let loose a little bit in front of the cameras and on the microphone. I also let loose while I enjoyed the nightlife in Orlando, and at one point, I enjoyed it a little too much and had to take a break.

The people who worked for the company worked really hard. Dixie Carter treated me very well. TNA's schedule gave me a lot of flexibility, which was something I liked. It gave me time to plan a life with my new bride, though at the time, I didn't think being at home would present so many problems.

From the second I met Jackie, one of the things I liked about her was that she didn't know anything about me—who I was or what I did. It just didn't matter to her. If she wanted to have dinner with me, she just wanted to share a meal and spend time together.

In a small, private ceremony, Jackie and I got married in November of 2009. This time my best "man" was my agent, Melinda.

Within a few months of our marriage, I saw a side of Jackie that I had never noticed before. Her way of handling a disagreement was to become combative. One night, we got into an argument, and she attacked me like someone on the street. It concerned me a great deal, and I tried to work on it with her.

I knew Jackie had a difficult childhood. She grew up in a foster home. Jackie had a tough side to her. I didn't expect it to be physicality projected on me when we got into an argument.

Thankfully, work always stepped in to quiet the waters of a turbulent home life, and my matches at TNA helped calm those stormy seas.

TNA taped its programs at Universal Studios theme park. The wrestling is almost treated as an attraction at the park. People who are walking through the park can come in and watch the show for free. WCW did that for a while too.

It's different performing in front of a crowd that's paid. You have to have paying fans see your product. They invest their time and money into your characters and into your story lines. As a performer, that's when you're able to see what's working in your performance and what's not. You're receiving real reactions. Someone I worked with that summer certainly had his share of authentic crowd reactions: Jay Lethal.

One of my favorites at TNA was Jay Lethal. Jay's Black Machismo character picked up a ton of steam when Jay became known for his dead-ringer imitation of Randy Savage. When I got to TNA, I heard Jay did a great impression of me in the locker room. I suggested I work with him.

We began our story line in the spring. In a matter of weeks, we were full steam ahead. Fast-forward to the summer of 2010. I was introducing my new group, Fortune, and Jay came out in a suit and did a spot-on impression of me. He did me better than I did. There were times during the almost ten-minute segment that he made me break character and laugh. Jay was another person I hoped would make it to WWE and someone I wished I worked with when I was in my prime. He's a tremendous talent.

I continued my work with AJ and added some fabulous talent to Fortune—namely, James Storm and Robert Roode, the team known as Beer Money. They were the best team in wrestling. I hoped they would move up to the WWE, but their contracts were over. Frankie Kazarian was part of the group—another excellent talent.

In working with young talent, I wanted to emphasize the importance of having confidence in themselves and their ability, to know who they are. I wanted them to realize how crucial it is in this profession to know how you're different as a talent from everyone else in the locker room.

I thought the company made a mistake trying to have their characters resemble my look. I didn't think they were fully comfortable in the suits and robes and jackets. I wanted them to be themselves, because that's when you get the best performances from people.

Toward the end of my first year with TNA, the way the company was structured and the way the lines of communication traveled became frustrating. As a talent, I felt like you could never get anything approved so you could move forward. Management would tell me one thing and then do another. You would think something was happening, and then someone would speak with a different executive and the objective would change. You didn't find out what the new, approved direction was until moments before you were in front of the cameras. That's challenging for even the most experienced performer. People had good ideas. I felt it was very difficult to get anything moving. It was a reminder that there's nothing like the professionalism and dedication of working for Vince

McMahon and WWE. I learned that after I finished up with WWE in 1993 and returned to WCW.

When I heard that a friend who worked for WWE was coming to TNA, I hoped he'd be able to facilitate change. Bruce Prichard joined TNA as an executive in the talent department. I wished that Bruce's track record of success during his more than twenty years with WWE would add structure to TNA's corporate environment, bring excitement to creative plans, and help develop characters.

The end of the year also brought me into the middle of the ring with someone I've had quite a history with: Mick Foley. I first met Mick in 1991; Jim Cornette and Jim Ross introduced us. Mick came into WCW. I left the company about six months later to go to WWE. We were on the same roster again, and I was backstage in Germany when Mick's ear got ripped off in a match against Vader. Mick went to ECW and then debuted in WWE in 1996. I didn't see him again until my return to WWE in 2001.

Things took a turn in 1999 after Mick's first book was published. For almost three years, wherever I went, people came up to me and asked for my opinion about what Mick said about me in the book. I didn't read it. To paraphrase, Mick mentioned that I was a great wrestler but a terrible booker, referring to our time together in WCW during the '90s. There was that misconception again, that I was the booker or in charge of the booking committee. Those notions bothered me for a long time.

When I came to WWE, I thought Mick and I worked well together. WrestleMania XX will always be a fun memory for me: Batista, Randy Orton, and myself versus Mick and The Rock—Evolution against The Rock 'n' Sock Connection.

When my first book came out in 2004, I responded to Mick. In brief, I gave my opinion on the hard-core wrestling style and genre. I called Mick a "glorified stuntman." I never took away from Mick's success in our business, but things escalated quickly. We got into an altercation backstage at a WWE event in Huntsville, Alabama.

Mick approached me while I was sitting at a table with Arn Anderson.

I extended my hand to shake Mick's. He wouldn't shake. He asked me to sign a copy of my book to him. I took that as a show of disrespect. I got up from my chair, and I punched Mick. Other members of the roster came and kept us apart. That was something we both regretted. Shortly thereafter, any ill will between us was forgotten.

As fate would have it, we ended up sitting next to each other on a flight back from a WWE tour. Before everyone took their seats for the fourteen-hour flight from the Philippines to Los Angeles, Paul and John Cena came up to us separately and asked if either of us wanted to switch seats with them. We both said no and that we were fine. Were we? Saying hello and shaking hands at an event is one thing, even working together in a match is another, but sitting next to each other for almost fourteen hours in an airplane flying halfway around the world? We were better than fine.

Shortly after takeoff, we started talking about everything but wrestling. We had more in common than just being wrestling fans as kids. We both were devoted to our children. I told Mick he certainly had a better track record at being married than I did. By the time we landed in Los Angeles, it was like we were old friends. We looked forward to the next six hours flying back to New York.

One of my favorite matches in my career was my "I Quit" match with Mick at SummerSlam in 2006. I was always up for trying new things. I had never done anything with barbed-wire-wrapped baseball bats and thumbtacks. I thought we put on a heck of a show that night in Boston.

Because our past issues became public knowledge, when we shared a locker room in TNA, some people in the company thought we still harbored anger and resentment toward one another. They didn't know that Mick and I were past that and had become friends.

One night on *Impact!*, we were backstage preparing to go out for an interview on TV. Terry Taylor told Mick, "You and Ric go out there and do that thing between you that only you guys can understand." Mick told me he was going to challenge me to a match. I told him I was going to say something about him being a good father and he should keep it that way. That was the premise we agreed on. Over that ten-minute span, we had one of our most intense face-to-face interview segments ever. We wanted the audience to feel like they needed to see the match between us. We knew we could bring out the best in each other and that fans would talk about the match after it took place.

I think our Last Man Standing Match delivered. Whether it's in the ring during a match or on the microphone, Mick always gives it everything he's got. And the fans love it.

I kept up with WWE and what my friends were up to on TV. When I heard that Shawn Michaels was announced as an inductee to the 2011 Hall of Fame, I knew I had to be there.

When I got off the plane in Atlanta for WrestleMania weekend, I had a lot of different emotions. Atlanta's one of those cities that I'll always feel close to. So many years of my career were spent in Atlanta— performing at the Omni, working at WTBS, and going to CNN Center. Those memories continued as a WWE Superstar: working in a match against Vince at the 2002 Royal Rumble and setting up the match between Evolution and the Rock 'n' Sock Connection for WrestleMania XX.

I couldn't wait to arrive at Philips Arena during the Hall of Fame rehearsal. Going through the building, I saw so many friends I missed working with. This would be the first time in two years I'd see Shawn in person. Every day when I look at the Rolex that Shawn gave me, I'm reminded of my retirement and the special friendship we share.

To commemorate Shawn's induction, I wanted to give him a gift. Knowing he's a Texan at heart, I gave him a sterling silver belt buckle with *HBK* engraved on it. We hugged. I told him I'd be in the audience that night for his induction. I think there were some people at WWE who were surprised that I was there. There was no way I was missing Shawn being inducted into the WWE Hall of Fame.

That night marked the first time since the 2007 Hall of Fame ceremony in Detroit that I had the opportunity to enjoy the event from the audience; I couldn't be on camera because of my contract with TNA.

I marvel at the Hall of Fame production every year. It was tough not to have a great night because I sat next to Pat Patterson.

Shawn's speech was very moving. I was grateful to be there and happy for my friend, who I believe will go down as the greatest performer in the history of our profession. I was so proud of Shawn. I'll always have a difficult time articulating what my relationship with him means to me.

A couple of days later, I went back home to Charlotte. I reflected on the weekend, but I had no idea that a year later I'd be back at the WWE Hall of Fame, this time onstage as an inductee—again.

In the beginning of 2012, WWE announced that the Four Horsemen would be inducted into the Hall of Fame. I remember right after we got a call about the induction, J. J. Dillon called me and said, "Are you coming?"

I would be the first two-time WWE Hall of Fame inductee. Once again, I was overwhelmed with gratitude. I was also under contract to another company. While I didn't think this would be a problem, I had to have the conversation.

Dixie Carter was very gracious. She understood how important it was to me to receive this honor in person. She congratulated me. I was off to Miami.

I was excited because Ashley and Reid were going to join me on the trip. Reid kept training and was scheduled to meet with WWE executives to see what he needed to do to be considered for another tryout. Ashley built an incredible personal training business for herself at a private studio in Charlotte and was doing great. It took her a little while to get settled after graduating from college and getting married. I was so proud of them both and wanted to have them share this experience with me.

When I arrived in Miami, I was greeted by the familiar feeling of excitement when WWE and WrestleMania take over a city.

After the storybook ending to my career at WrestleMania XXIV, I didn't think I'd return to the Hall of Fame as an inductee. It was surreal

to make that familiar trip through the talent entrance in American Airlines Arena and be backstage wearing a tuxedo at the WWE Hall of Fame.

When I saw Arn, Tully, J. J., and Barry, it felt like I had just seen them at *Raw* in Orlando the night after my retirement match. Now we were backstage together. I fought back tears looking at the Horsemen career retrospective video that played for the audience.

To remember how we looked back then and to see these men now—well, it was a special moment. When I listened to Dusty

Rhodes, our greatest on-air rival, sing our praises, I thought back to our battles with the Dream. And poor J. J., the night the Road Warriors hit him with their Doomsday Device finisher in the War Games match, he dislocated his shoulder.

Dusty's induction speech was the type of magic that only the American Dream can deliver. I never thought that one of my idols, who helped break me into this industry, would one day induct me into the Hall of Fame.

When we took the stage as a unit, it was like being transported back in time. It was fitting that J. J. Dillon, our manager, was the first to speak.

J. J. Dillon was the perfect man to lead the Horsemen to the ring. And he really was our manager in so many ways. J. J. was there for us every step of the way: making travel arrangements, setting schedules, confirming travel, and giving us advice. He looked out for us like we were his kids.

In front of the cameras, everything J. J. did meant something. Everything he said had a purpose. J. J. Dillon is a true student of the game who has an incredible history in the business. When J. J. was a kid, he loved wrestling so much that he was the president of the Johnny Valentine fan club. After he graduated high school, he got his break in the business as a referee for Vince McMahon Sr.

When J. J. said, "Naitch, come on up here and tell them what's causing all this," it felt like I was where I should be, on WWE's beautiful stage, before a packed house of so many friendly faces.

I had to tell a funny story, or the emotion of the evening was going to get to me. I told everyone how I was remarried since the last time I was inducted in 2008. I shared with the audience the story about how Tiffany started an argument with me over the phone because I was going to the bar with John Cena. Tiffany asked, "Are you ever going to grow up?" I told her, "I'm not thinking about it anytime soon. Why?" Tiffany followed that up with, "What do you have in common with someone thirty years younger than you?" I paused, thought about that, and said, "I don't know, but I'll tell you this, you won't find out tonight." And I hung up the phone. Cena and I had a blast in that hotel bar in Indianapolis and stayed until 3:00 in the morning. Cena's another one. It took him a little while to go out with me and enjoy a few drinks, but he could've run with the Horsemen!

I have so many memories with Barry Windham. His father, Blackjack Mulligan, was a huge influence on me. I first met Barry when he was a kid. When he was fourteen, I told him to get a tuxedo and a chauffeur's cap. I paid him to be my limo driver. Barry's the most naturally gifted athlete I've ever been in the ring with. Barry stood six foot six and weighed 275 pounds. He could do anything in the ring, and that included going for an hour with me in the main event. Working with Barry was like working with Steamboat. He was that good. I was so proud to see Barry put his Hall of Fame ring on backstage. Now he has one just like his dad's.

Tully Blanchard was another second-generation performer. His dad, Joe, ran Southwest Championship Wrestling. Tully was a master technician in the ring. He was the type of villain who was not afraid to get the crowd riled up. In fact, Tully may have loved doing that more than the rest of us. And the team Tully formed with Arn is one of wrestling's greatest duos.

As respected as Arn Anderson is, as unanimously highly regarded as he is within our business, it's not enough. Arn deserves more recognition. That night, he took his rightful place in the Hall of Fame. I can't say it enough: Arn Anderson is the brother I never had. For more than twenty-five years, people have come up to me and said that Arn was their favorite Horseman. I've said the same thing to each person every time: "He's mine too."

I think the Horsemen will go down as the greatest faction of all time. We loved the business. We couldn't wait to get to that arena every night and perform, and we couldn't wait to go out and party after the matches. I was honored that our work was recognized by WWE. That night served as another reminder that there's nothing like the respect of your peers.

After the Hall of Fame ceremony, the kids and I had dinner with John Laurinaitis—or, as some fans know him, Johnny Ace. I've known John since he was a performer in the NWA and WCW. To fans of our industry who follow what goes on in Japan, John was a top star for All

Japan Pro Wrestling in the '90s. He's also the brother of Road Warrior Animal. After John retired from the ring, he worked behind the scenes in WCW and came to WWE in 2001.

At dinner, Reid told Johnny what he had been doing: training, getting booked on more independent shows, and using the internet and social media to contact promoters to book more dates outside the Carolinas. John knew how much Reid wanted another opportunity to try out for the company. They continued to talk about what Reid needed to do, and Johnny gave him some suggestions on how he could get more experience.

Then all of a sudden, Johnny asked Ashley why she wasn't in the business. I didn't know what to say. She was never attracted to it, but for some reason, she seemed interested in hearing more about what Johnny was saying—that they were always looking for people with great athletic backgrounds and that she should consider it if it was something she might want to become involved in.

I tried telling him that wrestling was not Ashley's thing. Then Reid encouraged her to consider it and said they could train together. I couldn't believe the conversation I heard. I thought we were having dinner to talk about Reid getting back for a tryout. Now my daughter's suddenly thinking about it? What? I told her that I knew she had the athleticism, but she couldn't do this half-assed.

Being at the WWE Hall of Fame reaffirmed what I had been feeling through much of my time away from the company: I should've stayed with WWE. The way my retirement was handled, the Hall of Fame induction, the match with Shawn, and the reverence people continued to show me really struck a chord. With everything WWE did for me in making that possible, WrestleMania in Orlando should've been the final time people saw me walk that aisle in my robe, trunks, and boots. I never should have left WWE and worked for another company. I was given the once-in-a-lifetime opportunity to go out on top, and I didn't take it. That's a regret I'll always have.

The next morning, which was the familiar day after WrestleMania, I didn't feel right. I felt like I should've been going to the building that afternoon for *Raw*—not to the airport to go home.

When I returned to TNA, there were still communication issues with management. There were times when checks were late. During my time there, I received calls at the last minute to show up at events. I would get a call on a Wednesday to go to an event the next day—and there was no advertising in place to announce my appearance. I'd get to the building, and people in the locker room and other TNA employees didn't even know I was booked to be there.

The people at TNA were very nice, and they tried hard to build the company. I had a great time working with many of the people there. I wanted to do more with Fortune since the group was so talented. I made some great friends. I gained enormous respect for people like AJ Styles, Bobby Roode, James Storm, Frankie Kazarian, Jay Lethal, Samoa Joe, Christopher Daniels, and others. Like many young stars I worked with in WCW, I hoped they'd all get the chance to make it to the big time before their careers were over.

The day-to-day dealings at TNA became more tedious than anything else. It's impossible to experience the same level of professionalism and commitment as you do working for WWE. I called Bruce Prichard. I thanked him for everything TNA did for me and expressed my gratitude to him for his personal efforts on my behalf. I had to be honest. I just said, "I need to go home."

7

ON MY WAY HOME

*I never thought I'd have two children training to get
into the business at the same time.*

January 2013

The year 2012 was marked by a series of highs and lows. I never
dreamed that I'd be a two-time inductee into the WWE Hall of
Fame. Having a Hall of Fame ring for each hand didn't seem real. It
was another moment that WWE and the fans supplied me with enough
adulation to last a lifetime.

I asked Paul if Ashley could call him about entering WWE's developmental program. I knew he would be honest and a little tough with her
over the phone. He always made sure that people knew what to expect
when they decided to pursue a wrestling career. I just wanted him to
know how much I appreciated it and that it was okay if he took a hard
line with her. I really had no idea what to expect from Ashley.

Paul described the countless obstacles that Ashley would have to
confront: the constant physical pain and exhaustion; the isolation from
family and friends; the damage to her marriage; and the difficulty of
being Ric Flair's daughter. He told Ashley that she'd be starting from
the bottom and that she shouldn't expect to receive credit for anything
positive. For someone just beginning, it couldn't have sounded much
bleaker. But Ashley couldn't be deterred; she still wanted to try it.

I had mixed feelings about my daughter entering this business. It wasn't a matter of her being successful with the right preparation and dedication. I didn't want her to get hurt. The physical toll wrestling takes is indescribable. I know I'm fortunate to wake up every morning pain-free. That's rare.

Emotionally, I didn't want her to face the inevitable criticisms and comparisons because she was my daughter. I know that was a factor that both my sons had to deal with. People did not give them the chance to develop. They were immediately compared to me. Reid handled it the best way he could, but I knew it was difficult for him. Negative comments in the early stage of his career along with the anonymity of the internet and social media just made it worse. I didn't want Ashley to endure that kind of undeserved—and unjust—scrutiny.

Not to be discouraged under any circumstances, my daughter reported to WWE for training in Tampa. Before she left, we had a crash course at a facility in Charlotte so she would not be completely unprepared when she got there: five hundred free squats, conditioning drills, and learning the basics.

During one of our sessions, I stood in the corner of the ring and watched her and Reid work on something together. I couldn't believe that both my kids were going to give it their all so they could be in the wrestling business.

Unfortunately, not everything in my personal life was this positive. The incident that took place with Jackie a few months after we got married was not a onetime occurrence. In April of 2012, shortly after my induction into the WWE Hall of Fame, Jackie was pulled over for reckless driving and driving while impaired. She blew a 0.21 on the Breathalyzer. Since the car was in my name, I couldn't get automotive insurance for a period of time.

Roughly two months after that, there was another domestic incident in our home. Jackie and I got into an argument. She went down a line of martini glasses and smashed them into her head. She said she was going to make herself bleed and then call the police and tell them I beat her up. That's when I realized that when she was angry, she was capable of anything. Her violent, unpredictable behavior triggered a very disturbing, unsettled feeling. We separated the next day.

All told, Jackie had gone to jail three times. These incidents, and the circus-like media attention they attracted, did irreparable damage to my personal and professional reputation. Product endorsements came to a halt. A representative from Coca-Cola informed me that even though I was not at fault in this situation, the decisions I made could adversely affect the Coca-Cola brand. The company terminated our relationship.

By the end of the year, my fourth marriage was over. Signing the necessary paperwork made it official. I couldn't believe I had rushed into marrying Jackie. Why did I marry her? When it came down to it, I walked down the aisle with a woman I didn't really know. It had been a terrible mistake.

After my relationship with Jackie ended, I slipped into a downward spiral. I couldn't be by myself. I didn't like the person that I had become. And when I look back, I don't know how I ended up in that place. The only antidote was to go out and party, be with other people, and escape my insecurities.

Being around the bar and restaurant scene was a way for me to break free from reality and the mess I had created.

When I was younger, wrestling was always easy for me; it was what I did from 11:00 p.m. to 3:00 or 4:00 a.m. that sometimes caused an issue. Many of my contemporaries are either really hurting after years of punishment in the ring, or they're no longer with us because of the choices they made. This was a time during my career that I started to hurt myself.

I went out every night for a month. Each evening, a different woman spent the night with me in my home. Some people may think that's a dream come true or really impressive. It's not. While I had a wonderful time with each of them, I never felt more lost in my life. It was like I didn't have an identity. I tried to fill a void. It was a coping mechanism. I was not making good choices. I soon realized that it didn't pay to be the Nature Boy the way it did in my younger days, especially in the '80s, when I lived by the mantra of ladies, ages eighteen to twenty-eight, no boyfriends, no husbands, the Marriott. That was a wonderful way of life.

Thankfully, I refocused on work and on my kids. That's when I saw a friend who I hadn't seen in a long time.

I met Wendy Barlow in 1993 when I returned to WCW. She was cast to play the character of "Fifi the French Maid" for my talk show segment, *Flair for the Gold*. Wendy was gorgeous . . . she reminded me of Elizabeth Taylor in the film *The Last Time I Saw Paris*.

Before Wendy entered the wrestling business, she studied at the prestigious Sorbonne School in Paris, France. She was fluent in French. Wendy brought a special level of cultural authenticity to the role of "Fifi."

When the lights were on and the cameras were rolling, Wendy played her part so well that fans wondered if she spoke English. She escorted me to the broadcast area for interview segments, and accompanied me to the ring for my matches. Wendy was awesome.

We worked together for a year and became great friends. In 1994, Wendy left the business to start a family and pursue other interests.

Twenty years later, and after some divorces, Wendy and I found one another. We got to know each other again. Wendy has four incredible children: Sophia, Sebastian, Paris, and Summer. She understood how important my children were to me. Wendy also knew how large of a part my career played in my life. She was so instrumental in helping me beginning to make certain adjustments and becoming more comfortable with life outside the ring. We started to see each other.

Before we got back in touch, Wendy returned to wrestling. She made select appearances at independent shows and autograph signings. At some events, she was Reid's valet for his matches.

At the end of the year, I surprised fans with my return to WWE TV. A week before Christmas, I presented the Slammy Award for "Superstar of the Year" to John Cena on *Monday Night Raw*.

The Philadelphia crowd received an added bonus when CM Punk and his manager, Paul Heyman, arrived on the scene. Punk was in the midst of his WWE Championship reign. It was fun mixing it up with him on the microphone. His work was always very good. I liked Punk. He always treated me well. He was always very respectful of my career. I had a good time tagging with him on an episode of ECW during my retirement story line in 2008. The segment concluded with me slapping the Figure Four on Paul Heyman, whose on-air persona was always perfectly summarized by Jim Ross as "easy to dislike."

It was great getting back to *Raw*. As far as WWE and I were concerned, we returned to the understanding that we'd had before I left: the company was going to use me for different things, and that for now, it would be on a pay-per-appearance basis, which was perfect, given where I was going a month after I left the City of Brotherly Love.

A few days before New Year's, I had a follow-up call with a good friend of mine about wrestling in Japan. This time, I was going to make it to the match. Or so I thought.

I first met Keiji Mutoh, also known as the Great Muta, in the '80s. His debut as Muta on WTBS featured him along with his managers Hiro Matsuda and Gary Hart in an interview segment with Jim Ross. As Muta, he was billed as the son of Japanese legend the Great Kabuki. Muta was a tremendous performer. He blended the athletic, physical Japanese style with the charisma and performance nuances that the American style often required for a talent to be successful in the States. He returned to WCW several different times in the '90s. I loved working with him.

During this period, Mutoh oversaw the All Japan office. It was Mutoh who contacted me in the summer of 2008 after my match with Shawn in Orlando. He made me an amazing offer: wrestle him as part of a ten-day All Japan tour. I turned it down.

When he called me in the fall of 2012 to see if I wanted to be his tag team partner for a match in the new year, I gladly accepted his offer.

I always had a wonderful relationship with All Japan Pro Wrestling, going back to when Shohei "Giant" Baba owned the company. I had performed many times for All Japan in the '70s and '80s.

The fans remembered my matches against Baba, Steamboat, Genichiro Tenryu, Jumbo Tsuruta, Riki Choshu, Kabuki, the Funks, Bruiser Brody, Stan Hansen, Harley Race, and a Champion-versus-Champion match when Rick Martel was the AWA Champion for Verne Gagne and I entered the ring with the NWA's ten pounds of gold around my waist.

Many of those matches were two-out-of-three falls. Those are just some of the great memories I have of competing in an All Japan ring.

In those days, the relationship with All Japan was so strong that I wrestled Brody in St. Louis for exclusive broadcast on Japanese television.

As Reid and I got ready to go to the airport for our trip to Japan, I thought about a period when I didn't want to tell WWE if Reid was in the hospital or in treatment. I knew they'd help us. They wanted to help. I wasn't sure if that would prevent them from hiring Reid when he got better.

At one point, I confided in Paul and Shawn about Reid's situation. They spoke to him like he was their own son. I know how much that meant to Reid, because he idolized them both.

There was a time when I believed that my son wasn't going to beat his addiction. I tried to mentally prepare myself for that phone call, when I would hear someone's voice telling me that my son had passed away. Our family didn't give up. Reid didn't give up. He wanted to keep fighting and doing whatever he could to land on the right path and stay there.

The medical bills for Reid kept coming. It seemed as though when one was paid, another one appeared. When I totaled all of them, they added up to more than $300,000. I didn't care about the money. I cared about my son. But you need money to keep things going.

You're not given advance notice when someone relapses. You go through another sleepless night, another chilling day, trying to figure out why your son didn't come home and where he is and hoping if, God willing, you find him, he's still alive. You have to get help—right away. And you need that money available immediately. Our family lived with this every day. As Reid's father, I was in a perpetual state of anxiety. I know his mother was too. We all tried to do our part in helping Reid beat this.

The staff at these rehabilitation centers do incredible work in helping people fight against the disease of addiction. Those services require money that's paid up front. Some of these treatment centers averaged between $30,000 and $50,000 per stay.

There was one instance when we made plans for Reid to go to rehab. I was about $13,000 short. I was running out of time. Hulk happened to call me to see how Reid was doing. I told him what was going on. He made a call and then phoned me back. Within thirty minutes, that money was in my account. That helped save my son's life. When I think of Hulk Hogan and the type of friendship we've had over the years, that's what I think about. No cameras, no microphones, no story lines, no audiences— just someone who helped a friend. I'll always remember that.

Reid and I boarded the plane. I thought about Vince, Paul, and Shawn. They helped me at different points along the way in my professional and personal lives and with Reid. That type of help brought my son to this point.

We were leaving for Japan. I was going to perform in a tag match, my first match in sixteen months. I wasn't happy with my last match in TNA versus Sting. The fans never let me down, but with that one, I felt I had disappointed them. I looked forward to this event in Tokyo so I could show the fans I could still deliver. Reid was going to perform in an opening match on the card and begin training in the All Japan dojo. I was eternally grateful for this opportunity.

I arranged for Reid to train in the dojo. I realized over time that Charlotte was a trigger for him. Our family was constantly under a microscope. The media had a history of partially true reporting. Their criticism of Reid's wrestling and his not being given a chance to learn hit him hard. He was friendly with so many different kids, but there was one group he fell in with that was trouble. I thought if I removed him from that environment and put him in a place where he could focus on doing what he loved—as Reid, not the son of Ric Flair—he could return to the path he was on and remain there. If all went well like I knew it could, Reid would be in Japan for three months.

Once we landed in Tokyo, it was all business. Reid and I attended a press conference hosted by All Japan. We were with Mutoh, Masahiro Chono, Akebono (who had a sumo match at WrestleMania 21 with Big Show), and their champion Masakatsu Funaki. Mutoh and I were there to talk about our tag match against a man I knew very well: Tatsumi

Fujinami and the young star Seiya Sanada, who was All Japan's TV Champion.

The Japanese culture and media have always treated our profession with a tremendous amount of reverence. When an organization like All Japan hosts a press conference in its country, members of the Japanese mainstream and sports press cover the event. I was proud to be there and so proud of Reid. Everyone was impressed with how he carried himself, especially since he was in the early stages of his career.

Before the match, a blood clot was discovered in my leg, and I couldn't wrestle. Understandably, Mutoh was very worried. What could he do to keep the match on the card? Who could he get at the last minute to fill in for me? I felt terrible. A lot was put into promoting this match and me being a participant in it.

I told him, "My son can do it."

Mutoh said, "No, no, he can't do this. He's too young."

I said, "Yes. Yes, he can. He was an amateur wrestler. He's been in a ring. I know he can do it."

Mutoh finally agreed to put Reid in my place.

I knew Reid understood this from studying the business, but I wanted to remind him that the crowd in Japan is different. They're not loud like the audiences in the States. I didn't want him to do something during the match and expect a reaction, and when he didn't get it, think he did something wrong.

A few minutes into the match, I arrived at ringside and stood in their corner.

It was fun playing off my history with Fujinami and playing up the possibility that we might have an altercation. The crowd enjoyed it. I didn't get in the ring. This wasn't about me. At one point, Reid and I took turns chopping Sanada outside the ring. I was so proud to see Reid excel with a young star and with legends Mutoh and Fujinami.

I worked with both men many times. I wrestled Fujinami before more than sixty-four thousand people in the Tokyo Dome in March of 1991. That was during WCW's working relationship with New Japan Pro Wrestling and the event called Starrcade in the Tokyo Dome. I was the

World Heavyweight Champion, and Fujinami was the IWGP Champion. Our rematch was at WCW's first SuperBrawl pay-per-view almost two months later.

During this tag match, when they saw Reid move around the ring, I think Mutoh and Fujinami realized his enormous potential. They saw how agile he was and, thanks to his amateur wrestling background, how he followed that up later in the match with rolling German suplexes that ended on a great-looking bridge into a pin-fall attempt.

The match was well received by the audience and by All Japan. As a sign of respect, we all shook hands. I felt great watching the postmatch interview backstage and seeing Reid next to Mutoh with cameras flashing and members of the press around them. He was going to do very well in Japan.

I was so proud of Reid. Most importantly, he was proud of himself. People in the locker room congratulated him and shook his hand. He deserved that. It was a phenomenal way for him to begin his tenure with All Japan.

The next day, they told me that Reid would be in the dojo for two months before having a match and that it was going to be tough. I didn't think he'd be in there that long, but I didn't say anything. What would've been the point of me telling them he'd be out of there in two weeks?

Before I left for the airport and home, I told Reid, "Stay focused. You can't get sidetracked here. In this country, they put Paul McCartney in jail for smoking a joint. Stay focused so everyone here can see all the potential you have. I know you can do it."

Reid began training in the dojo. When I left, I thought Reid would be out of there and have matches in two weeks. I was wrong. My son was out of there and in the ring in five days.

He loved the structure of the environment and immersed himself in wrestling. Reid was also enamored of the Japanese culture. He loved teaching kids and began instructing young children in the fundamentals of wrestling.

He and his sister were posting about each other's training on social media. Reid was in All Japan, and Ashley was in NXT, Paul's WWE developmental program of the future.

Reid's work was so well received and his work ethic was so highly regarded that his stay was extended for another three months. Even on his days off, he still trained in the gym. Our family was so proud of him. An expanded stay also meant that his talents would be featured in matches as part of his first tour with All Japan.

Reid continued to receive high praise for his work. He performed well in singles, tag team matches, and in six-man tags. He learned how to perform and have compelling matches with opponents of different shapes, sizes, and in-ring styles. Reid was thrilled. He couldn't wait to go back to Japan in April to continue his work. And I knew he was going to miss his young wrestling students in the dojo.

Reid's last show in Tokyo was on March 22. I made arrangements for him to come home so we could go to WrestleMania 29 in New Jersey together. Ashley was selected to be part of the NXT roster, performing in matches during Axxess, the fan experience that runs during WrestleMania week.

Reid made it home to Charlotte. Once he settled in with his mother, he saw family and continued his workouts. He was so excited about showing the people he worked with back home what he'd learned while training in Japan.

On his first day back in Charlotte, Reid continued his training. He was completely focused on what he was doing and wanted to make sure he returned to Japan in better shape than when he left.

I saw him the next day, and he looked great and sounded even better. It was wonderful to hear the experiences he'd had in Japan. We were all happy that his girlfriend, Whitney, visited him during his final two weeks there. She was considered a member of our family and was devoted to my son. He was devoted to her too.

The following night, I took Reid to dinner at Del Frisco's Steak House. I could tell he was going to keep to his training regimen and diet for his trip back to Japan. He drank water all night.

We were heading out in the morning to work independent shows in Maryland and Pennsylvania. Then we were going to New Jersey to meet up with Ashley. We couldn't wait to see her perform at Axxess.

I so looked forward to this weekend. Of all the years I brought my kids to WrestleMania, this year it felt like I was going to be watching them: Ashley performing in the ring and Reid reconnecting with people at WWE and sharing with them everything he did with All Japan.

A part of me still couldn't believe we were going to WrestleMania. I knew that this was my son's dream from a very young age, from wanting to go to every show with me to amateur wrestling and being a four-time national champion to training with amateur great T. J. Jaworsky. He worked with personal trainers—you name it: if it involved professional wrestling, Reid was all about it. But Ashley?

After a couple of weeks of training, I asked her how it was going. She said, "I love it. I should've been doing this all along."

Ashley and I had an appearance the month before in Melbourne, Florida. When I heard her greet autograph-seeking fans and say her ring name, it took me back to when she'd called and told me what her ring name was going to be.

She said, "Dad, my name's going to be 'Charlotte.'"

I said the first thing that came to my mind. "That's perfect."

PART II

GROWING UP FLIEHR

March 29, 2016—Dallas/Fort Worth International Airport

The wheels just touched down on the runway. It's the greatest time of year for people in the sports-entertainment industry—WrestleMania. Before I can get out of my seat, so many emotions seem to be converging at one time. How should I feel? I'm overcome with anticipation . . . excitement . . . happiness . . . sadness . . . and perhaps the strongest of all, the fear of uncertainty.

I've been to WrestleMania many times as a spectator, most notably to watch my dad's final match in a WWE ring and, on two separate occasions, to see him inducted into the WWE Hall of Fame, an honor only he has received.

I remember the first time I set foot on WrestleMania's sacred ground. It was WrestleMania XXIV. I was just twenty-two years old when I took the stage with my siblings to greet the crowd on my dad's behalf as the 2008 Hall of Fame Class was announced. I was so nervous. Being in front of more than seventy-four thousand people at the Florida Citrus Bowl was like standing on a beach and looking out at the ocean—all you saw was a sea of people. It was awesome. It meant so much to us to stand together to celebrate my father's life's work. I never envisioned that one day I'd be the one to perform in front of such a large crowd.

What some people don't know is that since that night in Orlando, Florida, I appeared once before at a WrestleMania as part of Triple H's grand entrance. It was at WrestleMania 30 in 2014. As a goddess, I wore an extravagant gold mask and a skirt of flowing crimson silk as the King of Kings entered into battle against Daniel Bryan. Though it was an uncredited role, I was sure it would've made Cleopatra green with envy. But that was then— and this is now.

This year, 2016, is the thirty-second WrestleMania, and I'm the reigning WWE Divas Champion. Sunday will mark one of the select times in WWE history that a women's championship is being defended at WrestleMania and only the second time the Divas Championship is on the line. The match for the Divas crown is one of the most anticipated of the show, and I couldn't be prouder to be part of it.

The music of Guns N' Roses has been one of the sound tracks of my life. As I thread my way through the airport to pick up my car, the song "Patience"—my current anthem—is playing in my head. Being here and knowing what Sunday means reminds me that sometimes I still can't believe where I am in my life. I was my dad's biggest fan, but I never wanted to be a WWE Superstar. This is a far cry from the roads of Charlotte, North Carolina, where I once called home. It's not anything like the volleyball courts I thought I would compete on forever.

This trip to Dallas represents an unlikely journey to WWE. It's all coming back to me—the relationship with my dad, a marriage I shouldn't have been in, the fear of the unknown when I first reported to Tampa, Florida, for training, establishing myself in the rings of NXT, and the hurt when someone who I looked up to professionally said I wasn't ready to be on WWE's main roster. I wonder what would have happened if this had gone another way, if someone else—not me—was chosen to end Nikki Bella's historic Divas Championship reign.

It's now, when I'm in the car, that I can see my picture along with other WWE talent posted outside of AT&T Stadium. I know there's more work to be done, but I can't help but feel a sense of achievement. I think about the people who believed they should've been holding this championship instead of me, the people who thought I was a joke and just another wrestler's kid looking for a handout, and the people who tell me the only reason I'm doing anything noteworthy is because of who my father is. But that doesn't take away from this moment. I won't let it.

I wouldn't be here without the work of the Four Horsewomen; without Nattie (better known as WWE's Natalya) believing in me, without support from my parents and family, and Dusty Rhodes, and Becky Lynch being there every step of the way, and most of all, without the encouragement from my brother and best friend, Reid.

It wasn't long ago that we both, in our own way, were in such dark places. Reid pushed me to pursue a WWE career, and now I'm living his dream. I sense his presence most when I'm performing—walking to the ring, feeling the canvas underneath my boots and the ropes across my hands. WrestleMania week is when I get the strongest sense that Reid is by my side. I think it will be that way for the rest of my life.

Even now, days away from the biggest date on the WWE calendar, I feel a sense of uncertainty about my match.

Backstage this past week at *Monday Night Raw*, Stephanie McMahon and Triple H laid rumors to rest: as of this Sunday at WrestleMania, female competitors would no longer be called WWE Divas. The Divas Championship would be retired. Instead, we would be referred to, like the men, as WWE Superstars. They unveiled the stunning white, gold, and diamond prize, which would be worn by the new WWE Women's Champion. I don't know if I'll be the one leaving Dallas with that beautiful title or if I'm performing at WrestleMania to hand the championship over to someone else.

There are a lot of questions that will be answered in the coming days. I will make sure that I do what I always have to ensure that my story continues—and that's to work hard. One thing I already know—before I go anywhere or do anything—is that the journey that's brought me to AT&T Stadium and the path I will travel after it mean everything to me.

8

A BEAUTIFUL LIFE

Our life may have seemed like a fantasy to other people.

October 1996

I can still hear myself saying, "I'll race you to the back door, and you'll never beat me!" My little brother's infectious laugh matched the sound of our small feet. We ran as fast as we could to get through the wooden gate that fenced in our backyard. If we weren't pushing each other out of the way during our sprint, we'd run to the front of the house to climb our favorite tree. It had the perfect branch to lie across like we were in *The Jungle Book*.

Our neighbors were a German family named the Lindenbecks. They had three children: Axel, Michael, and Caroline. I named my short-hair Siamese cat after Michael. The cat became so infamous in the Fliehr house that he was included in one of the oil-painted murals my mom gave my dad as gift. It hung above the fireplace. The Lindenbecks' house was overwrought with trees like a cottage tucked away in the woods from *Hansel and Gretel*. Every morning at dawn, Reid, whom I called Reider, and I made trails from their house to ours. We either ran on foot or raced across on our bikes. These were epic adventures into an enchanted forest, and it was up to us to find our way home—and the trails were too scary to run through at night. But that was only the beginning. With the

back of our brick house on the horizon, our determination propelled us through our backyard, across the sprawling lawn, past my dollhouse, through the swing set, around the pool, and up the deck stairs into our house. Every moment was dedicated to wreaking havoc on the Lindenbecks' yard. Whatever risks we thought we took during our explorations were worth the reward. It was breakfast time.

When I think of those mornings, I can see my mom's face in the doorway so clearly. My mother had long, natural brown-and-blond hair with bangs and crystal-blue eyes. Her smile was brighter than any star in the sky, and she had olive skin. Those mornings, she'd have on an oversized yellow cotton T-shirt that hung past her knees. It had a giant Mickey Mouse face on the front of it. She was so beautiful, she didn't need to wear makeup.

My mother was born at Fort Jackson Army Base in Columbia, South Carolina, and was raised in Havana, Florida, a suburb of Tallahassee. She was the oldest of six children, and her natural maternal instincts were honed helping raise her five siblings. My mom always dreamed of having children of her own.

My parents were married in 1983. My older siblings, Megan and David, were in my parents' wedding party, as were Jim Crockett, Ricky Steamboat, and Roddy Piper. Roddy Piper became a confidant to Reider later in life. My mother's best friend, Susan Beck, was also in their wedding party. Early into their marriage, my mom had a difficult time staying pregnant and suffered through several tubal pregnancies. When I was older, it was explained to me that a tubal pregnancy is when a fertilized egg attaches itself outside the uterus and can't survive. Left un-treated, it can be life-threatening to the mother.*

My mom endured a great deal of physical and emotional pain, and she faced an enormous amount of uncertainty, wondering if she could sustain a pregnancy from conception to delivery.†

After four years of marriage, my mom's dream came true: she was pregnant with me. While her doctor approached each appointment with extra caution, she had a normal pregnancy and gave birth to me without complication. I was told that after my mom gave birth to me, she wouldn't put me down. I slept on her. She wouldn't let me go.

Twenty-two months later, another blessing. This time, it was a boy. The pregnancy was fine until the doctor discovered something during the delivery.‡

We were my mother's miracle children, and she loved us every day

---

* Ric: "The question was, could Beth have a normal pregnancy? The egg would grow in the fallopian tube and could not sustain itself. The egg would eventually burst, and she'd start bleeding internally. Back then, there were not tests to see if you had a tubal pregnancy. You had symptoms, like feeling like you were going to faint, throwing up, and bleeding. My dad had an OB-GYN practice in Minnesota and helped her during this time. His partner per-formed a surgery on her to repair her tube, and she was told it had only a 10 percent chance of being successful. After the surgery, we waited several months before being able to try to become pregnant again. She went through a lot."

† Ric: "I was on the road so much back then that Beth would travel with me. I was coming back from Japan, so she met me in Hawaii. We found out she was pregnant again. We were so happy, we started to celebrate. Suddenly, she started to get familiar feelings and thought it might be another tubal. She was right. The doctor wanted her to stay in Hawaii for sur-gery to remove it. We were so upset. Against doctor's orders, she flew home with her friends to Charlotte to see her doctor. By the time she landed, she felt dizzy, started throwing up, and was bleeding. I came home immediately. Her doctor rushed her into surgery to save the tube. After she recovered, he told her the small chances of having a normal pregnancy were getting smaller. That was the first time she started to lose hope."

‡ Ric: "Beth was in labor. I got very emotional and ended up choking. I went into the bath-room. Beth told the doctors to make sure I was okay, but they refused to leave her. She continued to push, and the baby was delivered. The doctor and his team took the baby and immediately brought him behind a curtain. I didn't know what was going on because I was

like precious gifts from heaven. My mom worked hard to make sure the house was in order, that my dad's schedule was set, and, most of all, we were together as a family as much as possible. She wanted the best for her children, and she wanted us to be the best we could be at anything we pursued. I can hear her telling me, "Ashley, always do your best. Always be the best that you can."

Every day, my mom and grandmommy made magic for us in the kitchen. No plate went unfinished in our house. In the morning, the aroma of pancakes filled our home. Reider and I would run to the kitchen table, sit next to each other, and plead, "Grandmommy, please make Grandmommy's pana cakes." My mom and grandmommy smiled at each other because they were already making them for us. Grandmommy's "pana cakes" were made with Bisquick. What made them so special was the large skillet that was used. They always came out perfectly round and thin.

To enjoy pana cakes, Reider and I needed two things: Land O'Lakes butter and Aunt Jemima syrup. We always argued about who would get the next pana cake. A bowl of batter was always next to the refrigerator.

We shared so many wonderful meals as a family at home. I see my mom and grandmommy making chicken and dumplings. The dumplings were the size of baseballs, and the chicken was pulled by hand and placed in a huge pot that sat on top of the stove. Plates of fried okra lined the table, and squash casserole made with Philadelphia cream cheese was topped with crushed Keebler Club crackers. My dad made his ground beef chili when he came home.

Our family used these times as a way to be together among our hectic schedules between school, sports practices and games, piano lessons, and my father being on the road each week for work.

Although we'd try to delay the inevitable and create reasons why we couldn't go to school, when it was time, we bickered about whose turn it was to sit in the front seat and filed into Mom's giant black Mercedes before the long roll down the driveway. We loved the heated seats in the

---

still choking. The delivery team said, 'It's okay, We'll be right there.' It turned out, Reid's umbilical cord was wrapped around his neck."

winter. The opening notes to "The Great Migration" from *The Land Before Time* and, my favorite, the chorus from "I Just Can't Wait to Be King" from *The Lion King* always made us smile. We'd hit the same line of traffic on Sardis Road every morning. Once we hit the neighborhood known as Lansdowne, reality set in—we were a few minutes away from school.

If you were a child living in south Charlotte who went to private school, chances were you attended Providence Day School. Since it opened its doors, Providence Day has been one of the finest private schools in the country. Like the city of Charlotte back then, Providence Day was beautiful and felt like a community. The school offered classes from transitional kindergarten through twelfth grade, and it was expected for kids to be there all thirteen years and then go on to college. Everyone went to college. For some kids, it was predetermined from birth where they would go to college and which sorority or fraternity they would join, and it wasn't up for discussion.

In many cases, children at Providence Day were part of the same social circle: we went to the same school and played sports together, and families hosted different functions at Providence, Ballantyne, and Piper Glen country clubs. Some of us went to the same church and frequented the same restaurants. We'd run into friends at Harper's and the Palm at Phillips Place.

After graduating from pre-K at St. Stephen's United Methodist Church in 1991, I became a proud member of Providence Day's kindergarten class. Despite my spirited efforts to stay home, once I got to school, I was fine. In the afternoon, Grandmommy picked me up, and sometimes we'd go straight home. I'd put my book bag down and take my seat at the tabletop in the kitchen to watch TV shows like *Family Matters*, *Designing Women*, *The Nanny*, and *The Golden Girls*. Other times, on the way to gymnastics practice, we'd go to Back Yard Burgers, one of my favorite restaurants.

My grandmommy lived with us and helped raise Reider and me. She spoiled us with unconditional love and amazing food. On any evening, the smell of chicken and dumplings, "perlo," a.k.a. chicken and rice, and fresh spaghetti drifted through the house. Most nights, Reider and I could be found sitting on the steps just off the kitchen, anticipating when

her wonderful culinary creation would be served. Then we'd run to our chairs to eat. My parents and grandmommy always made sure we ate, and that included a struggle to eat our steamed broccoli— even if we put one square of Kraft Singles cheese on every stem. We also had to finish each meal by drinking a tall glass of milk.

Whether I went home after school or came home after an activity, there were two places I wanted to go: my dollhouse and the playroom.

My parents had a dollhouse built for me. I don't mean the Barbie Dreamhouse in my bedroom with a pink Corvette next to it, or something with a handle that I could take with me, or even a scale model of a Victorian home. This was my own house. Just off our deck was a little white wood house—something off the pages of my mom's *Southern Living* magazine.

Once you passed the planted flowers in the front, you'd open the door and walk on Italian marble floors, stroll under elegant ceiling fans in each room, and see a ladder that led to a second-floor loft that was a bedroom. I would host my family during "dinner" and "tea parties" and push my cat, Michael, in a stroller for my dolls. He was part of our family too.

The playroom room is where Reider and I watched movies. The room had beautiful beige leather couches that were so comfortable it was like resting on a cloud. We liked to wrestle on them, do flips off them, and make tents extending from one couch to the other. In the corner was a huge leather chair that my dad would sit in when he came home. One night, my parents, Reider, and I played a board game where each player took a card and had to act out a scene from a famous movie in a certain amount of time.

We all just laughed at each other, and one Fliehr looked sillier than the next.

The TV screen took up almost the entire wall. It felt like we were in our own movie theater.

The feature presentation could be any number of films, and sometimes I'd have a double feature. Disney classics like *101 Dalmatians*, *Cinderella*, and *Snow White* were always in the rotation—as were newer Disney films of the time like *The Little Mermaid*, *The Lion King*, *Aladdin*, and *Pocahontas*.

There were movies that I loved so much you could come to our house any day and one of them would be playing: *Ghostbusters*, *Forrest Gump*, *Steel Magnolias*, *Cool Runnings*, *Mrs. Doubtfire*, *Batman*, and all-time favorites—*The Land Before Time* and *Jurassic Park*.

Jurassic Park was released in June of 1993. My dad was traveling for work, and we waited for him to come home so we could all watch it together. He called to tell me that he and my uncle Arn were preparing for a big match in Virginia the next week but that as soon as he came home, we'd all go to Arboretum Cineplex to see it. I didn't understand what made this trip more important than the others. I patiently counted down the days.

My dad came home. By the time I knew it, we each had our bucket of popcorn and were in our seats as the theater lights slowly dimmed. I loved the previews. I'd turn to my mom and say, "Yeah, that looks so good," and then turn to my dad and say, "I think that looks so good. Don't you?"

The music, the story, the enormity of the dinosaurs . . . Steven Spielberg had me gripping both armrests from the opening credits. Even now, I get chills thinking about the kitchen scene and the ingenuity and agility of the raptors. I was scared, but I knew I had to be brave and keep watching. I looked on both sides of me and saw the look on my parents' faces and the shock on Reider's face. It was like we were on the Tower of Terror ride at Disney World. We all hoped that Lex and Tim Murphy would make it out of the kitchen alive. I kept picturing Reider and me in the scene and wondered if we could outsmart the raptors and make it out. To this day, I think we would've bested the bloodthirsty beasts.

Jurassic Park is one of my favorite movies. That night at the Arboretum Cineplex will always be dear to me, because it's one of the few movies we watched in the theater together as a family.

On a side note, what I learned years later was that Dad and Uncle Arn were in Virginia for the main event of Clash of the Champions XXIII, in a two-out-of-three falls match against Steve Austin and Brian Pillman, the Hollywood Blonds. So now I'll agree with my dad—that was pretty important.

At a young age, I had some health issues. In kindergarten, I had a persistent problem—strep throat. After the third time I got it, the doctor told my parents that if it happened again, I'd need to have my tonsils taken out. Shortly after that appointment, strep returned, and my parents decided to have my tonsils removed.

Following the surgery, I needed to be watched closely, because I was throwing up blood. Ultimately, the procedure was a success; the strep throat never came back. My mom was so proud of how I handled everything, she bought me a purple mountain bike, but by the time all that was over I'd missed so much school that my parents decided to keep me back a year.

In first grade, I experienced one of the rights of passage to growing up—chicken pox. After a couple of days, what was thought to be a mild case became worse. I ran a fever, my body ached all over, and the itching was so bad that wearing clothes seemed like cruel and unusual punishment. I was moved to my parents' room so I could sleep in their bed. It was so high off the floor, I needed help getting into it. My two favorite stuffed animals made the move with me: a small velvet dog my parents brought me back from Japan, who I called "Doggy," and a two-and-a-half-foot bunny I named "Floppy" because of his arms and legs. They went everywhere with me. I had to take baths in Epsom salt twice a day. I can still see the pure white southern shower curtain lining along the tub. I remember looking up at the white wallpaper with pink ribbons printed on it. After I'd dry off, my mom covered me in calamine lotion. It felt like a papier-mâché project gone wrong all over my skin. I battled against the virus for almost two weeks. Thanks to my mom, I made a full recovery and was able to keep up with my school assignments.

After saying goodbye to first grade and hello to summer, things took an unexpected turn.

I was playing baseball with my parents and Reider in our backyard. While I was running, my back locked up, and I fell to the ground. I couldn't move, and my entire body was in pain. I was terrified and didn't know what I had done. After seeing a spine specialist, I was told my back went into a spasm—a spontaneous contraction of a muscle. After undergoing tests with two different specialists, it was discovered that I had a cracked fifth lumbar, also known as spondylolysis, where my vertebrae kept rubbing against each other—something very common for gymnasts. Though I didn't know it at the time, the doctor and my parents were worried that surgery would be the only solution. That was something no one wanted, especially at my young age.

After a follow-up appointment, my parents were told that surgery was not necessary. The only way for my back to recover was to be put in something that had to be fitted for my body and I couldn't take off once it was on—a body cast. So, for the entire summer of 1994, I was in a body cast while my back healed. One afternoon, I fell while I was running and broke my arm.* For a couple of months, my arm was wrapped in addition

---

*Ric: "We knew Ashley was not going to stay still for the whole summer. She eventually found a way to run while in that body cast. Can you believe that? In no time she was running as fast as Reid. She kept all of us on our toes. It drove Beth and me nuts."

to the body cast. I was so upset that I couldn't go swimming that my dad bought a huge safety raft so I could float around while everyone swam around me.

Overall, I was a good kid. I played by the rules. I used to love to play in my parents' cars—something they allowed me to do, since I enjoyed pretending that I could drive their Mercedes-Benzes too. I would sit in one of their cars, pushing buttons on the radio and imitating how my parents would open and close the glove compartment. I'd move down in the driver's seat to press on the gas and brake pedals. One day when I was looking through the glove compartment of my dad's Mercedes, I found something that looked like a miniature walkie-talkie, but I wasn't sure what it was. But being a good kid, I put it back and never mentioned what I had seen to either of my parents.

When the edict of early bedtime was established, Reider and I joined forces to beat the system. Like good little children, we endured the evening rituals of bath time and brushing our teeth before retiring to our respective bedrooms. My mom, dad, or grandmommy would tuck us in and made sure to read us a story. Grandmommy would always say a prayer with us.

"Now I lay me down to sleep, I pray to you, Lord, my soul to keep. If I should die before I wake, please take my soul to keep. God bless Mommy and Daddy, Reid, Megan, and David, my grandmommy, granddaddy, grandma, and grandpa, and all those that I love. Please let them know I love them. Please forgive me for my many sins. Amen."

Some nights we'd ask for "special treatment," which meant Mom or Dad lightly massaged our faces until we fell asleep. Reider liked to have angel wings drawn on his back. We loved it. Then we'd give big hugs and kisses and go to bed—or so they thought.

The minutes pretending to be asleep were excruciating.

Each night, when the coast was clear, we took turns tiptoeing into each other's rooms to watch TV. (I preferred Reider's room because he had a race car bed.) We had to handle this delicately. The key was to make sure the volume was high enough for us to hear but low enough so that the adults in the house didn't suspect what we were doing. If we heard someone coming, one of us rushed to turn the TV off. While we made our night moves, I always had to tell Reider not to laugh, but he couldn't help it. Like so many great ideas, our strategy had to be meticulously planned. Like the perfect caper, we needed a secret weapon, and we had one—Grandmommy.

She'd sneak upstairs and bring bowls of Breyers chocolate ice cream for the three of us to enjoy while we watched *Buffy the Vampire Slayer*, *Felicity*, or *Dawson's Creek*. Reider and I would play thumb wars and sometimes punch each other for stealing the covers. Grandmommy stayed with us every night until we went to sleep. I never knew if my mom was aware of our late-night tradition and let it go, or if we really pulled off what we thought was the best covert operation of the twentieth century—at least in the greater south Charlotte area.

During many of those nights, separately, Reider and I migrated into our parents' room and slept in their bed when my dad was away for work.

I loved being around my family and friends, but I didn't like being the center of attention. I didn't like going to sleepovers, because I always wanted to be home with my family. There was one exception: the Helms family. Sybil and her husband, Mike, and their daughters, Mika, Sheila, and Molly, helped take care of our house. They became family to us. Reider and I spent nights in their home. The Helmses lived on a pasture about an hour away from Charlotte.

They'd boil peanuts for us and let us eat as much cereal as we could eat. My favorite was Lucky Charms. We were not allowed to have that at home because of all the sugar in it. They treated us like we were their children.

One time, I brought Randy Savage to school for show-and-tell. He walked into the school in full Macho Man attire. He came back to our house and threw Sybil in the pool—it was like an impromptu pool party.

I gravitated toward exercise and playing sports. I remember being three years old and doing squats with my dad on our deck.

He had a separate gym built on our property that was so big, people thought it was a second house. Once you stepped through the door, you were inspired by wall-to-wall, state-of-the-art Cybex equipment.

I remember sitting on the teal leather seats and walking on the tread-mill. I loved going on the stair-climber and feeling like I was getting my cardio in for the day. Just like my dad.

He was away for work a few days a week every week. On television, in arenas, and all over the world, he was famous for being the Nature Boy. When he was just forty years old, and by the time Reider and I were born, he was considered a living legend in sports entertainment and one of the greatest, if not the greatest, performers of all time.

He'd come home with his matching black TUMI luggage, dressed in a suit from Taylor Richards, a button-down shirt, and leather shoes that gleamed. He brought a silver briefcase with him whenever he traveled for work. My father was handsomer than any Hollywood leading man. I'll always remember when he cut his hair at the behest of a WCW executive. He brought me to his hairstylist that day. I didn't know what was going to happen. All of a sudden, huge pieces of his gorgeous blond hair were being chopped off. I started crying and picked up the hair off the floor with my hands and tried to give it back to him. As children, we had no idea the struggles he went through in WCW when they wanted to change his image and give him a new name.

I think some people had this idea of my dad at home in his diamond-studded robes, flashing the symbol of the Four Horsemen, and answering the phone saying his signature, "WOOOOO!" catchphrase. Later, I learned this idea took on a life of its own after WCW's 1994 Spring Stampede. During the main event match between my dad and Ricky Steamboat, Bobby "the Brain" Heenan said on commentary, "You should see the robe he wears at home." I don't want to disappoint my dad's fans, but that couldn't be further from the truth—that was just for the show.

For all the "stylin' and profilin'" that he was famous for, when my father walked through our door, all he wanted to do was spend time with his family. He wanted us to have the best of everything and anything we wanted. To us, he was "Daddy." I was so proud in the third grade when each student had to bring in a shoe to decorate in class. I brought my dad's wrestling boot and put gold and silver sprinkles around the *RF*.

When he was home and my parents had plans, my mom and dad looked like they were the president and the First Lady. They always hosted dinner parties with their friends the Becks, attended community and business functions, took us to Charlotte Hornets games. They loved being with one another. I can still see my dad's immaculate blond hair and smell my mom's Boucheron perfume when she'd kiss us good night. One year, my parents bought the main street in front of Providence Day to support a fund-raiser for the school. The green street sign read, "Ric Flair Blvd."

My dad grew up in a suburb of Minneapolis, Minnesota, called Edina.

He moved to Charlotte in 1974 and quickly became a local celebrity. Something people may not know is that, starting in the early '90s, he became a well-known member of the Charlotte business community. He owned Gold's Gyms.

What he took pride in, and what the Nature Boy may not have wanted people to know, is that from day one, he was a great dad.* He did an excellent job of following Grandmommy's recipe for pana cakes and even bought a waffle iron to make waffles with the batter. He'd take us to school and pick us up, go on backyard adventures with us, bring us to Sports Authority every week to buy us new athletic equipment, play H-O-R-S-E with us in the driveway, and take us to restaurants for family dinners.

Sushi night at Nakato was a major event. We'd all sit at the sushi bar for hours while amazing sushi rolls and sashimi were passed around on big wooden boats. Megan, David, and I used to laugh when Reider would say, "I like the boats. You like the boats." We'd get takeout too. I can still taste the Snow White Chicken from Chia Best as those tall brown paper bags, stuffed into plastic ones, covered our kitchen counter.

When I think back, I realize that people recognized my dad everywhere he went. They were always very respectful of his time with his family. Rarely did anyone come up to us, but anyone who asked for an autograph or a picture with him was always very nice—and because we were his kids, people were kind to us everywhere we went. We had no idea that our dad was a celebrity. He would drive up to a storefront to stop in quickly and leave the car running. Sometimes people would say, "WOOOOO!" in passing. We just thought people were being friendly, especially since we were regulars at so many places. Except in one bizarre instance.

After a family night out, we came home and found that our garage had been broken into and vandalized. A wrestling fan, who eventually

---

*Ric: "I was away from Megan and David so much during my first marriage to Leslie. I learned that you can't make up for lost time. That's why I was so glad I was in a position with WCW to take weekends off and be able to spend so much time with Ashley and Reid. I thanked God for it then, and looking back now, I cherish those times even more."

became a family stalker, had embarked on what would become years of psychotic behavior directed at my father and our family. This person spray-painted obscenities on my dad's Mercedes and smeared paint all over the garage's interior walls. The stalker also called our house and pretended to be other people. We never gave information out over the phone unless we knew the person calling. One night, the stalker called and told my parents that voodoo dolls were made and needles were being put in them to curse my parents' lives.

Whether it was a major threat to us or something as simple as a bicycle accident, my father was very protective of us and always had a solution. One morning, Reider and I were on our bikes, and I fell over the top of the handlebars. When I got up off the ground, my four front teeth were on the ground, and my mouth filled with blood. I left my bike and ran into the house as fast as I could. My mom and grandmommy couldn't tell what happened. My mom called my dad on the phone, and I was crying, screaming, asking him to come home. He came home that day. We found two of the teeth that the dentist could put back. A rod was placed over my front teeth so the roots could grow back. I felt like my nickname was going to be "Snaggletooth" or "Bucktooth."

After that ordeal, my dad proclaimed, "Let's get them go-carts with helmets!"

We grew up with Dad's work friends as fixtures in our house. Out of all the wonderful people that were part of our life, there's one name, one voice, one face that will forever be a special part of our family— Uncle Arn.

Arn Anderson rose to prominence as a member of the famous Anderson wrestling "family," my dad's TV "cousins." Uncle Arn was a founder of the famous Four Horsemen and gave the group its iconic name. He had a TV persona so intimidating that his nickname was "the Enforcer." Away from the ring, Uncle Arn was the kindest, sincerest person you could ever meet. He and my dad were like brothers. Our families spent holidays and vacations together, and Reider and I were close with his son Barrett. When I think of my childhood, I realize a huge part of it included

Uncle Arn and my dad sitting on our deck, talking, and enjoying a few beers.*

Other stars from WCW we frequently saw included Bobby Eaton, who rose to fame as part of the Midnight Express tag team; referees Tommy Young and Pee Wee Anderson; stars like Terry Taylor, Kevin Sullivan, and his wife, Nancy, who was Woman on TV; and of course, Dusty Rhodes, whose son Cody was in my class at St. Stephen's. Most fans didn't know, and I learned later, that dating back to the '80s, Dusty was an executive and was as substantial an influence behind the camera as he was in front of it.

For a few years, we took trips to Lake Norman to visit Ricky Steamboat and his family. Reider and I were friends with his son, Richie, who I'd meet again in FCW, but we'll talk about that later.

When I was five years old, I studied jazz, tap, and ballet at Fancy Feet Dance Academy. The recitals were major events held at Ovens Auditorium in Charlotte. I had three outfits and was a lead for three dance numbers. Grandparents from both sides attended my recitals. There was an excitement all year to see which costumes we'd be wearing and what dance numbers we'd perform. This was also the one time of year that I was allowed to have lipstick, blush, and mascara on. My mom loved styling my hair and applying makeup for my recitals, and I loved wearing her red lipstick. After the final number, my parents greeted me with an enormous bouquet of flowers. Dance was a lot of fun, and though I didn't realize it at the time, it built a strong foundation for the life that was to come.

When I entered first grade, I began competing in gymnastics. From my first practice at International Gymnastics, it was intense. Practices were eighteen hours a week after school: Monday, Wednesday, Thursday, and Friday from 4:30 p.m. to 9:00 p.m. On Saturday, I trained from 9:00 a.m. to 1:00 p.m. It was here, under Coach Suzie Sanocki, that I had

---

*Ric: "The Horsemen were so close back then. Everything we talked about on television—the jets, the limousines, the all-night parties—they were all true. One of the reasons it worked was because we were so close. From that, my family and Arn's family grew up together. It was wonderful."

principles from home reinforced: work hard, prove yourself, and earn people's respect. We traveled all over the southeastern United States to compete in gymnastics events. Coach Suzie was very strict, emphasized discipline, and motivated us to be our best not only as gymnasts but as people too. She also treated her gymnasts like they were her own children.

The holiday season was the most exciting time of year in the Fliehr house: days off from school, family and friends coming to our house, including my dad's parents, Grandma and Grandpa, and the best part, visits with my older siblings, Megan and David.

From my earliest memories, Megan and David have been a huge part of my life. They are my dad's children from his first marriage to Leslie. Megan and David lived in Minnesota and came to Charlotte for holidays, summers, and family vacations.

Megan is the oldest of the Fliehr kids and the most intelligent. She was a standout basketball player, has a great sense of humor, and is the only one of us who never sought a life in the squared circle. As the oldest Fliehr child, she's had to be the toughest emotionally. Megan bottle-fed me as a baby and is someone I've idolized my entire life. Megan's been there for me every step of the way.

David is one of the kindest people I know. He is so genuine with his love and feelings for those who are close to him. Growing up, he was an all-star on the baseball diamond. To this day, David is the perfect big brother, providing a balance of protection, counsel, and lighthearted pranks. I know how much he loves me.

The fact that Megan and David lived in Minnesota never affected our relationship. The four of us were always close; we all shared the same sense of humor and could feel each other's pain. If they weren't in Charlotte, we'd talk on the phone. It felt special knowing that I had an older sister and brother I could count on. They were close with my mom and even called Grandmommy by that name. To this day, Megan and David are like parents, older siblings, and best friends. They've been an incredible influence on my life and are two of the greatest people I know.

Each of us had a nickname. In fact, it was rare that we used our real names when speaking to one another. Megan was "Meegs," David was

"Big Dave," I was "Winky," and Reid was "Reider." Proving to be the quintessential younger brother, Reider sometimes called me "Stinky Winky," to which I'd reply, "Reider, Reider, Pumpkin Eater."

Every year on the Saturday of Thanksgiving weekend, we decorated our house for Christmas. I remember running around in a frenzy to see how I could help my mom. Even writing about it now, I have visions in my mind of Reider and me working together to take lights and tinsel out of huge boxes as my mom unearthed family ornaments from layers of Bubble Wrap. We had the same ornaments, placed in the same part of the tree. My grandma created handmade stockings with our names on them. My mom dressed our mantel with them, and they rested underneath a mural my mom had painted of her, Reider, and me. We still use those stockings today.

Another fun part of decorating our house for Christmas included the sights and sounds that ushered in the spirit of the season. I remember all of us watching *Home Alone* and my parents assuring Reider and me not to get our hopes up, that they would never forget us before leaving on a vacation—ever. Two songs always take me back to the times we were together in our living room: Bing Crosby's "Silent Night," because it was my grandmommy's favorite Christmas song, and "The Chipmunk Song (Christmas Don't Be Late)" from Alvin and the Chipmunks. Reider and I loved yelling, *"Alvin!"*

On Christmas morning, my parents ran with us down the stairs to see what Santa had brought. Even when the gifts from Santa's sleigh were in sight, it didn't seem real. The entire living room floor was covered with presents—like a winter wonderland—and the flow of gifts extended into other rooms. I always asked myself, *How are we going to open all of these?* But we had to because before we knew it, guests would be arriving, and there would be more presents. Santa always left something for us at their house too.

My mom hosted Christmas dinner every year. Once we finished taking family photos around the tree, dinner was served. Shrimp cocktail was the appetizer, followed by filet mignon and baked potatoes. For many years, Uncle Arn's family celebrated with us, and our families exchanged gifts under our tree. One year, NFL great Kevin Green joined the festivities. You never knew who was going to be a guest at our home, and we loved that, especially during holidays.

Another wonderful memory from the season is my dad's Gold's Gym holiday party, which was held at the South Park Suites Hotel in Charlotte. The men dressed in three-piece suits, and the women wore flowing evening gowns. There was a live band, ice sculptures, and more food and drink choices than a royal banquet. Once the band Cherry Bomb started to play and the dance floor overflowed with people, that's when Reider and I went to bed. There was no sneaking back into the party.

I was so excited when Megan came to this. We had a slumber party in her hotel room and shared the bed. She was never annoyed that I wanted to be with her and that she couldn't spend all her time with her boyfriend.

Many guests stayed at the hotel, and our family always reserved a block of suites. One year, my dad came up to the room, gently woke Reider and me, and whispered, "Guys, wake up, wake up. There's someone I'd like you to meet." We went out to the living room, and my dad said, "Michael, these are my children Ashley and Reid." This very tall, well-dressed man crouched down, shook our hands, and spoke to us for a couple of minutes. He wished us a merry Christmas and shook our hands again, and then Grandmommy took us back to bed.

The next morning at breakfast, I asked my dad who that nice man was. He said, "Ashley, that was one of the greatest basketball players of all time. That was Michael Jordan."

I said, "Oh, okay."

Reider said, "He was nice," and we went back to eating our omelets. South Park Suites had great omelets.

Something similar happened in Detroit. It was Halloween Havoc '94, and my dad was facing Hulk Hogan for the WCW Championship in a steel cage match. Mr. T was the special guest referee, and Muhammad Ali was scheduled to present the winner with the WCW Championship. Backstage, Mr. T played with us, and Muhammad Ali did a magic trick. We all laughed together. When they left, we took our seats in the arena.

We had no idea that these men, especially Muhammad Ali, were cultural and athletic icons. Reider and I just thought they were my dad's friends and maybe they'd come to our house like everyone else. That night I also met someone he respected greatly, former AWA World Champion and on-air WCW commissioner Nick Bockwinkel.

There were times when our family appeared on television in segments with my dad. The first time I remember being on television as a family was for Starrcade '93. Starrcade was created by Dusty Rhodes in the early '80s and was WCW's largest annual pay-per-view event. In its early days, Starrcade was a precursor to WrestleMania and an event that was synonymous with my dad for many years.

In 1993, after a brief time with WWE, my dad returned to WCW. On television that December, he was facing a monster named Vader for the WCW World Heavyweight Championship. Vader weighed over four hundred pounds and could fly off the top rope. It was the tenth anniversary of Starrcade, and if my dad conquered this gruesome giant, he would be crowned champion. If he lost, he would have to retire from wrestling. What a way to spend a Christmas!

To add drama to the match, earlier that night, a camera crew came to our house and filmed my dad saying goodbye to our family. To provide that added sense of authenticity, legendary TV announcer and WCW commentator "Mean" Gene Okerlund was there. They both stepped into a stretch limousine and filmed an interview segment to build suspense for the match.

After what many consider to be one of his most spirited performances, my father pinned the Mastodon, Vader, in front of the hometown Charlotte crowd and became the World Heavyweight Champion for the eleventh time.* After the match, we were all in the locker room as part of a segment with "Mean" Gene. During our interview, Ricky Steamboat and Sting came in to congratulate my dad. No one knew this

---

*Ric: "I've always liked Leon [Vader], but the big man didn't want to lose that night. That match was so physical, it was like a war from the old days of our business. He hit me. I hit him back just as hard and vice versa. That intensity made the match look even better."

at the time, but I had a huge crush on Sting. He was my boyfriend—well, at least I thought so.

In front of the cameras, Gene and my dad had interviews that went from being funny and energetic to intense and emotional. At times, years later, they ended with my dad throwing down his suit jacket and performing an elbow drop on it in the middle of the ring. Away from the bright lights and cameras, they have always been close friends.

Whether it was December or April, Charlotte has always had beautiful weather. While we had four seasons, Megan and David liked to remind me that the winters in Minnesota were a bit different.

I remember pulling up to our house and seeing the sun shining on the tree branches that were dancing in the wind . . . the flowers in front of the house that led to the front door resembled something from *The Wizard of Oz*. Even as a child, spring's beautiful color palette spoke to me. There was one day in all its splendor that meant spring's brighter days were just ahead—Easter Sunday.

Each year, my parents hosted Easter dinner. But for the kids, it was all about the Fliehr Easter egg hunt. During the week before Easter, my parents secretly hid eggs all over our backyard. My dad took things to another level and put hundred-dollar bills into the eggs. One Easter, I planned to hop into my Barbie Power Wheels and comb the grounds looking for those eggs, but I didn't think that was fair to the other kids.

Regardless of the calendar, it was considered summer in the Fliehr house when my parents opened the pool. Reider and I spent hours throwing whatever we could find in the deep end to see who could grab it and make it back to the top first. Our diving contests were epic battles worthy of being included on Olympic broadcasts—or so we thought.

From slumber parties in her room with Reider and me to going to K&W Cafeteria for dinner and creating excursions that were more thrilling than anything Doc Brown and Marty McFly could've experienced in the DeLorean, another one of my mom's specialties was planning extraordinary adventures for us.

Since my dad traveled so much for work, we got to travel as a family in the summer—the best! During those days, WCW taped their TV shows at Disney-MGM Studios, which meant one of our most amazing trips each year was to the most magical place on earth—Disney World.

My parents always rented a Cadillac, and when we'd drive under the awning that said, "Welcome to Disney World," it was as though we were transported to a land where anything was possible. We'd stay in suites at the Yacht Club Resort and spend all day swimming in the sand-bottom pool and going down the waterslide until it was time to visit the parks.

Exploring the parks with my dad was always an experience. Our family had our own tour guide. One of our first stops was the *Indiana Jones Epic Stunt Spectacular!* Reider waited all year so he could sit front row and dress up like Indy: the hat, the shirt, binoculars, and a rubber snake around his neck. My parents got me a collector's Mickey Mouse watch with a leather band. At different points of our tour, they'd take turns asking me what time it was. We'd go on every ride as many times as we wanted. We'd always go on the Space Mountain ride two times in a row, though I didn't find out until I was older what my dad's references to Space Mountain meant. To say it was different is a bit of an understatement.

Going to dinner as a family was even more fun when we were on vacation, especially at Disney World. We had a view of the entire Disney skyline from our table at the Top of the World restaurant and incredible sushi dinners at the Grand Floridian Resort. We couldn't wait to stand under the stars together for the *Illuminations* fireworks show at Epcot.

Disney was only the beginning of our adventures.

I remember fishing on Mexico City Beach with my dad and Reider and making bonfires at night, building sand castles on the shores of Daytona Beach with Uncle Arn's family, snorkeling with Kevin Sullivan, and getting my hair beaded in St. Martin's with Anna Claire and Abby Murnick, whom Reider and I grew up with. Elliot Murnick was a TV announcer for Mid-Atlantic Championship Wrestling in the '70s and early '80s, a promoter, and a member of WCW's events department in the '90s. My parents were close to Elliot and his wife, Anne.

Since my dad owned a Gold's Gym there, we made trips to St. Martin's for many years. We went horseback riding on the beach, swam with dolphins, and went on cruise boats that had glass bottoms. The water was so clear we could see schools of fish swimming on the ocean floor.

My mom planned a dream trip to Colorado: white-water rafting and horseback riding in Aspen; climbing to the top of Pikes Peak in matching sweatshirts; and enjoying crêpes at a French restaurant in Vail. I remember how ridiculous my dad looked on a horse.

Of all my childhood memories of summer, there's one that stands above all the rest—spending days on my dad's boat, a thirty-six-foot Sea Ray called the *Sweet Elizabeth*.

The excitement of waiting for him to come home, knowing that the next day we'd be on the boat, was incredible. The next morning, we'd pack Jersey Mike's Subs, spicy salsa from Harris Teeter, and shrimp cocktail, beer, wine, and Gatorade into huge white coolers. We'd get into the car and drive to the marina. When my dad turned the key and we heard the boat's engine roar, we knew the fun was about to begin.

Lake Wylie was so beautiful. My dad would let us sit on the bow of the boat. He'd drop anchor so we could swim in the lake, take out the inner tube, and launch our Jet Skis. No one looked more beautiful sitting on the *Sweet Elizabeth* than the woman who it was named after, my mom. My mom taught me how to water-ski on that lake. I remember my family watching, cheering me on. I was so nervous but so excited. I can still hear her say, "You're doing it, Ashley. Stay straight, hold on. You're doing it!" I was so happy. All I could say was, "I'm waterskiing!"

Our life may have seemed like a fantasy to other people. Thanks to my family's commitment to create a "normal" life, everything was perfect for Reider and me. We thought our world was like everyone else's. Our home was filled with fun, love, and happiness, and there was no other place I wanted to be.

There was something genuine, a joyous innocence about those days. From time to time, something will bring me back to those tree-laced trails, sitting at our kitchen table, or watching late-night TV with Grandmommy and Reider. I can hear our feet running across the deck to hug dad and Uncle Arn before our next conquest in the backyard. I can hear us singing Alvin and the Chipmunks at Christmas . . .

It's funny what you carry with you as the years go on. I will always hold those days close to my heart. It was the best of times. It was a beautiful life.

9

A BLESSING AND A CURSE

The older I became, the more things changed.

October 1999

My dad pulled the car into the garage, and like always, he carried our bags in the house. That weekend, he was on the road with WCW, and I had a gymnastics competition. We landed at Charlotte Douglas International Airport around the same time. My flight arrived a few minutes early. I could see him in one of his beautiful suits with a pocket square. He walked quickly from the other side of the terminal. His recently changed his briefcase from TUMI to brown leather, and he had a large Band-Aid on his head.

I loved holding his briefcase and looking inside. It was filled with pictures of his most prized possessions—his children—and our family holiday cards from each year. You could always find one of my grandmother's silk handkerchiefs.

During my six years as a member of International Gymnastics, I achieved the distinction of being a Level 9 gymnast.*

---

*Coach Suzie Sanocki: "To put the Levels during that time into perspective, a gymnast couldn't move up to another level unless she was able to perform certain moves. Level 9 is two levels below what you see on television when you watch the Olympics."

At the time, Levels 5 and 6 were basic compulsory, which meant you did routines set to music; Level 7 meant you had your own routine and your own music. For Levels 8 and 9, the requirements were more challenging. You could only perform certain moves during longer routines and could change your music.

I was so proud of the individual and team awards I won. The awards that are closest to me were won at the team's end-of-the-year banquet. Coach Suzie recognized me with the "Hardest Worker" and "Most Determined" awards.

We had gymnastics meets every other weekend. That weekend, my team performed in one of the largest competitions in the country, the Buckeye Classic. Each year, girls from the team were selected to compete at Buckeye. We stayed at Coach Suzie's mom's house.* Outside of the competition, the weekend always was a giant slumber party. Air mattresses lined the basement floor. We played games like Monopoly and Sorry, watched movies, and enjoyed her mom's home cooking. Whenever the

---

*Coach Suzie Sanocki: "Ric and Beth were so involved. We'd get to an airport and Ric would quietly come up to me and put $500 cash in my hand and say, 'Please take everyone out to dinner tonight.' He never wanted anyone to know that. I don't know if Ashley ever knew her dad always did that for the team. If you didn't know who Ashley's father was, you'd have no idea of that based on how Ashley behaved."

2008 WWE Hall of Fame. No one else could have inducted me the way Paul did.

Being in Evolution was tremendous. It was one of the best times in my career.

Stylin' and Profilin' on *Monday Night Raw* with my man John Cena!

(*Above*) Having a few laughs backstage with The Rock. I've known him since he was twelve years old. So proud of him!

(*Left*) 1991: When the "Real" World Champion arrived in WWE.

Some of my fondest memories are nights like this, spending time with my sons.

No matter how old she is, Ashley will always be my little girl.

So what does your dad do for a living? My dad is the World Heavyweight Champion.

Always by my side . . . always teaching me . . . always having fun.

Custom made from head-to-toe. The special "Ric Flair" edition sweatshirt that was only available at his Gold's Gyms.

My favorite childhood memories are the ones where my family is together.

My parents have always been my biggest fans. They came to every event.

Hooray for Hollywood! The only time I was a flier with cheerleading.

On the road with Charlotte Elite Volleyball.

Senior year, 2005. My last home volleyball game at Providence High School.

(*Left*) One of my favorite shoots from my days in NXT.

(*Above*) Before I was the Queen, I was a goddess for the King of Kings at WrestleMania XXX.

The Four Horsewomen: Driven to change the game.

TLC 2015. Champn' with my dad.

My dad won the 1992 Royal Rumble match. He never thought I'd be in the ring in 2016 defending a WWE Championship.

The Thelma to my Louise . . . my best friend . . . I wouldn't be here without you.

With Wendy at the WWE Hall of Fame . . . I'm the luckiest man alive!

Another successful corporate event with my Legacy Talent agent Melinda. Don't let her looks distract you—she's the smartest person in the room!

WrestleMania: The first WWE Women's Champion. I didn't choose this path. It chose me.

team had new leotards, we'd have pose-offs before going to bed. Her mom taught us how to play a card game called Russian Banks that was like Go Fish. I loved traveling for gymnastics. It was one of the few times that I spent the night away from home.

That Sunday evening, I had a lot of homework from social studies to math that was due the next day in school. I always spent extra time checking my math homework. That year, I set a reading record for the number of books I read.

My parents told me that I could participate in any activity as long as I earned good grades. I wanted to be exceptional in school and as an athlete, and my parents instilled that in me. When I had an assignment due after a competition, I had to start working on it before we left town.

At that time, I was still adjusting to my new surroundings. The summer before middle school, we moved into a new house in the Piper Glen section of Charlotte. I remember when I saw the house for the first time.

We turned into the circle driveway. I got out of my dad's Mercedes and walked up to massive columns and a brick exterior with my head tilted back. When my parents opened the giant glass door, I couldn't believe my eyes. Our house in Providence Plantation was a beautiful home on a cul-de-sac in a neighborhood—this was a mansion. We were only five miles away from our old house, but it felt like another world. Everything was changing.

Reider and I argued over who would have which bedroom. Knowing her children, my mom decided that for us well in advance. Since I was older and the girl, I got the large bedroom on the third floor of the house. Reider had his choice between two other bedrooms on that floor.

Once a truce was reached, Reider and I ran through all the rooms and yelled so we could hear our voices bounce off the high ceilings. My parents smiled and said, "Slow down," but we didn't listen. We couldn't. We saw a never-ending living room for our Christmas winterscape, a billiard room, and a playroom with giant beanbags and a huge TV screen built into the wall. When we saw the staircase, I looked at my brother and said, "Wanna race? First back here wins." We flew up and down three flights of stairs in record time.

My parents stood in the entryway to the living room. Their arms were around each other. They pointed to different areas and described where new furniture and paintings would be placed. Mom and Dad showed us where another master bedroom was going to be added and where the gym on the first floor would go; it would have all the equipment from his original home gym along with several new machines, including rubber floors and mirrored walls. My parents couldn't wait to host their first dinner party in the new house.

Once you stepped through the back door, you were on the deck. Beyond the gardenias and roses my mom would plant, and the mist that rested on top of the lake, was the eighteenth hole of the championship Piper Glen golf course. The course, designed by legendary golfer Arnold Palmer, had rolling hills, rocky terrain, and tranquil lakes as far as the eye could see. My parents showed us where the new in-ground pool was going and where the outdoor marble bar with built-in stove would be. A balcony was added to the plans. While my dad proudly unveiled his new grills on the bottom and main levels, I had to ask where my trampoline was going to live. This was not a resort—this was our new house—and it came with a membership to the Piper Glen Country Club.

Each week when my dad came home from the road, we all got dressed in our best evening attire and had pasta night at the club. This was a wonderful family tradition. The dining room overlooked the beautiful Piper Glen landscape that we saw from our deck, but from our table in the dining room, it was like we could touch it. We enjoyed all different types of pasta: linguine, fettuccine, penne, fusilli, and rigatoni. It was like we were on a tour of Italy. I always created my own masterpiece with alfredo sauce, red bell peppers, mushrooms, and onions. My dad loved having red sauce; Reider loved his white sauce; and my mom loved the meatballs.

Each week, Reider and I felt like part of my parents' glamorous nightlife. One evening, we were in the car on our way to a Carolina Panthers football game, and I said, "We're older now. We're ready to go out at night with Mom and Dad." I didn't know how revered my father was on a global scale, but soon I realized by the responses he received at Hornets and Panthers games that he was a celebrity and one of the Queen

City's favorite sons. The Panthers incorporated my dad's "WOOOOO!" for their Jumbotron. We were so proud that he was our dad.

Brass bannisters, crystal chandeliers, mahogany wood . . . Piper Glen was a beautiful place. My mom surprised my dad with a fiftieth birthday party at the club, and it's one of my most cherished family memories. Mom couldn't wait to curl my hair, and I couldn't wait to wear the bridesmaid's dress I wore to Megan's wedding. I remember taking pictures with all our close family and friends during cocktail hour. I was always amazed the ice sculptures didn't melt. Everyone was there to celebrate, including employees and business partners from his Gold's Gyms. My mom took her creative passion and love of family photography to the next level.

After dinner, everyone's attention was called to a screen at the front of the dining room. Before we sang "Happy Birthday" and cut the cake, my mom played a video montage she'd created of different photos of my dad and our family through the years: pictures of him growing up in Minnesota with Grandma Kay and Grandpa Richard, yearbook photos from Wayland Academy, photos of him throughout his career, their wedding, graduations, holidays, and vacations. With each new period of his life shown, a different song played. You could feel how much my parents loved each other and how much this meant to everyone in the room. There wasn't a dry eye in the house. I was so proud to be my parents' daughter.

The winds of change swirled around Piper Glen. Grandmommy did not come with us to the new house. I think she felt her job was done. She moved to help my aunt raise her son, Dylan. Grandmommy made it a priority to visit and always came to Thanksgiving and Christmas. It took a little while to adjust to being apart. When she left, she said, "Say your prayers. Jesus is always listening." Thankfully, my parents knew the recipe for pana cakes, so we didn't miss out. One morning when I told my mom I missed Grandmommy, she told me to remember what Grandmommy always said: "When God closes one door, He opens another."

When I think of our Piper Glen house, I think of my mom's Aunt Francine. She had family who lived twenty-five minutes away in a town called Davidson. Aunt Francine visited us for a few days at a time and on long weekends.

Whenever she stayed with us, she and my mom would retire after dinner to the enclosed patio to play a card game called Rummy Cube. One night, they taught Reider and me how to play when we got back from dinner at K&W Cafeteria. I smile when I think of the time Aunt Francine and my mom decorated my bedroom. The duo spent hours in furniture shops, looking at area rugs, and matching paint swatches with the Bermuda blinds that filled the entire house. They brought me in with my eyes closed to show me the amazing décor, which included marble flooring. Aunt Francine was always smiling. She was a ray of sunshine in our lives, and she gave the best hugs.

Even though we moved to a new house, we still went to Providence Day School. My mom drove us there in her new silver Mercedes as hits from Britney Spears, Christina Aguilera, *NSYNC, and 98 Degrees played on KISS 95.1 FM. Sometimes we'd listen to the Delilah show on 102.9 FM.

I started to become interested in a variety of sports, and Reider did too. He played football and baseball, and by the time he was ten, he was one of the top amateur wrestlers in the United States for his age group— and a national champion.

Something happened that I never expected. I had just won a race against one of the boys during recess, and I heard somebody yelling. I looked around but couldn't understand what the person was saying or why it was being said. The bell rang, and recess was over, so I ignored it. The next day, I crossed the finish line in another race, and I heard it again, this time clearly and from more than one person. It was being repeated like a chant, and as I looked around, it was getting louder. I said to myself, *Wait, they're talking about me. They're pointing at me.* I put everything together and felt a burning sensation in the pit of my stomach. For the past two days during recess, the boys had been calling me "Beast."

Whenever I stepped up to the starting line for a race, walked to home plate, or shot a basketball, I heard a chorus chanting this word. I promised myself I wouldn't get upset in front of everyone. I'd use it as my motivation to do even better, to beat them at their own game, and I did.

But away from the high fives and cheers from my friends, it really hurt. I always did what my parents taught me. Say "Good game" or "Nice race" to the other person. Besides, this was recess. We were supposed to be having fun.

I learned that in a school environment, this could take on a life of its own. It was tough being in the same class with these kids and seeing them with their group of friends in the hallway. What I hoped would pass over a weekend or school vacation carried over into the next week and the week after that. Weeks turned into months. Any time I saw those boys on the playground, I'd hear the chants of "Beast! Beast! Beast!" I tried to be positive. This was just happening at recess. That changed too.

Each year, I received the President's Challenge Physical Activity & Fitness Award, which was given to students who placed in the ninety-eighth percentile of all national participants. When my name was called, I walked to the front of the auditorium and received my award. There was that voice again. It managed to transcend the applause, and there was that word, *Beast*. I ignored it and went back to my seat where my friends congratulated me. That's when I asked myself, *Will they always call me Beast?*

The next week, one of the boys started to make fun of me because I had hair on my arms. He ended his litany with the familiar chant. I made sure that he didn't see how much I was hurting. Reider fought with him after school. Later that day, my mom got a call from the principal. Reider was suspended from school for three days. It was one of the few times I saw my parents argue. My mom understood why Reider did what he did, but she was upset that he got into serious trouble at school. My dad, on the other hand, thought Reider did the right thing and shouldn't have gotten into trouble for defending me. After that day, I never heard that word again. All thanks to my brother.

I was teased. I know worse happens when kids are bullied, but that experience created a layer of insecurity that still clings to me. I've always felt the most comfortable playing a sport or being in a gym, and yet there were times when I hesitated to push myself too much. I wondered, *Will I become too muscular? Will someone think I'm a beast?*

Girls are not less attractive because they're talented athletes or are in phenomenal physical shape. Even thinking about it now, it's upsetting that happened because I was the tallest kid in my grade and I was skilled in sports. I think of what would have happened today with the tidal waves of negativity that can be created on social media.

The next month, after a meet in Savannah, Georgia, I realized I didn't love gymnastics in the same way. I asked Coach Suzie if I could speak with her after practice.

As I've said before, it's funny what you remember. I was wearing my favorite practice shorts—red Umbros with the pockets on the side. I told Coach that I didn't feel the same about gymnastics anymore. I was getting so tall and knew I was going to keep growing. Even though she and the girls were so special to me and I loved being on her team, I didn't think I could continue as a gymnast. And I fell in love with volleyball. The next day, with full support from Coach Suzie and my teammates, I went to the other side of the gym. The years being a gymnast under Coach Suzie gave me a discipline that has stayed with me and helped create a skill set that makes me unique as a WWE Superstar.*

When I was thirteen years old, I went to the same building as gymnastics but moved to the other side of the gym. I became the youngest member of Coach Kevin Brubaker's Charlotte Allstar Cheerleading. I fell in love with the sport right away. The physical strength, speed, balance, and timing that were required to do something that looked so easy to someone watching fascinated me. Cheerleading was similar to gymnastics. What drew me in even more was the continuity required of the entire group to create an amazing routine. As a member of their team, the Teal Squad, I wanted to work extra hard to make sure I caught up with the other girls and knew the routines as well as, if not better than, they did.

The Charlotte Allstars competed all over the country. Before I knew it, I was a seventh grader on a plane headed to Nashville, Tennessee, on

---

*Coach Suzie Sanocki: "Ashley was a wonderful kid with a great personality. She was super tenacious when it came to getting something right and was an excellent teammate. Since she was getting so tall, gymnastics became more difficult. In twenty-one years of coaching, Ashley's determination and athleticism still stand out."

the all-girls senior squad. The night before a competition was exhilarating: practicing our routine until it was perfect, feeling the music and moving to it on beat, and right before bed, getting our hair and makeup ready.

The competitions were part rock concert, part sporting event, and part live theater. When the music started, I felt like I was shot out of a cannon. Hearing the crowd roar during our performance was like nothing I'd ever felt before. I thrived on the challenge of contributing to a perfect performance, knowing that months of dedicated practice boiled down to a two- or three-minute chance to shine brighter than the opposition. The ultimate sense of accomplishment was when we ran back to our bench and Coach Brubaker high-fived everyone and said, "You nailed it!"*

As a team, we traveled together, volunteered in the community together, and went to church together. From someone like me, who was thirteen years old, to the oldest girls on the team, who were eighteen, we were all sisters. The team rules were similar to gymnastics. Coach had a strict travel dress code. We had to wear black shorts. They couldn't be torn or have holes in them, and they couldn't be revealing in any way. Our team shirts had to be clean, pressed, and tucked into our shorts. If you were late to practice, the airport, or a competition, there were penalties in terms of added conditioning drills.

I'm proud that when Coach Brubaker led our team into a building for a competition, the other teams from around the country knew what they were going to get: a machine that won three national championships. I remember our brush with local celebrity in Charlotte when we performed the halftime show at a Carolina Panthers game.

Looking back, it was during this time that I began to grow up a little faster than most people my age. I wasn't doing anything wrong or bad, but when you're thirteen and you're around girls who are seventeen and eighteen years old, you're not talking about the same things. They were

---

*Coach Kevin Brubaker: "The best cheerleaders are often ex-gymnasts. Ashley had a high level of what we call 'acrosense,' which is how you move in the air. Teal Squad is our highest-level team. Ashley reached a level in two years that most people don't reach until they're doing this for ten or twelve years."

talking about what boys they were going out with on dates, going to parties, curfew, and having sex—and that's a different type of education. I couldn't contribute anything to the conversation, so I'd just listen.

Once I found a pair of women's underwear rolled up in a Ziploc bag in the laundry room in our house. I didn't understand what it was or how it got there. I just figured that it had to do with stuff that the girls talked about during our cheerleading trips, so I put it back.

I was always comfortable around older people. Those girls took me under their wing. They never made me feel like I was younger or an outsider. The girls on my teams thought I was cool because I dressed like them and did well as a member of the team. In some ways, I matured very quickly. This resulted in my having a difficult time relating to the kids in my grade at school. I wanted to be with the older kids and do the things they were doing. I still had my friends at school, but physically, mentally, and emotionally, I was often somewhere else.

During spring break, all the older girls were going to Myrtle Beach, South Carolina. I begged my mom to let me go. After several sessions of trying to justify why I, as a seventh grader, should be allowed to go, she offered an interesting proposal. My mom told me that I could go if my sister, Megan, drove me, stayed in a hotel room with me, and drove me back. I also had to agree to be picked up by the 10:00 p.m. curfew. To this day, it's one of the quickest agreements I've ever entered into.

Being a Charlotte Allstar wasn't without some bumps and bruises. One day in practice, I fell and knocked my teeth out.*,†,‡ Coach Brubaker

---

*Coach Kevin Brubaker: "Ashley was not worried that she had her teeth knocked out; she wanted to make sure no one else was hurt. We went with her parents to the dentist that night so she could have surgery. She wanted to return to practice the next day. When we told her she had to wait a few weeks to be cleared, that seemed to be more painful for her."

†Ric: "Ashley's always had a high tolerance for pain. If she turned her foot, the coach would have her sit out and ice it. She couldn't stand having to be on the bench while practice was going on. She wanted to get back out there right away."

‡Coach Kevin Brubaker: "Ric wanted to make sure everyone was okay. He always treated us so well. He brought the whole team and staff to WCW *Monday Nitro* when they came to town, would have flowers given to all the girls. He even helped pay for uniforms and travel when

ran right over to me. My teammates circled around us. The next person at my side was Coach Suzie. She rushed over from the other side of the gym.

I didn't realize it at the time, but working under those coaches and competing with those girls taught me self-discipline and teamwork. It reinforced how important it is to have pride in what you do and strive to be the best. I also created lifelong friendships.

It was time to add another sport to my seasonal calendar. As a seventh grader, I laced up my Nike high-tops and stepped onto the hardwood as a member of the Providence Day Chargers junior varsity high school basketball team.

I didn't want the fun to end there. After basketball, I wanted to try a sport that I enjoyed watching on TV but never played before: tennis.

My family was so excited that I wanted to try out for another school team. My dad took me to Sports Authority and bought me a white-and-blue Prince tennis racquet. The first day of tryouts, I showed up ready to play. Or so I thought. To put it nicely, my lack of experience showed from the opening serve. I was terrible. I got cut in the first round. It is the only team that I didn't make. As I left tryouts, I could hear Grandmommy's words about God closing one door and opening another.

The school volleyball coach, Mrs. Stockton, asked me how tryouts went. When I told her I got cut, she said, "Why don't you come over and give volleyball a shot?" She called my dad and told him I should try volleyball and that I needed knee pads, sneakers, and high socks. So I went into the gym and started learning the fundamentals. From the moment I saw the team run a play from the sidelines, I thought this was the ultimate team game. I had to get out there. Volleyball moved fast. The sport combined speed, power, and athleticism. I liked the equal emphasis on playing great offense and playing great defense.

I went back to tryouts the next day. As the new kid on the court,

---

certain people on the team had difficulty affording it. The number of pictures and autographs he'd stay for at competitions was unbelievable. Ric and Beth were so appreciative of our work."

I held my own and made the team. I couldn't wait to get home and put on my uniform. I was so excited about my rookie season.

During this time, we attended even more WCW shows. My dad's close friend Doug Dillinger was the head of WCW security and always made sure we had official WCW shirts and hats if we wanted them. I remember Ted DiBiase asking me how I was doing in sports and telling me about his sons. We couldn't turn a corner without Curt Hennig playing a joke on Reider and me, and J. J. Dillon wanted a full update on how I was doing in school.

When we weren't at WCW events, we watched my dad and all our friends each week on WCW's *Monday Nitro* and *Thunder* television programs and every month on pay-per-view.

We loved sitting around the TV together. I used to get chills when I'd hear his music. Reider loved getting up from his beanbag to emulate my dad's strut. Sometimes we'd do it together, and he'd want to make sure we did it in stride. His favorite was reciting my dad's "Meannnnnn, by God, Gene!" greeting that he'd begin his interviews with when he spoke to "Mean" Gene Okerlund. Of course, we joined the fans from home in saying, "WOOOOO!" at the appropriate times, which seemed like any time my dad was on TV. Reider wanted to grow up to be just like him. I was so proud of him. He was our hero.

There were times when our family returned to WCW programming. One of the most popular segments was when Reider walked to the ring with Uncle Arn on *Nitro* and confronted Eric Bischoff.* Dressed in his wrestling singlet with his gold medal around his neck, my brother took the microphone and said he was there to "take care of Dad's light work." He then brought Eric down to the mat twice with amateur wrestling takedowns. We were so proud of him.

Today, when someone sends me a YouTube link or I'm watching the WWE Network, it's funny to look back at me storming the ring on *Nitro*

---

*Ric: "That was a great segment. We were so proud of Reid. He was a little nervous, but he did great. I know he loved that his uncle Arn was right behind him. For all the problems Eric [Bischoff] and I had during my time in WCW, he always treated my family very well."

to give Vince Russo what he had coming to him. I remember certain events, but I was so young and involved in so many different things. It never crossed my mind to try wrestling or to ask my dad if I could go to WCW's training school, the Power Plant, in Atlanta and enter the ring. That was his job. I was just his biggest fan.

There were times when things happened on WCW programming that involved my dad or David, and we'd get questioned about it at school. It became more of an issue for Reider. Kids went up to him and said that the nWo was going to beat up the Four Horsemen, and they'd tease him if my dad was doing something on TV that was unflattering to him, and people thought was real. He dealt with it as best he could, but I know it was hard.

Sometimes I'm asked what it was like being Ric Flair's daughter and living through the Monday Night War—the battle between WWE and WCW over signing talent, television ratings, pay-per-view buy rates, and merchandise sales. Some people have a hard time believing me when I say I didn't know. In fact, I didn't know until years later. I didn't know anything about WWE. We watched WCW.

Birthdays in the Fliehr house continued to be historic events. The morning of my fifteenth birthday, we all walked to the garage. I thought my mom was taking us to school as usual. When I opened the door and turned the light on, I saw a brand-new forest-green Land Rover with balloons tied to it. My dad recorded the proceedings with the family camcorder, and my parents and Reider sang, "Happy Birthday."

I couldn't believe what was in front of me. I looked at my parents and they said, "It's for you. Happy birthday." My dad added, "You have to learn how to drive in something," and he gave me the keys. I walked around the car twice before I opened the driver's-side door. I turned the key and saw the dashboard light up. One of the first things I noticed was something was blinking. My parents got me a five-CD changer in the dashboard. We all got in the car, and I drove us to Providence Day. Since I could only drive with another licensed driver, my parents would be with me, or sometimes one of the older cheerleaders would drive us to practice.

That night, I drove everyone to the Melting Pot for a special dinner. We had a big table with my parents, Reider, my dad's parents, and Grand-mommy. As servers brought out different types of cheese fondue and breads, we laughed and took pictures the whole night. The adults enjoyed pairing different wines with the menu. No sips for us. Reider and I raised our glasses of iced tea and lemonade and toasted a wonderful night.

10

ADVERSITY COMES IN MANY FORMS

I never said in my heart, "This is where I should be."

June 2001

One afternoon after school, I walked into the kitchen and said hello to my mom and her friend Susan Beck. I wanted to ask about a summer trip, but once I saw that she and Susan were busy talking, I thought better of it.

I decided to go to my room, and on the way upstairs, it sounded like they were both crying. I got to my room and stayed in the doorway. I could hear them talking, but I couldn't make out what they were saying. All the while, my mother just kept crying.

I wanted to help my mom feel better. I went downstairs and asked her what was going on. I saw something that looked like a tape recorder—like the one I'd found in my dad's car when I as a kid, but this one was a different color. She hesitated and looked at Susan.

I said, "Mom, tell me. What's wrong?"

My mother said that my dad was having an affair.

"With who?" I asked. "How did Dad meet her? Did she work for WCW?" I couldn't understand how he could possibly meet someone since he was so busy traveling all the time. When he wasn't on the road, he was home with us. He took Reider and me with him everywhere. Either that or he was out with my mom.

My mom explained that Tiffany, the woman from Dad's Gold's Gym in South Park and the person who trained Reider and me every so often, was the other woman. I just stood there, stunned.

I said, "What? What do you mean?"

All I kept thinking was that my dad was my hero, our protector. He would never do anything to hurt our family.

Hearing more about this and seeing my mother inconsolable made it feel like walls were closing in on me. My heart started racing. I couldn't make sense of it. Should I be mad at my dad? We'd never had a conflict before. But how could I not be angry? How could I not feel betrayed?

My mom explained that my dad had bought her a Mercedes. I never had any idea that there was a problem with my parents' relationship. For the first time in my life, I was torn between my mom and my dad. I had to get to the bottom of this.

I swiped the cordless house phone from the kitchen counter, ran up the stairs to my room, and called him. When he said, "Hello," I couldn't hold back my tears anymore. Everything poured out. "Dad, where are you? Who's Tiffany? What's going on?" I didn't give him a second to answer me. "Come home, Dad. Please just come home." I hung up the phone. I stayed in my room and cried.

That night, somewhere around 8:00, I heard someone pull into the garage, walk through the kitchen, and up the steps. It was my dad. He came into my room, hugged me, and said he was sorry.* He went back downstairs and talked with my mom. That was the last time we ever discussed that day.

What made it more hurtful to my mom was that in addition to Tiffany being my brother's trainer, she was a guest at my dad's surprise fiftieth birthday party at the country club. This woman applauded with everyone

---

*Ric: "I went back because of the kids. When I was home during my lawsuit with WCW, and during this time, after WCW closed, things changed between Beth and me at home. I wanted to try to make it work for the kids."

after my mom's video played. She joined us in singing "Happy Birthday" to him and saw all of us together as a family.

After that night, my dad came home, and I never imagined I would hear the name *Tiffany* again. It didn't dawn on me to ask about it either. I was so focused on athletics that if something didn't directly affect me or if something happened and it was resolved, I turned my full attention back to sports. But whenever I heard the song "Breakfast at Tiffany's," I thought of her.

My parents went to counseling. They returned to hosting their dinner parties and attending events throughout Charlotte, and they went on a private cruise in Tahiti with another couple. Our summer family adventures continued. It felt like everything was back to normal. My parents sent me to see a therapist too. I remember speaking to him in his office. I molded clay. Around that time, all the girls on the Charlotte Allstars cheerleading team had their belly buttons pierced. I argued with my parents to let me do it, but they said that wasn't appropriate for a girl in middle school. The therapist told them they should let me get it done, so they did. At least I could fit in with the girls on the team!

Over the previous few years, many of the WCW families we grew up with moved from Charlotte to Atlanta. Thankfully, Uncle Arn's family didn't move, and we continued to enjoy more holidays and summer vacations with them. His son Barrett and I were boyfriend-girlfriend for a few months in middle school.

Since WCW changed TV taping locations from Disney to Universal, we got to spend even more time exploring Orlando before I went into high school. We left no stone unturned when it came to enjoying the rides at Universal Studios: *Back to the Future* and *Jaws* were two favorites. Reider and I got slimed at Nickelodeon Studios, and we loved the shows at Sea-World. We have pictures of all of us petting Shamu, and we were picked to hold fish up for the dolphins and whales to eat during the live shows.

Back at "the Happiest Place on Earth," we couldn't wait to return to the Yacht Club. Once we settled in, we met our tour guide and hopped on the monorail to the Magic Kingdom to eat the giant turkey legs. Whenever I smell turkey legs, I think of how much my dad loved eating them. Disney offered something called a FastPass, which meant there was no waiting in line to go on our favorite rides. It was incredible.

Even though I was surrounded by my precious family and the fantasy worlds I loved, volleyball began to consume my thoughts. You hear stories of athletes sleeping with their football or basketball or having their baseball glove under their pillow. I didn't add volleyballs to my bedroom's décor, but I understood the mentality.

I still loved cheerleading, but volleyball, more than any other sport I played, became a part of my DNA. It became my passion. I wanted to take my volleyball skills to another level. I wanted to know how I'd fare against a wider range of competitors.

The summer before ninth grade, I went to two camps that had top players from all over the United States. One was the Nike camp in North Carolina, and the other was at San Diego State University in San Diego, California.

Each camp lasted one week, had three sessions per day, and included a player evaluation. Based on your grade, you'd be assigned to teams of appropriate skill. The top player from each class was put in the all-around game at the end of the camp.

I had to work harder because, one, I had to catch up to everyone else at the camp. Most of the girls were dedicated to volleyball—no cheerleading, basketball, diving, track and field—just volleyball twelve months a year. Also, everyone saw my dad drop me off and watch from the stands. I had to prove that I belonged, that he didn't pick up a phone and call someone to get me into these camps. I wanted to be known as a great athlete and a great teammate, not someone who received special treatment because her dad was famous.

By the end of both camps, I made it into the all-around game. It was another reminder for me to always work hard, strive to be the best, and earn people's respect. After many of the girls shared their routine with me throughout the year, I knew a tough decision was on the horizon.

Once my week at San Diego State was over, my dad drove up the 405 to Los Angeles. The way the sun shone along the mountains and reflected off the Pacific Ocean was like looking at a piece of heaven. We talked about volleyball, how much I loved going to these camps, and what movies we were going to see when we got home. He was so happy taking me to camp and being at my games.

The traffic in the Los Angeles area was like nothing I had ever seen before. It reminded my dad and me of *Independence Day* when everyone was trying to get out of New York—though this was LA—and Jasmine Dubrow was not along for the ride. That didn't deter us. First stop, Rodeo Drive in Beverly Hills and the Salvatore Ferragamo store. When I walked through the doors, I thought I was at a fashion show. When I walked out, I felt like I was ready for the runway. He bought me a $2,000 bright red leather bag. Only a limited number of these came to the States from Ferragamo's flagship store in Rome. I saw one of the camp instructors who played at San Diego State carrying one, and I wanted to be just like her. Before we flew home, Dad took me to his favorite sushi restaurant in LA.

A few weeks later, I began training with Jeff George—not the NFL quarterback at the time but a top trainer who worked for my dad at the Crown Pointe Gold's Gym. Jeff inspired me with his complete approach to fitness, which included sessions at his personal training studio in the Ballantyne section of Charlotte and which required a new level of commitment on my part. Regardless of vacations, birthday parties, or hanging out with friends, I trained with Jeff every Monday, Wednesday, and Friday. I looked forward to raising my level of training.

Since I was a middle school student who played junior varsity volleyball and had two years under my belt as part of a senior cheering squad, I knew the kind of intensity I could expect in the ninth grade. I was determined to use my experience to be the best volleyball player I could be. After the kind of training I'd had during the summer, I felt confident that if I played well, I'd make the team. I wanted the pressure of having to make a new team, to be someone teammates and coaches depended on. Plus, I figured I'd fit in with the older girls, because I always played sports at a level higher than my age and I was comfortable around older people.

By the time school started, cheerleading and volleyball were in full swing. I knew how to manage schoolwork and a team sport, and I was beyond ready to get my driver's license in April. During the fall, I rode

with the high school girls in their cars. The Land Rover my parents bought me just sat in the garage unless I had a girlfriend drive it or my parents allowed me to take it to school with my learner's permit tucked in my wallet. I was the only fifteen-year-old who had a brand-new car, but I couldn't drive it. It was torture. I counted down the days to freedom.

The Charlotte Allstars continued to travel the country and, as I like to say, "collect hardware." More awards filled the trophy case back at our gym.

But as a ninth grader, my sights were set on another goal: to be a starter on the Providence Day varsity volleyball team—the only freshman who played varsity.

I wanted to outhustle everyone. I looked forward to showing what I could do on the court. When it came to high school sports, it was all about playing on varsity teams.

On the first day of tryouts, I met Ashley Flohouse, the standout senior on the team. Ashley was the top female volleyball and basketball player at our school. She was tall, blond, athletic, and intelligent. When she drove me home in her 4Runner, we listened to JLo's "Jenny from the Block" and

Nelly's "Hot in Herre" together. It was then that I realized that I started to have a lot more fun with older girls than the kids my age.

Even though I wasn't on the team yet, Ashley and I talked about how the team was going to have a great season. She told me about the spandex shorts that were part of the varsity uniform and the tie-dyed socks we'd be wearing. She also told me about the teams who were good in our conference.

On the last day of tryouts, the group headed to the track. Coach Coffee was timing the mile. My dad had come to tryouts every day and was so proud that as a freshman, I was competing for a spot on the varsity team. He couldn't wait to see me fly off the starting line and leave everyone in the dust.

None of the senior girls wanted to run. Since I wanted to hang out with them, I ran casually, joined them in singing songs, and basically goofed off. As I came up on the first row of bleachers, along the fence on the straightaway, I saw my dad's face when he realized what was happening. He stood up, ran to the fence, and started pointing at me to "get my ass going." I looked at him, totally embarrassed by his reaction. I gritted my teeth and pretended he wasn't there. I clowned around on the rest of the laps. I knew I disappointed him. He was so angry he left me at practice.[*]

Despite that showing on the final day of tryouts, I made the team and was the starting middle hitter on the Providence Day varsity girls' volleyball team. It was time to work. The sport really ignited the competitor in me. The thought of losing a point, let alone a game, drove me to work even harder. There were times when losing a close game stayed in my mind more than a thrilling victory. It was either first place or no place. Now when I was at practice, I wanted to run the fastest, jump the highest, and be the best in every drill. I also liked cheering my teammates on

---

[*] Ric: "When Beth and I were married, she'd tell me I was too much of a friend to the kids and not enough of a father. I knew they were working hard, and when I didn't think they were working hard, I let them know. That day I let Ashley know. What she didn't know was that I was at home ready to get her if she called me."

and encouraging them to be better. One of the coaches at Carolina camp said, "Iron sharpens iron."

Toward the end of the season, one of the players' parents told my dad about a new travel team. His daughter was the starting setter at Providence Day and had played on club teams for a few years. He told my dad that this team was going to be the best to come out of our area and featured the top high school players from all over Charlotte: Charlotte Elite.

The idea of trying out for a team like that made me nervous, but the anticipation of stepping on the court and seeing how I'd do against players from all over Charlotte fueled me to train harder. I couldn't wait!

The first day of tryouts, I saw a girl hitting balls that sounded like they were going to implode. I heard the coach say, "Good job, Brittany, again. Just like that, one more time. Let's go." I played against her once that season and expected her to be at tryouts. Her name was Brittany Zahn.

Brittany was a junior at Charlotte Catholic High School. Charlotte Catholic had one of the best volleyball programs in the city. Brittany was considered one of the ten best players in the country; she was known for being one of the hardest hitters in the game. All you needed to do was see her play to realize that distinction was well deserved. She had played volleyball since she was in the third grade and had a great mind for the game. Brittany's presence on the court was intimidating. I was more than happy to have her on my side of the net.

Once the team's roster was set and we started practicing, we decided to ride together to and from practice, which meant Brittany let me ride with her and a couple of other girls, since I didn't have my driver's license yet.*

Brittany didn't care about what anyone thought of her. She didn't know who my dad was, and she wasn't interested. Sometimes I felt that other coaches and players were interested in me as an athlete because they really wanted to interact with him. Brittany just cared about playing volleyball.

---

*Brittany Zahn Arnold: "Ashley's one of the most athletic people I've ever been around. In comparison to the rest of us, volleyball was new to her. For Ashley to be as good as she was, playing at that level in the amount of time she was playing volleyball, it was incredible."

One night after eating dinner at my house, before I could ask her what she wanted to do, she was on the patio playing Rummy Cube with Aunt Francine. She fit right in with my family. Brittany and I became best friends.

Travel teams were more intense than school teams. The level of competition was higher. One of club team players' goals was to get recruited by college scouts while playing in the big tournaments. Club teams were a huge commitment in terms of time and money. You had to pay to try out and pay thousands of dollars in registration fees if you made the team. There were additional club fees, as well as coaches' fees, and you had to pay for the uniform. That didn't include travel expenses, hotels, and food.

The commitment included driving an hour to UNC–Charlotte's campus in north Charlotte for practice. We'd do fast-paced drills to perfect movement patterns, ball control, team chemistry, and basic fundamentals.* Practice ended with conditioning drills. Every time.

Right now, I'm reminded of running suicides in the gym and hearing the sounds of everyone's sneakers on the gym's wood floor. Picture being on the baseline of a basketball court: squat down like a catcher in baseball; shuffle from the ten-foot line on the court and then back to the baseline; shuffle to half-court and back; go to the ten-foot line on the other side of the court and back; and finish by shuffling the full length of the court and back to the baseline. It worked my core and my legs, and it built my endurance. Running suicides felt like second nature to me because of my training regimen. I wanted to finish first every time we ran them.

Practice was two hours. We'd drive home, and I'd go straight to bed after dinner. Our games were on weekends. Once tournaments began, our team spent a lot of time out of state. I loved being a part of Charlotte Elite and playing volleyball at such a high level. Being able to travel with Brittany made all the long hours worth it.

---

*Brittany Zahn Arnold: "One of the things everyone respected about Ashley was that she didn't want to be known as Ric Flair's daughter. She wanted to be known as Ashley. She didn't talk about her dad's wrestling career, the house she lived in, the cars they had, or trips she took. She was dedicated to being a great athlete and teammate."

I never thought about how leaves changing color in the fall could be a metaphor for the changes in our lives.

This was the first time that Reider and I were getting dropped off at different schools in the morning. I was in the ninth grade, and he was in the seventh grade. My brother did well in school when he applied himself. As he became well known as an athlete, his dedication shifted to sports, especially wrestling. My parents would argue about balancing school and sports. He and my parents talked a lot about how doing well in school was as important, if not more important, than sports.

Reider also brought his mischievous nature into the classroom. While a few teachers didn't always appreciate his fun-loving antics, he was a favorite with many of them. Reider had a kind nature, always stuck up for kids who were picked on, and had a natural charm. No one could stay mad at him. He finished middle school a few minutes down the road in a less strict environment while continuing success as one of the top amateur wrestlers in the country.

At Providence Day, a senior boy who was part of Ashley Flohouse's group of friends asked me to go to homecoming with him. I went to Ashley's house beforehand to get my hair and makeup done. All the parents took pictures. This was one of the most exciting days of the year and one that all the girls from Charlotte Allstar Cheerleading used to talk about. There was the varsity football game, where the homecoming king and queen were crowned; a halftime show with floats that celebrated the history of the school; and class reunions. And now I was going to be there. Nothing happened for me to contribute to the conversations the older girls had during cheerleading trips, but I was proud of my "upperclassman" story as a freshman. Being in high school definitely had a different feeling to it.

I continued to play by the rules at home. On occasion, I'd push the envelope and argue with my parents about a fair curfew time or debate if I spent too much time on my laptop or cell phone. I was dedicated to one sport, so I had a little extra time, but one night, something got into me after I came home from a school football game.

After my parents left to go out for dinner, I called one of the girls from volleyball to see what everyone was doing. Add a couple of calls between friends, and suddenly, all the seniors were at my house. In what felt like a few minutes, my parents' house resembled a scene from *Can't Hardly Wait*. All types of music blared through the surround-sound speaker system. People were swimming in the pool, sitting in the hot tub, hanging out on both levels of the deck, and taking self-guided tours of the house. Kids kept pointing at the lights that lined the shape of the pool and changed color.

I felt really comfortable, like my first high school party was a huge success. I figured I could do this whenever my parents had weekend plans. It was almost too easy. Then came the crash back to earth.

I was on the deck, and someone asked, "Who drives a silver, four-door Benz?" I looked and saw the distinct shape of the headlights. I knew who it was right away: my parents.

People started to file out the front and back doors of the house. A group of kids scaled the deck. The music suddenly faded from the speakers. My dad turned everything off, including the hot tub. My mom burned a hole right through me with her eyes. My dad combed the house for any stragglers. Everyone left. He took away the cases of beer cans that were in his memorabilia room and on top of the pool table. Despite the shocking discovery that I had thrown a party of this size while he and my mom were at dinner, he was furious but surprisingly calm and composed.

He told me how irresponsible it was to have a party and that this was not the behavior of someone who wanted to play Division I college athletics and whose goal was to be the best athlete she could be. He took the twenty-four packs of Icehouse beer and poured them down the drain, two at a time.

Unless it was a party for one of my teams, hosted by my parents, I was forbidden to have large groups of people at the house. This was the first time that I had really broken any major rules, but I wasn't concerned about suffering any consequences. I fit in with the older kids. Everyone had fun.

My parents didn't ground me, but I got the feeling that I was skating on very thin ice and that the next thing I did would have far worse consequences. I kept a low profile and certainly didn't ask if I could go shopping for a while.

My dad was home more than usual during this time. The previous March, he'd had his last match in WCW on *Nitro* against one of his greatest opponents, Sting. When he came home from that event in Florida, he explained that WCW was gone.* It had been taken over by a company that he worked for when we were small kids—WWE. Beyond that, Reider and I didn't know anything about the details or the historical significance of the buyout.

We were used to my dad being home almost every week. To us, it meant he was home a little more. We thought it was great. He'd bring my lunch to school every day—a grilled jumbo shrimp salad and a bottle of Evian water—from my favorite place: Dean & DeLuca. He'd always put a few Gatorades and a couple of protein bars in my bag for practice. He was always there for me.

We spent the weekend getting our house ready to host Thanksgiving. My dad had been in his office a lot the week before and said we might stay home from school on Monday. We had to keep that a secret. We didn't know what to think: Were we going on a special family trip? Was one of dad's friends coming to stay at our house? What could be so special that we would get to stay home from school?

Monday morning came, and my mom told us the news—we weren't going to school. After lunch, we all got into the car and drove to the Charlotte Coliseum. My dad was going to his first day of work at WWE . . . since 1993. He was so excited. He was in one of his custom-made suits and handmade handkerchiefs. Reider and I asked if he was sure he had everything he needed. We didn't see the bags for his robe and wrestling gear.

---

*Ric: "WCW closing was one of the happiest days of my life. I was sad for people who lost their jobs, but the company was so dysfunctional and became so unbearable that I said good riddance long before WWE acquired it. The only way I survived was by being at the hotel bar with 'Mean' Gene and Arn drinking dirty martinis. The match with Steve [Sting] was not our best. He came off surgery, and I hadn't been in the ring in months. I performed with a T-shirt on. I didn't want to have a match, but Shane McMahon asked me. If I had to perform in a match, I'm glad it was with Steve and that we closed out the final program together."

We went back that night for the show, our first *Monday Night Raw*. We didn't know what to expect and didn't know anyone who was in the ring. When we heard my dad's music, we jumped to our feet. I'll always remember the cheers from the crowd when he appeared. It gave me chills. Dad announced he was Mr. McMahon's "business partner." The segment ended with my dad in the ring with someone who was new to Reider and me, Stone Cold Steve Austin.

Together, they enjoyed what he dumped down the sink a month earlier at my party. I learned in WWE they were called "Steve-weisers." I didn't know this was the same person my dad worked with years earlier in WCW. I never saw anyone like Stone Cold Steve Austin. He was so cool. He did whatever he wanted. It took me a little while to adjust to WWE and learn who everyone was. *Monday Night Raw* was nothing like *Nitro*. This was a whole new world.

Just like that, my dad was back on television. In classic fashion, the next day at school, we were asked if our dad really owned half of WWE. That was such a special night for him and our family. It began a great tradition of attending WWE events, especially when *Raw* came to Charlotte.*

By the end of cheerleading season, I stood about five feet eight inches tall. During my annual physical, my doctor told me I should hit another growth spurt during high school. I said to myself, *Gosh. I'm a freshman. How tall am I going to be?*

As a cheerleader at that level, the goal was to be recruited by an NCAA Division I coed cheerleading program. I was confident in my ability, especially my tumbling, but I had to objectively look at what I was doing as an athlete and what could help me achieve my goal. I was already too tall to be recruited by a Division I coach for a coed squad.

I didn't think there would be enough time to devote to volleyball and continue cheerleading. I needed time in the summer to attend volleyball camps. I had to get as much time on the court as possible. Almost all the girls I competed against dedicated all their time to volleyball. I couldn't bring myself to leave Charlotte Allstars.

Every year during Christmas time, we had an end-of-season banquet. When awards were given out, there were a few I thought I could be in the running for: "Hardest Working," "Best Attitude," or "Best" at a certain aspect of cheering. There were so many hardworking, deserving girls on the team, I really didn't think I was going to win anything. When Coach Brubaker announced the final award winner of the night, the team MVP, we all sat on the edge of our seats.

Coach said, "And . . . our MVP for the 2000 season is . . ." Then

---

*Ric: "I almost appeared on WWE TV in 1997. I had Reid with me in a limo. I was on the phone with Jim Cornette, and the limo was circling the Greensboro Coliseum before a WWE pay-per-view event. Reid just won the AAU wrestling nationals. We were going to sit in the front row. Jim Ross was going to announce on the air that WWE was going to interview 'a great wrestling champion' and then walk over and speak to Reid on camera. WWE's attorney decided it was too risky, because I was still under contract to Turner. [Laughs] After WCW closed, I waited all summer for that phone to ring. 'Are they going to call? Are they going to call?' Jim called me and said, 'Ric, we'd like you to be part of this company.' I was told I wouldn't be wrestling but rather be an authority figure on TV. My return was official. I couldn't wait."

he called my name. I looked around and thought, *What?* Everyone started clapping. I was a little embarrassed. I couldn't believe I won. Coach Brubaker and my teammates made it possible for me to develop into a cheerleader who was capable of winning that type of award. It was one of the times that what my dad said on television applied to real life: "There's nothing like the respect of your peers."

I felt like I had just come off my best season. The rest of the night I asked myself, *How can I leave this team? How can I say goodbye to a gym that—combining cheerleading and gymnastics—has been my home since I was five years old?* I didn't know if I was making the right decision. I tossed and turned all night.

The next day, I said goodbye to Charlotte Allstars. Walking out of that gym was one of the toughest decisions I ever made. I knew if I looked back, I'd want to stay. Bigger things were ahead if I was willing to put in the work.

After all these years, my eyes still well up when I think about saying goodbye to Coach Brubaker and that team.* Some of my favorite memories and most important lessons were learned from Coach Brubaker. They will stay with me forever.

Once the ball dropped on New Year's Eve 2002, I had my own countdown: sweet sixteen—and my driver's license! The winter dragged. I was so close to my birthday, I could blow out the candles on my cake. My truck that sat dormant in the garage was going to be set free! My dream car was the yellow Land Rover, the Defender 90, that Freddie Prinze Jr.'s character Zack Siler drove in the movie *She's All That.*

I was in the car with my parents, and we drove past the Rea Road shopping center. They waited for me to notice the Defender parked on

---

*Coach Kevin Brubaker: "It was heartbreaking to see Ashley leave Charlotte Allstars. She was a wonderful cheerleader and teammate. She always had the drive to be the best. Ashley was also an amazing volleyball player, and I knew that was best for her. In twenty-seven years of our program, Ashley's one of the toughest, hardest-working athletes we ever had, and a top-ten all-time cheerleader."

the side of the road. It was the only one in town. We pulled into the shopping center, and I freaked out! I got my dream car for my sixteenth birthday. At that moment, my transition to adulthood, I thought, was complete. My birthday was on a Friday that year, so I immediately thought of what I was going to do once my training and volleyball were done. Unbeknownst to me, my dad had one of the best sound system technicians in Charlotte install a custom-built surround-sound system. The car was tinted out front to back with limousine tint. I was the only freshman at school who had a car. I had to make sure my music was ready. Some of the artists you'd hear blaring from my car when I stopped at a red light were the Red Hot Chili Peppers, 50 Cent, Eminem, Nelly, the Dixie Chicks, Hootie & the Blowfish, Uncle Kracker, and Kid Rock. There's nothing like the way a song sounds when you're in the car.

When a new CD came out, I drove to the SouthPark Mall to buy it. For some reason, those trips reminded me of my childhood. Grandmommy took Reider and me to the Eastland Mall to skate at the indoor ice rink after we watched the Winter Olympics. We used to love watching the Zamboni clean the ice and thought it would be fun to hop behind the wheel and go for a spin. The following year, I would start on my own clean slate.

My dad was taking Reid to Providence High School to train with AAU wrestlers. He met the volleyball coach and started talking about me and the teams I played on. Providence had the highest-ranked 4A girls' volleyball team in North Carolina. Its program was built by one of the most respected coaches in the country, Coach Zoe Bell.*

After several conversations with my parents and feeling that I was outgrowing my environment, I decided to leave Providence Day in the fall and transfer to PHS as a sophomore. It was time for something new!

---

*Coach Zoe Bell: "I knew of Ashley's athletic background and her level of play at Providence Day. This was a different environment. At that time, Providence Day had a total of about 1,500 students from kindergarten to twelfth grade. Providence High School had more than 3,500 students from ninth to twelfth grade. We'd have more than fifty girls try out for the volleyball team ever year. We carried a roster of fifteen players."

I knew that after being in a more close-knit, private-school setting for more than ten years, going to a larger, public school was going to be an adjustment. One positive note was that PHS was down the road from where I went to school, so I felt like I was in the same neighborhood.

By this time, I started to build a name for myself as a volleyball player. I looked forward to joining a new team and playing against tougher competition. I looked forward to learning with such a highly regarded coach.

Even as a sophomore playing on the varsity team, I was determined to make an impact and show Coach Bell that I could be one of her best players, but things didn't get off to a great start. I ended up having to dig myself out of a hole.*

I found that whatever sport I played, at every level, what my parents taught me about working hard, treating people well, and earning their respect was the best way to be part of a team and be a good teammate. Since I knew my dad would attend practices and games and sometimes be vocal from the stands, I didn't want the fact that he was famous to bother any of the girls.† I didn't want any distractions.

My first year as a member of the Providence Panthers was a success. We won the All-Conference and NCHSAA 4A State Championships. This was a tremendous way to set the tone for my junior year, which, for a high school athlete, was so important from a college recruitment point of view.

My family continued the great tradition of going to WWE shows

---

*Coach Zoe Bell: "Ashley was late the first day of practice. The team's expectation was to be on top every year. If we lost a match, it was a big deal, and in the newspapers. Practice at 8:00 p.m. means I want you there by 7:50, not 8:01. Ashley always worked hard and was always respectful. She was raised right. But she tested me a little bit in the beginning with small things like that."

†Ric: "I was very involved with Ashley's and Reid's schooling and sports. I admit, sometimes a little too involved. I was so happy that I got to be there with them. It upset me so much to miss Megan's basketball games and David's baseball games when they lived in Minnesota. I didn't want to miss out on this second chance. [Laughs] I know I went overboard by delivering meals to school, but I wanted to look out for their diet. I just wanted them to be healthy."

with my dad. When WWE was in Charlotte, we went to the arena early because my brother David performed in matches that were not televised. He was training in OVW, which was WWE's development system. Very often, wrestlers who performed in matches before televised events like *Raw* and *SmackDown* were trying out with WWE.

The year 2003 will always be memorable. My mom told us that we were starting the New Year by traveling to Hawaii with my dad for his WWE shows. We were going as a family, and my boyfriend at the time was allowed to come with us.

I can still remember Honolulu. Our family ate dinner at an amazing seafood restaurant. There was a luau and gorgeous Polynesian women in handmade skirts with leis around their necks. We had leis around our necks too, and we tried to dance with the dancers. Looking over the cliff on the north shore side of the island was breathtaking. It was a kaleidoscope of colors, like something out of a dream. We sipped our drinks out of coconuts and took family photos together with the sunset as our backdrop.

I remember taking our seats at the arena later that night. Howard Finkel's iconic voice wished everyone a happy new year. The crowd chanted, "We want tables!" during the Dudley Boyz' match. Shawn Michaels was there, and my dad introduced his team of Batista and Triple H. They were in the main event against Rob Van Dam and Kane. At the time, my dad was in a new group called Evolution, with Triple H, Batista, and Randy Orton. In a way, it paid tribute to the Four Horsemen. I thought it was cool, and it was one of Reider's favorite WWE segments. He knew the similarities and differences between the Horsemen and Evolution. I just knew I wanted to see my dad perform in front of the live crowd.

Even though he was a villain, the crowd showed him such admiration. Other individuals were very popular for a certain period of time or in different personas in different companies. Some left sports entertainment for Hollywood and came back. I remember returning to that building the next night, and my dad received the same ovation from the audience. It was then I realized that my father epitomized wrestling. It's not just something said on TV; his is "the man" in the ring and in life. At home, he was our best friend.

In the beginning of my junior year, I saw additional proof that my decision to transfer to Providence paid off. I was no longer considered the new kid on the block; I was known as a leader on the team. After two years of playing varsity and two years playing on Charlotte Elite, I felt more confident than ever on the court. I started to own the game; I could anticipate the other teams' moves before they happened. I was able to understand defensive formations and direct my teammates by saying things like "Go line" or "Go cross-court" during games. I was selected to the 2002 and 2003 *Charlotte Observer* All-City Team and became a three-time All-Southwestern 4A Conference selection.*

I started to be recruited by NCAA Division I programs for volleyball.

Over the next few months, I received more than thirty letters from schools across the United States. My parents and I made trips to more than a dozen colleges and universities, meeting with coaches, going on campus tours, and meeting members of the women's volleyball teams.

My first official visit was with Atlantic Coast Conference (ACC) powerhouse Wake Forest. Wake was close to home in Winston-Salem, North Carolina. The school had an excellent volleyball program and an academically prestigious reputation. I can still picture walking through the beautiful campus with my parents. I felt a bit self-conscious because I was getting that familiar look from people we passed because they recognized my dad. Future NBA star Chris Paul mentioned in an interview once that he remembered seeing my dad during our tour of the school. As I walked around the campus and through different buildings, I could see myself there. I spent the night with one of the girls on the volleyball

---

*Coach Zoe Bell: "In the beginning, it was tough for Ashley to fit in. Every day, Ric brought her lunch from Dean & DeLuca to school. During practices and games, people asked Ric for autographs and pictures. This was the first time someone on the team had a famous parent. I never saw anything like it. He was so kind to everyone. Ashley wanted to be recognized for contributing to a successful team and for her talent as an athlete. Some schools, like Riverside, had home fans taunt her. She never let it bother her. She just used it as motivation to be better. She adjusted perfectly."

team and two of the field hockey players. I had a good time, and I liked the coaching staff. But there was one issue—they wanted me on the team solely for defense. I liked playing front row and wanted to continue playing that position.

The next trip was to a school my parents didn't think I was serious about attending: Appalachian State University in Boone, North Carolina. Boone is a town in the Blue Ridge Mountains about two hours northwest of Charlotte. We took a tour of the campus on a Friday morning and met the head coach that afternoon. I was a homebody growing up. Looking at schools, even if they were in North Carolina, where I'd have to live on campus, felt like a big step. This wasn't a long weekend with one of my sports teams or a week away from home at a camp—this was living somewhere else and "visiting" home.

After touring the athletics facilities with the head coach, he took us into the locker room. And that's when I saw it—my number six on an Appalachian State jersey hanging in a locker. I felt like a draft pick who signed with a professional sports team and put her jersey on at a press conference. To think, three years earlier, I was getting my legs under me learning the game of volleyball. Now, I wore the uniform colors of an NCAA Division I volleyball program. The coach said he wanted me to play the position of outside hitter. I felt that this was starting to come together, but I still needed to meet the girls on the team and spend the weekend there.

I said goodbye to my parents and met the girls on the team. That night, I attended my first college party. The football team knew how to host a party. It was phenomenal. I felt like I connected with the girls on the team and almost forgot that I was away from home. Within two hours, I decided that this was where I was going to school and this was where I wanted to play volleyball.

No one expected me to pick Appalachian State, or as some called it, "Happy Appy." It was an odd choice. It was a Division I program, but the school and the area were laid-back. People roped in their yards. There was one shopping mall and a small strip of local shops and restaurants. I was going to be a big fish in a little pond—the exact opposite of the schools I wanted to attend, especially for volleyball. In the end, I didn't care if no one saw me going there or what they thought of the school as my choice. I wanted to attend the school and play volleyball there because I left with a great feeling, and I was being recruited to play the position I wanted to play.

My parents picked me up on Sunday around lunchtime. I signed my commitment letter when I got home, and my dad faxed it to the coach from his office in our house. Sometimes you find the right thing when you least expect it.

Five months later, I was back on an airplane with my parents.* This time it was just me. WWE had events in Dublin, Ireland, and Manchester and Birmingham, England. It felt like an eternity since the last time I was on the road with my dad for a WWE tour. My volleyball schedule intensified with each year of high school, and like many teenagers, I felt that my social calendar was very precious. My parents wanted to take me on a trip for selecting a college and for being recruited by a Division I volleyball program. I knew this was going to be a wonderful experience.

My first night at the arena in Dublin was my first real time being in a WWE locker room. I met Fit Finlay's wife, Mel, and she showed us around. I turned a corner and bumped into Stacy Keibler. I gave her a hug right away. I filled her in on everything going on in my life since we last saw each other. Stacy and my brother David dated when they worked together in WCW. I saw WWE Divas Lita, Trish, and Victoria getting ready for the show. They looked so glamorous sitting in their chairs getting their makeup and hair done. I was mystified standing there but did my best to look natural.

After the show that night, my parents let me "go out with the kids." I was with Stacey, Randy Orton, Victoria, Hurricane Helms, and Torrie

---

* Ric: "I wanted to take Ashley on a trip as a congratulations for picking a college. I remember the kids taking Ashley out. She was so happy. I also remember later seeing pictures they took of her jumping on the beds and walking around the hotel with the Hurricane's superhero mask on. If this was the kind of fun she was having, I was all for it. Ashley's always been the epitome of what a father wants his daughter to be."

Wilson. Since I was in Europe, I was legally allowed to enjoy drinks with them. They watched over me like I was their little sister, which was unfortunate for me because, in high school, I had a crush on Randy. I hoped, as a high school girl would, that he'd see me in another way, not as his little sister. What high school girl wouldn't? That didn't happen.

I met my parents back at the hotel bar.

The group showed them that I made it back in one piece. Since I was having fun—but not too much fun—I was allowed to have a couple of drinks with my mom and dad. We had a great time, and I looked forward to seeing Manchester.

My mom couldn't wait to take me exploring through England. We went shopping and had lunch at amazing cafés. At night, we'd go to the WWE show and have dinner afterward with my dad. My mom told me stories about what it was like traveling with him when he was NWA World Champion, before Reider and I were born.

We extended our trip a few extra days and finished in London at the Conrad. I had my own room that overlooked the water. I remember putting on my personalized white robe and meeting my mom in the spa. We got massages and then went shopping with my dad. He bought my mom and me matching Fendi purses, and we took pictures with Beefeater guards. After the three of us went to dinner, we went to the hotel bar and proceeded to call my friend Brittany's cell phone. We filled her voice mail with funny messages from across the pond. Oh, what a night!

I loved spending time with my parents, and I couldn't help but think about how exciting things were going to be for my senior year in high school and all the fun we'd have as a family when I was in college.

The overseas tours helped me to understand the enormity of WWE productions. The number of trucks, backstage crew, pyrotechnic teams, lighting crews, catering professionals, medical staff, the roster of Superstars . . . to see the shows in Dublin two nights in a row and then to experience the shows immediately following in Manchester and Birmingham with the same grandeur was all incredible.

Heading into my senior year, I was getting ready to be the captain of the Providence volleyball team. It was an extraordinary honor. I took my leadership responsibilities seriously. If the team did well, I felt like I contributed to a job well done. If the team didn't play well, I held myself responsible. Being the captain of a team is a huge responsibility. When you're the captain of a team that's expected to win the championship every year, you feel a certain kind of pressure. I wanted that challenge.

My training with Jeff George continued. The gym in our home went from something Reider and my dad used to a place where I could be found every day—sometimes twice a day—to make sure my workouts pushed me to the level needed to be as an athlete and a captain. The stair-climber was a machine I saw my dad use all my life. It was the first thing I headed for when I stepped through the door.

It was an amazing season. For the third year in a row, our team reached the state finals. For the second time, we won the NCHSAA 4A State Championship. It was a fantastic way to end my volleyball career with my teammates and Coach Bell at Providence High School. Before I could think about the rest of my senior year, the coach told me there was one more thing I needed to do: receive my award for player of the year. Senior year at Providence was one of the most special of my life. I was really looking forward to going to Appalachian State the next year, but I wanted to make sure I enjoyed everything in between.

Just as my family was thrilled to hear the PHS crowd cheer for me at one of my volleyball games, we all felt a sense of pride when the Charlotte crowd roared for my dad, even if at times he was supposed to be a "bad guy." One *Raw* from Charlotte stands out.

It was December of 2004. My dad was performing toward the end of the show. He was in Triple H and Batista's corner in a tag team match against Chris Benoit and Chris Jericho. It was always exciting seeing Dad work with people we knew.

The main event that night was Lita versus Trish Stratus for the WWE Women's Championship. I overheard people sitting near us asking why that match was going to be the main event. Sometimes when I saw Lita and Trish perform, it was in "Bra and Panties" matches, where the first woman to be stripped down lost the match. Reider always had a smirk on his face when this type of match was on, like he was seeing something he was not supposed to see. The bell rang. The way Lita and Trish locked up with each other to start the match—ending up on the arena floor— showed everyone that this was a different story.

These women put it all on the line. There were high-flying moves, exciting back-and-forth exchanges of offense, and different times when it seemed like the match was over. I was worried about Lita after she took a dive out of the ring and landed on her neck. Trish enjoyed breaking the rules, especially when she showed that her protective face mask was not to prevent an injury but to be used as a weapon. It was then that I wondered if I performed in the ring, would I be a "good guy" or a "bad guy"? I was my dad's biggest fan, but I watched matches like everyone else. I didn't know all the things that went into the performance aspect of sports entertainment.

In the end, Lita won with her signature flip from the top rope—the moonsault. When I saw her execute that move, I said to myself, *Hey, I can do that too*, but not with the type of sex appeal that Lita had and not in front of thousands of screaming fans. The people in our section who questioned why women were in the main event before the bell even rang turned out to be some of their loudest supporters. It was an incredible performance by both women.

That week, my dad surprised me with an early Christmas present. He said there was something he forgot to mention about the WWE February tour—that I was going with him to Hawaii, Japan, and Alaska! He wanted to take me on the road because, one, I always had so much fun, and two, it would be the last time I would be able to travel like this before I went to college. This trip was coming at the best time. By junior year, I was looking ahead to college. My closest friends were away. They'd come home, and I felt like I was floating between them, kids at school, and the girls on my teams.*

Except when I was with my family and playing volleyball, I never felt like I truly belonged. I never said in my heart, "This is where I should be."

Other girls were athletic and worked out. I didn't feel like the beauty queen. I wasn't going after school for dress fittings for a cotillion or to weekly manicure and pedicure appointments. I trained with Jeff George three times a week and ran forty-yard wind sprints with a parachute tied to my back, and I loved it!

I felt conflicted driving to school every day. I was torn between a world of high society, the status of the "cool crowd," and the fact that I felt more comfortable in the gym, with my family, and with people who were older than I was. I liked being around kids who didn't care what anyone else thought about them. I admired that. They knew who they were. I wished I did.

This trip was an unforgettable way to spend my final year of high school. I couldn't have scripted anything more amazing.

I felt so fortunate touring Europe with my parents, meeting so many interesting people, and seeing so many incredible things. To know that

---

*Brittany Zahn Arnold: "It was hard for Ashley, because so many of her close friends were always older than she was. There were times I'd come home from school and she'd have her friends over from her grade, and maybe people who were a year younger than she was. They were fine, but there's not much you can do with that crowd when you're in college. I'd go upstairs and play Rummy Cube with Beth and Aunt Francine. Ashley and I hung out later."

I'd be traveling in the other direction was surreal—and that this trip would be just my dad and me! Not everyone was able to bring their families on tour with them. I also cherished this time I spent with him, because my other three siblings did not have this opportunity. Most kids went on a trip here and there, maybe annually, but I was able to travel the world. I loved spending time with my parents. My dad and I became closer each day. This trip would be even better. I couldn't wait to pack my bags.

II

WHERE DO I GO NOW?

Suddenly, I felt empty.

May 2005

I didn't realize it at the time, but seeing the top of Mt. Fuji on our way from the airport to our hotel in Japan was a sign. This WWE tour was going to be incredible. I immediately fell in love with Japanese culture: the people, the food, and the pride they took in everything they did. This was a once-in-a-lifetime experience. To be there with my dad was truly a gift.

Once we checked into our hotel, he insisted that we go to a Korean BBQ restaurant. I had no idea what that was, but once we were there, I didn't want to leave. Any time we were at the traditional Japanese restaurants, I couldn't help but think of Reider, how he and I loved having miso soup before our main course at Nakato in Charlotte. We always sipped the soup from the wrong end of the big white spoons—though I did not do that on this trip. In Japan, miso was served with breakfast, lunch, and dinner if you wanted it. How could you turn that down?

On that tour, my dad worked in matches versus Shawn Michaels, and he was at ringside with Triple H during his World Heavyweight Championship defenses. Since my dad had gone back to WWE, he had become such close friends with them and Batista. He loved working with them too.

I enjoyed hearing about his first trips to Japan during the 1970s, along with familiar names like Dusty and Ricky Steamboat. He talked about going from All Japan Pro Wrestling to New Japan Pro Wrestling and how much fun he had teaming up with Uncle Arn during a New Japan tour. They worked with Sting and a Japanese star named Keiji Mutoh, who my dad explained was also known as the Great Muta. He wore face paint like Sting. I said, "Oh, okay." I didn't know the significance of those things the way a dedicated wrestling fan would, but I loved learning about my dad's career and all the events in his life, especially when they included people I knew. I loved feeling his excitement when he spoke about these experiences. Reider went to Japan to compete in a wrestling tournament when he was a kid. It was awesome that I got to be there now with my dad.

At the WWE shows, I beamed with pride when I heard the reception he received from the Japanese audiences. I didn't realize how special that was until he told me that normally Japanese crowds are silent for most matches in comparison to North American and European audiences. He said that when a lot of wrestlers go to Japan to perform for the first time, they think they're doing something wrong, because the crowd gives a minimal reaction at best.

Another memorable experience was going into the Roppongi section of Tokyo. Just like when I went on the European tour, he let me go out after the show. I had such fun hanging out with everyone: Victoria, Torrie Wilson, Rey Mysterio, and Undertaker. And once again, I could not have felt safer. It was like being somewhere with my mom and dad with just more eyeballs watching out for me. The time went by so quickly. I think Undertaker felt it was time to call it a night, and before I knew it, I was in a cab with him and Rey Mysterio. I can still see the taxi driver's white gloves on the steering wheel during our trip back to the hotel.

The next morning, we were off to Alaska. I stayed at the hotel, but I knew that if the Heartbreak Kid against the Nature Boy was anything like what I'd seen in Japan, the fans in Anchorage would be on their feet from the moment the bell rang.

———

Once we left Alaska, we made a connecting flight to New York and finally landed in Charlotte. Moving through the airport with my dad was like walking around our house. We knew the best ways to get in and out of the terminals, where to wait at the baggage claim, and the quickest way to get to his car. Going to the airport and flying out of town was as regular for us as people running weekend errands. Traveling had always been a part of our lives.

We talked about the week ahead and everything that was going on. I knew I still had time, but I was counting the days to graduation. I couldn't wait to start college. I was nervous, but I was excited about the future and how I would do as part of an NCAA Division I volleyball team.

Looking back, my final volleyball season at Providence Day was especially memorable. Everyone loved attending the women's volleyball games. On game day, the electricity ran through the entire school. The gym overflowed with people—it was like being in a sauna. And the senior fan section created the most raucous atmosphere of all. Opposing teams knew what awaited them when a game at Providence was on their schedule.

There was nothing like feeling the rush from a kill at a playoff game, and the best part was having my whole family in the bleachers, cheering me on. It was really rewarding to succeed at such a high level with teammates I worked hard with every day. It was bittersweet. I felt sad knowing that in a few months that chapter would come to a close, but I was energized thinking about the exciting times ahead.

My dad turned onto our block and pulled into the driveway. He stopped there and opened the garage. Before I could ask him what he was doing, he told me that he wasn't coming into the house. After a few seconds of silence, the only thing I said was "Why?"

He said a lot of things had been going on between him and my mom,*

---

* Beth and I grew apart as the years went on, and the differences that we had continued to build. When I returned to WWE in 2001, the company offered me a contract that included a downside guarantee of $500,000. That meant if nothing else, I would earn $500,000 a year. That didn't include royalties from the sale of consumer products and merchandise. I was fifty-one years old and not contracted to be an in-ring performer.

I was grateful to WWE for the offer. Especially given the stage I was at in my career.

that he wasn't leaving Reider and me but leaving my mom, and he'd be back at the house to get his things.

A numbing feeling came over me. I fought back tears, but my eyes began to well up when I asked him questions. "Why? What happened? Why can't you work it out? Where are you going? What about the rest of the year? What about graduation?" He promised me he'd be there and that everything would work out.

Dad helped me bring my bags into the house. I stood in the kitchen alone. When I asked my mother what was going on, she told me that my dad was leaving her and then said a name I never thought I'd hear again: *Tiffany*. At that moment, I was transported back to the eighth grade, and everything that happened that day after school. I felt sick.

Questions swirled through my head. How long had this been going on? Was my dad leading a double life? Why didn't he talk to me about this during our trip? I didn't know what to think, and—even worse—I didn't know what to do. The last time I heard that woman's name, I grabbed

---

When I told Beth about the contract I thought she'd be happy. But she had a different opinion on the matter.

Beth became hostile toward me. She raised her voice and said I should've received "[Steve] Austin money." She added that I was an "old, insecure motherf*cker," and that I never fought for what I was worth. Beth continued by saying I cost my family millions of dollars by conducting my business in this way.

A part of me appreciated that Beth felt I should have a larger contract. I don't think she understood that given where I was in my career, and not an in-ring performer, this was an amazing contract. I was also disappointed in the way she communicated with me. Especially since throughout our marriage I helped support her father by giving him a job to manage one of my gyms, even though he did not have management experience or any knowledge of physical fitness. My mother-in-law lived with us for nine years and all they did was fight. I provided for our family well, and that included members of her immediate family.

I also felt it became increasingly difficult over time to ensure Beth was present for the kids. I didn't sleep in our bedroom for three years. When I was home, I slept in a guest suite. I tried to keep as much as I could away from the kids. By 2005, I felt it was time to end the marriage. I walked out the door and left all of my belongings there except for two custom suits and two pairs of alligator shoes. I didn't set foot in the house for a year.

the phone from the kitchen counter and called my dad. That night, I got into my car and went to find him.

I scoured south Charlotte and tried to figure out where he had gone. I turned down block after block and rolled at five miles per hour. I looked in people's front windows and driveways. I went through the neighborhoods that surrounded his gyms. This went on for hours. I must've gone through a quarter of a tank of gas. Somehow, I found him—well, I found his car. I wrote down the name of the street and the house number. I tried to make sense of what was going on. The thought of driving home and unpacking seemed pointless. The idea of going to school the next day was unbearable.

The following morning, I felt like I was in a daze. I did things that were part of my routine, but there wasn't any thought or feeling behind anything. I was just there. For the next two weeks, I came home from school and slept until I had to go to volleyball practice for Charlotte Elite. The thought of moving was overwhelming. Nothing made it better. But I had to pack for my next game.

My team flew to Colorado to play in one of the largest volleyball tournaments in the country. This was the first event that my parents attended as single people; they were no longer husband and wife. To put it mildly, I was off my game. For the first time in my life, I didn't know how to act toward my parents. Would I hurt my mom if I showed affection toward my dad? Would I alienate my dad if I spent more time with my mom? I didn't know what was right. It seemed like it was only yesterday that I'd had lunch with them at a café in London. Now that was gone.

Something was wrong. I knew it had to do with my dad leaving, but I couldn't pinpoint what it was.* When I got back home, my mom let me

---

*Brittany Zahn Arnold: "Ashley called me at school and let me know what was going on. I think something else that made her parents' breakup harder was that the relationship with Tiffany took place in Charlotte. She felt like this was being played out in public, because the family was so well known in the community. Things at home were really tough for them."

stay home from school for a week. I curled up in my pajamas and watched *Sex and the City* on DVD. Every episode.

Our home always felt full: full of life, full of energy, full of love. I woke up every day trying to cope with the fact that my father, my hero, wasn't there, and that this wasn't like the last time. This time, he wasn't coming back.

My dad told Reider and me that he was taking us to Los Angeles for WrestleMania 21. He also told me what I suspected, that Tiffany would be joining us. This was the first time I'd be spending time with her. Normally, I'd want to see my dad's schedule and mark down what things we were doing together. This time, I used his packed schedule to stay more to myself. I didn't say much during the trip. I know he didn't do anything deliberately, but it didn't feel right to see him with someone else, let alone be in her company for several days during a trip. I was in my own world for much of the weekend.

What should've been an exciting path to graduation day remained a blur. What I envisioned as one of the most joyous and memorable weeks of my life, my last week of high school, was now filled with uncertainty and sadness. It felt like everything had come crashing down on me.

My dad and I only spoke for a few minutes that week. He said he'd be at graduation. I knew deep down he would be there, but I felt so unsure of everything. I felt so empty.

Graduation day arrived. I woke up extra early to do my hair and make-up. My mom came into my bathroom and said how proud she was of me and that no matter what, today was a happy day. I knew my mom, Reider, Grandmommy, and Brittany would be sitting together. I found out the night before that Megan and David would be at graduation with my dad.

During the ceremony, I looked around and tried to see where he and my siblings were. When my name was called to receive my diploma, I wondered if they saw me get it. Earning that diploma was a milestone.

I'll always remember celebrating all my achievements and the incredible friendships I made at Providence High School. It's a special feeling when you can say you transferred into a school as a tenth grader and by the time you graduated you felt like you had been there all four years.

I hugged friends and people who rotated in and out and took pictures. People were missing: my dad, Megan, and David. They were on the other side of the gym. Tiffany was with them. As the cameras kept clicking, I hoped I'd see my dad, Megan, and David come through the sea of people. As the final photographs were taken, I smiled a little less for each one. I realized they weren't meeting us. I never saw them. It was the first major event in my life where we didn't have a photo taken of all of us, together, as a family.

I tried to inconspicuously look around on my way to my mom's car. I gave one last glance before I got in the backseat. I sat in the car and looked out the window. People were talking in the car, but I just heard noise, like if you put a seashell to your ear. I was in one car, going to dinner at Upstream at Phillips Place with Reider, Brittany, my mom, and our relatives on her side of the family. My dad was somewhere else. He left in a separate car with Megan, David, and someone who wasn't my mother, someone I only knew by name and face.

I wasn't sure when I'd see my dad next or what was going to happen to our family. I was still in shock about my parents' divorce. For the first time in my life, my father and I were traveling in two separate directions.

As we drove out of Providence High School's parking lot for the final time, I couldn't help but wonder, *Is this how it's going to be now?*

Right after graduation, my mom took me to the volleyball nationals in Salt Lake City, Utah. When I wasn't playing volleyball, she made sure we had a good time. But on the court, it was a nightmare. I played terribly. I found myself just going through the motions. I didn't want to be there. I didn't care if we won or lost. I begged my mother to let me leave the tournament before it was over. I never left anything early. I was so disappointed in myself, but at the same time, I just wanted to go home.

My focus shifted to the string of graduation parties that went on throughout south Charlotte. When those were over, Reider and I decided that our way of dealing with my parents' breakup was to keep the party going—literally. Almost every night, our house was the gathering place for our friends. My mom tried to recover from her marriage ending and tried to keep things going as best as she could. I think she figured since she knew we were a good group of kids and things would not go beyond a certain level, the parties were okay—and at least we were home. For those hours, we were distracted, and no one knew it. These were masquerade parties to hide our pain. But at some point, the party had to end.

I saw my dad once that entire summer. We met in the Promenade shopping center parking lot. We talked for about an hour. There were times during that conversation that felt like I was speaking with a stranger. I saw his face and heard his voice more on television at the time—*Monday Night Raw*, Spike TV, at 9:00 p.m. EST.

The summer flew by faster than any I can ever remember. Before I knew it, I was packing the car with a few final things and getting ready to leave for college. I looked out at the street and back at our house. I couldn't believe this was really happening.

I gave one last goodbye to Reider and got in the car. He was going to be home for another week. He was finishing high school at Blair Academy in Blairstown, New Jersey. Blair was a highly regarded boarding school with one of the top wrestling programs in the country. Reider felt a lot of pressure to do well in amateur wrestling, but he loved the sport, he loved competing, and he was considered one of the best in his weight class.

My mom pulled out of the driveway, and we started our trip to Appalachian State in Boone, North Carolina. This was different from all the wonderful times we spent talking in the car: no singing along to songs on the radio or talking about what our plans were for the day. I even missed the bickering with my brother.

Since childhood, Reider was always larger than life. No matter how old he was, he was always the hit of the party. He idolized my dad and was just like him: charming, witty, funny, and kind. Reider loved being around people, and people loved being around him. He loved making fun of how I looked when I cried, because it made me laugh. My brother always knew when to be lighthearted and bring humor to a sensitive situation. Reider liked making people feel better when they were upset. If you were Reider's friend, he'd never leave your side.

I knew I'd miss his imitations of people. He'd quote Grandmommy when she was on my dad's boat. She'd say, "Precious, there are alligators in that lake." At the drop of a hat, my brother could go into a perfect rendition of any of the spirited interview segments from my dad and Dusty's career. His favorites were from the '80s. I couldn't guess how many links he had bookmarked on his computer. I'd miss his rendition of Dusty saying, "I have wined and dined with kings and queens, and I've slept in alleys and dined on pork and beans."

The previous summer, my parents had gotten a bill in the mail from the country club. My mother almost flipped out when she saw it was for $5,000 and none of us had been to the club, or so we thought. During the day, my brother went to the club to teach the younger kids how to play different sports. After those sessions, he treated them all to lunch. Every day. My parents were not happy about having to pay the bill, but I knew, deep down, they smiled a little because of why they had to pay it. Classic Reider . . .

College meant this would be the first time we'd be living apart. I knew we'd talk, Reider would come to visit, and we'd be home together for holidays. Gone were the days of my coming home after school or volleyball and hearing the thunderous sounds of WWE on television, his Guns N' Roses albums, or scenes from movies like *Stand by Me*, *The Goonies*, and *The Sandlot*. I was really going to miss my brother.

Reider started to have problems dealing with my parents' divorce. It was hard on everyone. I know it was hard for them too. Everyone experienced it differently. We knew my dad was not gone forever, but it was such a difficult adjustment because we were so close. As a child, you don't think of yourself as the one who wants better for your parents. That was how we felt. Our mom had a hard time with the separation. We felt that Tiffany was my dad's focus. For the first time, we didn't feel close to him the way we always had. I think going to Blair Academy was a good way for Reider to focus on himself.

As we drove to Boone, my mom kept everything upbeat and positive. She wanted to make this a special time for me. She made all the arrangements to move me into my dorm. When we got there, you'd think she was the host of an interior design show. She stayed with me all day. She decorated my entire room so beautifully. If you took a picture of my dorm and didn't know where it was, you'd think it was a suite at the Ritz-Carlton.

Saying goodbye to my mom was hard. I worried about how she'd be once Reider left for school. She'd be alone in the house. It hurt Reider and me to see my mom in so much pain after her split from my dad.

I didn't get much sleep that first night in my dorm room. It was difficult adjusting to a new place knowing that this was where I'd be living. I got up the next morning and was excited because there was someone else who was coming to Appalachian State. She was also a new student and a new member of the volleyball team: Brittany Zahn.

Brittany played volleyball at the University of Tennessee. Before her freshman year, she suffered a terrible knee injury, tearing her ACL and meniscus. She made a full recovery and returned to her top form. Brittany wasn't pleased with how things were going at the university. When I committed to Appalachian State, she wanted to transfer there. During the spring, it was confirmed: she was coming to Boone to play on the volleyball team.

I had volleyball practice every day, Monday through Friday. Home games were on Saturday, and we were off on Sunday. Although I had to adjust to the fact that the college game moved much faster than high school, it was great playing on a team with Brittany again. There was a fifth-year senior who played the same position as I did. Some games I'd start. Other games I came off the bench. For the first time in my life, I was sitting on the sidelines. I didn't like it. You never want to be injured, but when you're not playing due to an injury, you may be sitting on the bench, but you're working to make it back on the court.

Splitting time as a freshman, which I knew was common, was a tough pill to swallow. When I was put in the game, I made the most of it and was glad that I played well.

Freshmen, especially members of a sports team, were supposed to live on campus. Brittany was starting her junior year. Her apartment was off campus. I was inside Brittany's apartment in Mountaineer Village for ten minutes when I decided to move in. It was an unexpected twist of fate that my best friend was now at the same college as I was and also about to become my new roommate!

Somehow, everything from my dorm made it into her apartment. From the time the last bag was unpacked, the fun began.

On Wednesdays, we'd pregame at the apartment and then go to Gino's Bar in Boone for Karaoke and Club night. We'd have some drinks, and I'd force her to get onstage with me and sing karaoke to Britney Spears songs. I'd joke with Zahn and say she needed to understand that each song from Britney's catalog could be considered a greatest hit.

We definitely enjoyed college life and balanced volleyball with schoolwork too.

One night, there was a big birthday party planned for one of the girls on the volleyball team. We were all supposed to go to her place. Some friends stopped at our place first. We just hung out. A few people's cell phones rang, and within a couple of hours, there were close to seventy-five people all over our apartment. The girls on the team were furious. We never planned a party. We told them they should've brought everything to our place.

I implemented my strategy from the summer before: party, have fun, and smile. But when I got home, it was difficult to hold it together. I kept thinking, *What is going to happen to my mom? Is Reider okay at school?* Sometimes I'd get upset and just want to be by myself. This was the first time I'd suffered severe emotional pain. I don't know what would've happened during that time if Brittany hadn't been there for me. She was the only person I trusted.

Living with Brittany was a blast, but I was in for some hard lessons. I was overwhelmed by the fact that I didn't know how to take care of myself: I had to do my own laundry, vacuum the living room, and clean my own bathroom. Every week! At home, we always had people who helped clean our house. I didn't know what a checkbook was, let alone how to balance one. I never used a debit card or went to the bank. Money was left on the counter for me every day. I had two credit cards. The statements were paid every month.

My parents gave me everything I ever imagined. I wasn't aware of just how much money was spent on us and the time and effort being able to do that required of them. I had it all. I took it for granted.

College independence was a whole new world. I needed to get on board. In some ways, Brittany raised me the first six months of my freshman year.*

I remember one day I was walking to class and someone asked me how to get to the student union building. I said to myself, *Why are you asking me? Last weekend it took me ten minutes to figure out how to find the correct settings on the washer and dryer.*

Looking back on those twelve months from the beginning of my senior year at Providence High School to my freshman year at App, I went from having everything—not a care in the world—to having nothing. The perfection of Piper Glen was a far cry from navigating my way around the Blue Ridge Mountains that surrounded Appalachian State's campus. I first walked the campus with my parents. They were together. Everything seemed fine. What happened?

My dad and Tiffany came to Boone for a few home games. Megan and Reider visited too. Seeing them was so much fun. It reminded me of

---

*Brittany Zahn Arnold: "I'd tease Ashley a little bit, especially when it came to cooking, but she did well with it. The fact of the matter was that she came from a different world. Everything was done for her at home. She just needed to learn how to be independent around the house."

home. When I went back to Charlotte for holidays, whatever progress I'd made in coming to grips with my parents' split was negated. The emotional wounds that showed signs of healing would be ripped open; someone I'd see would say something, or my mom would give me an update on the divorce proceedings. It was a cycle I felt I couldn't escape.

As my freshman year came to an end, I made plans with Zahn to stay at App. I wanted to train for preseason and regular season volleyball and take summer classes. I saw my siblings at the end of May. My dad and Tiffany got married in Grand Cayman. Triple H was my dad's best man. His wife, Stephanie, was there as were WWE Superstars like Big Show and Batista. As with every Fliehr family function, Brittany was there too.

Where Megan and David accepted the fact that our father was getting remarried, Reider and I made a different statement. We began drinking at the beginning of the afternoon like we were at a college keg party, not a wedding for our father on a beautiful Caribbean island. We went overboard with our form of civil disobedience, and it was obvious to the guests.*

After the wedding, Brittany and I went back to Boone. At this point, we moved into a house with a huge patio and two other roommates. My room was a giant studio off one corner of the house. My mom came and made it like a little apartment with all my favorite paintings and colors and some furniture from our house, including curtains and a new bedspread. She also added dishes, electronics, and everything I needed in the kitchen. It really felt like home.

My mom's always been great with decorating, and she loves to do it. This time, she couldn't wait to design my first college house. She came to visit a few times that summer before fall season started, and we had a

---

*Paul Levesque: "It was an honor to stand as best man for Ric. Grand Cayman was beautiful. In May, it felt like seven hundred degrees. Steph was about eight months' pregnant with our first child. She was exhausted from the day, the heat, and the pregnancy. I wanted to make an early exit to bring her to our room. On our way out, we saw Ashley passed out on the side of a walkway at the hotel. Steph took care of her. We knew her seeing her dad get remarried was not easy."

blast with Brittany, the two other girls from the volleyball team, and some of the football players who we were friends with.

My mom enjoyed herself in Boone. I saw her smile more than I had in a long time.

By the beginning of sophomore year, I felt that I had created a life for myself in Boone; I made more friends, got comfortable with my schedule, and was more comfortable dealing with what was going on with my parents in Charlotte.

On the volleyball court, I saw the benefit of staying in Boone over the summer and training with Brittany. I was more confident, my level of play improved, and I started in more games. When we had a Saturday night and the next day off, Zahn and I took a few road trips to visit her old volleyball teammates at the University of Tennessee. At App State, the football team won the Division II national title the year before, so we went to a couple of games.

I remember finishing my last final of the fall semester. I couldn't wait to get home to spend the holidays with Reider. One night while I was out in Charlotte, I went to a place where a lot of kids from our area hung out when they were home on break. I met a guy my brother knew. He transferred into Providence Day the year I left to play volleyball at Providence. I knew his friends and he knew mine, but we didn't know each other. His name was Riki.

Riki went to Ole Miss his freshman year. He was one of the most highly recruited football players on the Providence Day team. He told me how he transferred to the University of North Carolina at Chapel Hill and made their football team as a walk-on. He made me laugh with funny stories about what it was like rushing for a fraternity and how he was in Sigma Chi, one of the best-known fraternities in Chapel Hill. He was tall, had nice hair, looked great in a polo shirt, and was so handsome he looked like he'd walked off the set of a Brooks Brothers catalog shoot. And he was beyond charming.

For some reason, I was surprised he stayed around to speak with me. I had guys show that they were interested in me before, ask me for my phone number, or invite me out on a date, but this was different. From where I stood, guys like Riki only talked to sorority girls. All their friends and families knew each other. If you weren't "in," you were "out." He was from a group that I had been around my whole life but never felt completely comfortable with. I liked nice clothes, but I didn't have a relentless compulsion to go shopping all the time or only wear pieces from specific designers. Most of the sorority girls from south Charlotte were different in that way. Riki was certainly different from the friends I'd made over the last year in Boone.

We looked nice when we went to parties and went out, but it wasn't wall-to-wall polo shirts and Lacoste dresses. Maybe that's why I was attracted to him. He was everything I wasn't, except for the fact that he was part of a social circle that I had spent most my life with up until the tenth grade.

When we said goodbye that night, he told me he would call me the next day. That afternoon, my cell phone rang. It was him. I was more surprised than anything else. I went into my room, and we just talked. I was happy that he called. Most times, guys would say they'd call and then they'd play games about actually calling.

Whether we ran errands, went to get something to eat, saw a movie, or just because, Riki and I spent every day of Christmas break together. Seeing him didn't feel like a chore. Before I knew it, it was New Year's Eve. We raised our glasses to the year that was and shared a kiss for the year that was to come. From where I stood, I liked how 2007 looked.

When the holidays were over, Riki drove back to Chapel Hill and I went back to Boone. We didn't want to leave each other. We made plans based on our schedules and marked weekends when he'd come to see me at App and I'd drive to UNC.

I made it back to school and settled in for the new semester. I had to prepare for my classes and spring volleyball workouts. I couldn't wait to see Riki. We talked on the phone every night. The first weekend he came up, I met him at the door when he pulled up to our house.

I showed him around, introduced him to my roommates, and took him into town. Over that weekend, he met all my friends from school: classmates, volleyball team, and football team. Everyone had a great time meeting Riki and hanging out with him.

Just when it felt like we had a few minutes to relax, it was time to say goodbye. I told him I'd see him the following weekend in Chapel Hill.

12

LOST

I felt myself slip away more with each passing day.

February 2007

It was only a few days since Riki had left. I was talking in the kitchen with my roommates. We'd hang out there at the end of the night. They could tell how much I liked him, but it was something else to admit it. They were relentless. They wouldn't let me off the hook. I felt like Ted Stroehmann in the interrogation scene in *There's Something About Mary*. We all laughed and said how much fun we had over the weekend. I'd usually hear from him by then. I figured I'd text him before I went to bed. Around 11:00, I got a text from him: "My dad is dead." I ran to my room. I took whatever clothes I could grab and stuffed them into my bags. Brittany looked at me. Before she said anything, I told her, "I have to go. I have to take care of him."

I got in my car with my dog, Louis, and drove the two hours and fifteen minutes straight to Chapel Hill. When I got to Riki's house, his frat brothers were standing around the living room. Riki sat on the floor in his bedroom. He was quiet most of the night. An hour after I got there, his fraternity brothers left. From what I gathered, Riki's dad's passing was unexpected. We were together barely a month, but we became close in that time. I didn't want to overstep my bounds. I tried to console him but also give him space.

The next morning, we put our two dogs in the car and drove to Charlotte, a little more than a two-hour drive. I called my parents and let them know why I was coming home. They jumped to help Riki. They bought him and his brother tuxedos to wear at their father's funeral. They sent food to his family's home, made him trays of food, and were on call if they could do anything to help.

Those few days were awful. My heart broke for his family. Riki tried to figure out how to help his mom pick up the pieces. On Sunday, we drove the two hours northeast from Charlotte to Chapel Hill. I spent the night at his house. The next morning, I drove back to Boone in time for my first class. That week back, I texted him during the day and we talked at night. I tried to be there for him as best as I could even though I could not be with him in person.

The weeks following his dad's funeral, Riki was very attached to me. I was happy to be there for him, and we'd take turns visiting one another at school. Soon after, things started to change. His moods went from one extreme to the other—fast. I thought it was understandable, given what happened, and I knew he was worried about his mom and siblings, but these erratic shifts intensified over time. I found myself taking on his moods: if he was happy, I was happy; if he was sad, I became sad. Even if we spoke on the phone—I was in Boone, and he was in Chapel Hill—I adopted his mood.

At school, I had to make sure I was current on all my assignments despite being less than interested. I knew midterms would be there before I knew it, and volleyball's spring season was starting soon. Given how my sophomore season went, I had high expectations for my level of play in the spring, and 2007 was set to be my breakout year. I wanted to seize the opportunity. But mentally, I couldn't become focused. I didn't feel excited when I thought of playing volleyball in the spring. My thoughts revolved around taking care of Riki.

We talked every day. When I traveled for volleyball tournaments, Riki called me from the bars he was at with his friends. Everyone was having a great time and partied all night. There were always a few of his friends who wanted to celebrate that fact and scream into the phone during our conversations. I sat in the bed in my hotel room with the TV on mute and wondered what he was doing.

We'd text throughout the day. I'd call him on the phone to see how he was doing. If he called when I was in class, I left class to take his call. Even at home with the girls, I became distant. I thought Riki was in trouble and that I was the only one who could help him. I knew how much he loved his family, and in a way, I could understand what it was like being concerned for a parent and siblings.

Something was coming up back home that I looked forward to.

Birthdays continued to be a major event in the Fliehr family. Every year, even during this time of uncertainty with my family, was special. That year was a milestone—twenty-one! My parents organized a dinner at my favorite Thai restaurant in downtown Charlotte. Megan and David were there, along with some other relatives and some of my close friends. The life of the party, Reider, couldn't make the trip; he was at school in New Jersey. My parents gave speeches at the table. Megan and David also spoke. My mom saved the best for last. She read a letter from Reider that he'd emailed her. Once I heard her say, "To my beautiful sister on her twenty-first birthday," it was like someone turned on the waterworks.

Every word spoke to how close we were since childhood, how much he looked up to me, and how much he loved me. Reider wanted me to know that even though he couldn't there, that I was so special to him, and he kept all our memories with him while he was away and couldn't wait to make new ones when he came home. He was proud to be my brother. I was so proud to be his sister.

For that weekend, I felt like I was really home. I went back to Boone and got ready for finals week. I couldn't believe that in a matter of days, I'd be done with my second year of college. I woke up one day and made a decision.

I didn't talk to anyone about it. I didn't ask anyone for their opinion.

I just did it: I drove to my volleyball coach's office, walked in, and quit. He just looked at me. I thanked him for having me on the team and told him I wasn't coming back. I got back in my car and drove to the house.*

In a matter of seconds, I destroyed everything I ever worked for. All the years of sacrifice, hard work, training, attending camps—all of it, gone. It was like I took my scholarship letter, put it through a paper shredder, and walked away.

When I got home, I packed. I decided I was going to live with Riki in Chapel Hill. I told Zahn and the girls that I'd be back at some point to get my stuff and that I'd make sure to send my share for the rent.

I called my parents from the road. I got my dad on his cell phone right before he boarded a flight to Australia.† He tried to talk me out of it. It didn't matter what he said. My mind was made up. There was no speaking to me. The timing worked out for me since he couldn't stay on the phone long because his flight was taking off.

I called my mom at home. She told me I was making a huge mistake. She asked me to come home. She asked me to speak with Brittany—I wasn't doing any of that.

Then I thought of Brittany. I knew in a matter of minutes, I inflicted major damage to my best friend, and she didn't see it coming. She didn't deserve it. I'd call her when things settled down. I chose to ignore those thoughts, and I kept driving. In a couple of hours, I was going to have the life I always wanted.

The decision I made that day had consequences far beyond what I ever imagined.

I made it to Chapel Hill, and I moved in with Riki. I was ready to

---

*Brittany Zahn Arnold: "I told her, 'You're here on scholarship to play Division I volleyball. You're away at college. Enjoy it.' We just signed a lease for a new house. Beth and Ric called me separately. They thought I could talk her into staying. She made up her mind. We were all so worried about her."

†Ric: "I went into shock. 'You're doing what?' I was boarding a flight to the other side of the world, and this is what I was told right before takeoff? She wouldn't listen to anything I said. I was deeply concerned. I called Brittany, and she told me the same thing. Ashley said she was leaving. That was it."

start the rest of my life. I learned very quickly that it was one thing to visit a house for a weekend, but was another to live there. The party scene was very different from what I was used to. It seemed like every night there were major parties that I'd have thought would've taken place during the weekend.

I noticed there was a change in the way we communicated. Riki's mood swings worsened. What he said to me and how it was said also intensified. Why were we arguing? That was a question I should've asked myself. We saw each other on weekends, and I hadn't even been living there that long.

The incidents themselves became more frequent. I thought that the way he spoke to me was not what I was supposed to hear from someone who cared about me. I moved there. I didn't expect a parade for doing that, but I thought that showed a certain commitment on my part and warranted a certain level of respect.

Riki said these arguments were my fault because of something I did. I responded by being extremely nonconfrontational. I did whatever he said to defuse the situation. If he said something was my fault, even if it wasn't, I took responsibility and apologized. After being told so many times that I was stupid, I didn't do something right, or something was my fault, I started to take it to heart. I started to believe that I did something to bring him to this point.*

A dark element started to consume the house. Riki was Jekyll and Hyde. If he was happy, things were great; he was the man of my dreams. If he was angry, everyone knew it, and it would be taken out on someone or something. There was a frightening rage behind his eyes when he became angry. For the first time in my life, I walked on eggshells. I became insecure and developed strong feelings of loneliness.

The partying at Chapel Hill continued. It was almost like it was part

---

*Brittany Zahn Arnold: "Riki appeared fine on the surface. He seemed polite and could carry a conversation. To me, once you got deeper, it was easy to see his true colors. You could also see he had nothing going on and wasn't interested in making anything of himself. He was in a frat. I didn't see why Ashley was so attracted to him. I was never a fan of his."

of the culture of the area. I soon realized that Riki developed a substance abuse problem, though he said I was overreacting. His mood swings were unbearable. The codependent tendencies I developed did not help what was a toxic situation. I was away from my family, I was away from my friends, and I was far away from the locker that now held someone else's volleyball uniform. Boone was two hours away. It felt like it was on the other side of the earth.

I felt myself slipping away, and I couldn't do anything to hold on. I started to lose myself.

During the summer, I thought about going back to Boone. I thought about going back to school. Could I get my scholarship back? Could I call Brittany and see if there was still an opening to live in the house?

At home, Riki and I got into another argument. I found pictures of him on his phone. When I asked him about it and what he planned to do with them, he entered a fit of rage. He kept yelling. As his voice got louder, he got closer and closer to me. I kept backing up, hoping that if he saw the look on my face he'd stop. He kept coming toward me. And then it happened—Riki pushed me into the closet door. I moved from the door and ran. He followed me into the guest room. His yelling continued. He said that this wouldn't have happened if I hadn't annoyed him; if I hadn't egged him on, he would never have done that.

These types of episodes continued. The focus of Riki's anger, at times, transferred to his dog, Yonder. There were times when Riki got angry that he kicked and punched the dog. I can still hear the poor dog screeching. I couldn't help but cry. My dog, Louis, would hide under the table. What was I doing there?

I think about that girl now, and it brings tears to my eyes. How did I get there? Why was this going on? Why wasn't I strong enough, brave enough, to end this?

To the outside world, everything was fine. At parties, we looked like a happy, young couple. In photos, based on appearance, it looked like we were in love without anything to worry about. I kept everyone in my life at arm's length. Everyone remained on the surface. Everything was great in Chapel Hill . . .

I should've called my mom, my dad, my siblings, Zahn, any of them. Since I'd graduated high school, Uncle Arn's wife, Erin, had become like a second mom, sister, and best friend to me. All I needed to say to any of them was one word—*help*. I just couldn't do it.

I called Brittany. I told her that I was coming by the house. I think she hoped that I was coming back for good. I told her I'd see her over the weekend.

I knew that even if I didn't play volleyball again, it was important to earn a college degree. I could return to App. I also applied to both University of North Carolina and North Carolina State University.

I went back to Boone to formally move out, and Riki came with me to help me. I knew Brittany was upset and that this was not what she wanted. She tried to tell me so many times that this whole thing was not the way to go. I ignored her until she stopped bringing it up. That was probably because deep down, I knew she was right. This was the only time in our lives that we didn't communicate and that we disagreed with one another.*

I didn't get accepted into UNC, because I didn't have the language or math requirements. NC State said I could attend part-time while taking the required courses at Wake Tech, their community college in Raleigh, North Carolina.

I started at NC State as a part-time student and took four other courses at Wake Tech. I was a full-time student in terms of hours and credits, but split my time between the two campuses. Regardless of whether I went to NC State's main campus or Wake Tech's, my commute was the same from Riki's house: forty-five minutes there and back.

This schedule was a double-edged sword. It was good because I was in school and doing well in my classes. The bad part was because of the commute and schedule, it created a heavier sense of isolation. I spent most days by myself. Since I was on two campuses, I didn't feel a sense of

---

*Brittany Zahn Anderson: "The more I told her that she needed to get out of her relationship with Riki, the more she ignored me. I was so worried about her, but it was a simple thing: she chose to be with Riki over everything else in her life. I felt like I didn't know who she was at this point in time."

belonging at either of them. During the hours between classes, I slept in the car, went running, or sat in Bruegger's Bagels and worked on assignments.

I focused on my schoolwork and knew that if I continued to do well academically, in the end, I'd earn a degree from NC State.

Since I'd gone back to school, to anyone who was on the outside looking in, everything with me seemed fine.

In general, I think when most people hear someone say, "I'm in school," they think you're doing what you're supposed to do and you're on a good path. Couple that with the fact that I never took a semester off from classes.

Unless something happened in public or I had marks on my body, which I didn't, no one really knew what went on behind closed doors. My parents always taught us to be respectful and kind to everyone, especially because you never knew what someone was going through personally; you couldn't see from the outside. I tried to hide my pain and insecurity. I didn't know if anyone could see it or not. I never thought that one day, that "someone" would be me.

There were times I'd say to myself, *Oh, it's hasn't been that bad this week.* Or after a few decent days, I'd think, *Maybe this is the point where things turn around.* I'd try to escape conversations with people to avoid the risk of getting into too much detail. I needed help.

What I should've questioned was why Riki was the only person who didn't try to stop me leaving App, tell me not to quit my scholarship, give up everything for him, and not want me to start over.

People commented all the time on how happy we looked or how great we looked together. The physical portrait did not convey the inescapable living hell I found myself in behind closed doors. The fact that people couldn't tell added to the anxiety, because what would happen to me if someone did find out?

I didn't realize it was a façade. If people looked a certain way, then they must have a certain amount of money, or they must be successful, or they must be happy together. But soon, no matter how good we looked together at an event or how nice a photo of us appeared in a picture frame, everyone would know that something was wrong.

In the fall, I got a call from my dad. He told me WWE put a story line together that centered around him retiring from wrestling. That would be his last match, and it would take place at WrestleMania in Orlando. But he didn't know who he'd be in the match with. He added that he'd be inducted into the WWE Hall of Fame the night before the match.

I wasn't sure what to make of it. I felt my father embodied wrestling. I'd never pictured him retiring. In the same breath, I was so proud of him. He dedicated his life to this profession. If this was happening at WrestleMania XXIV in Orlando, I had to make plans to be there!

Oddly enough, these were the type of happenings that I never had to worry about Riki's behavior. Riki liked being around WWE events. He basked in the attention of being recognized as part of the Flair family: being backstage, meeting WWE Superstars and Divas, sitting ringside, and enjoying the comfort of a corporate suite at a venue. I knew that this would be another instance that Riki would put his best foot forward.

My mom helped me pick out dresses for the trip. Riki and Reid were fitted for tuxedos. I was also excited because Megan and David would be there. The four of us had not been together for four days like this in a very long time. When I spoke with each of them, they were excited too. My siblings and I experienced so many changes over the last few years. We all lived in different places now. Even though I didn't speak with everyone as often, they were always with me.

I never thought of this until I wrote it down, but over the last few years, my dad's life underwent changes too. I know how much he loved his second tenure with WWE. I'm sure that came with its share of adjustments. And now, the only thing he ever wanted to do with his professional life was coming to an end. How did he feel? I thought about that in the weeks leading up to making the trip to Orlando for WrestleMania.

We drove through the night from Chapel Hill to Orlando. I remember riding in the back of Riki's car. Reider was in the front passenger seat. Reider and Riki knew each other from the different social groups

from Providence Day and Providence High School. I knew my brother
didn't like that Riki and I were in a relationship. Reider was watchful of
how Riki treated me when we were all together, but he got along with
Riki, for my sake.

As we made our way under the bridge on Interstate 4, I saw the sign
that read "Orlando." Even though it was around 4:00 in the morning, a
collage of childhood memories flooded my mind of all the wonderful
summer adventures my mom planned for our family: the character breakfasts at Disney, the rides at Universal, and the shows at SeaWorld. I never
imagined that one day we'd be back there as adults for a weekend, celebrating my dad's career.

To mark the occasion, Riki, Reider, and I took a trip to go to SeaWorld
for the day. It was like we were kids again!

I had no idea what to expect in Orlando. I knew the grandeur of
WrestleMania and the prestige of the Hall of Fame, but this time, my
dad was being inducted. The match he was in was "career threatening."
Out of all the times we were going to see one of his matches and all the
times we had been to Orlando, we'd never felt something like this. It was
like everyone was there for the Hall of Fame ceremony and Wrestle-
Mania. Whether you were at one of the theme parks, at a restaurant
downtown, or along International Drive, everyone was talking about my
dad. It was like this was the Nature Boy's weekend.

Being in the front row at the WWE Hall of Fame felt like being at
the Oscars. We were seated beside Shawn Michaels and his wife, Re-
becca. The feeling in the arena was amazing. To hear so many people say,
"WOOOOO!" at the same time always gave me goose bumps. This was
such a proud moment for my father and our family.

The time had come for him to take his place among wrestling's elite
in the WWE Hall of Fame. I felt like if anyone deserved to be the first
person who was going to be inducted while still being a WWE Superstar, it was my dad.

Seeing the video of his career, which included photos of his childhood,
was unbelievable. The moving piece captured the heart and soul of his life.
Triple H's induction speech was the perfect combination of humor and

sentiment. It showed how much he cared about my dad. Triple H has been such a close confidant to him and a great friend to our family.*

I could listen to my dad tell stories for hours, but on this special occasion, it was different. He could've talked about his endless list of accomplishments and greatest matches, and I'm sure everyone would've loved it, but instead, he talked about how much people meant to him and about the people who helped him throughout his career.

He showed everyone the person away from the glitz and glamour, away from the breathtaking robes and limelight, and away from the incredible performances. When I heard him speak at the podium, it was the voice of the man who's been my hero my whole life. That night, the Nature Boy had a rare night off, and the world was introduced to my father.

The way he spoke about Leslie, Megan and David's mom, and Reider's and my mom was important. I was sad that my mom wasn't there, but I knew why. My parents were married twenty-three years, and my mom was with him through the ups and downs of his career. It didn't seem fair that Tiffany got to be there now, because she didn't deal with the hardships along the way.

I thought about the last few years and what happened to our relationship when he left my mom to be with Tiffany. I thought I had always been number one to him. Having to follow the rules of a woman who wasn't my mom was not an easy adjustment. I went away to college and never dealt with it. The guests at their wedding saw how I dealt with that happening. It was difficult coping with my parents getting divorced and then trying to deal with my dad being with someone new right away. On top of that, I was dealing with growing up, finishing high school, going off to college, playing a Division I sport, and experiencing all these new things.

---

*Paul Levesque: "I just kept asking myself, *How do I induct the greatest professional wrestler of all time?* I was so honored that Ric asked me. And it's true, Ric deserved to be in the Hall of Fame and should have his own wing. He's one of the great pioneers in our industry."

That first Christmas during college break is something I barely remember. My dad and Tiffany got me a pair of Ugg boots. I zoned out. I gladly spent that summer at App for volleyball workouts and classes. I didn't want to go back home. I'm sure quitting volleyball and moving in with Riki, and the way I did that, didn't help our relationship either.

Tiffany and I didn't say one day, "Hey, let's start getting along." It came over time. It was hard seeing my dad create this new life and my mom trying to pick up the pieces of the one she had for twenty-three years, but we did get along. There were times when Tiffany, Brittany, and I trained together at the gym. We developed a relationship over time, and she became part of our family.

Being at the Hall of Fame put the focus on my dad and our relationship. I was so proud to be there as his career was celebrated. When he reached the point in his speech where he looked at us and spoke about his children, I just said, "I love you, Dad."

I know Reider was just as proud, and prouder in a different way, because this was the path he wanted to take with his life. It was Reider's dream to carry on the Flair legacy as a wrestler. He knew the path would be difficult and that he'd have more work to do because of his last name, but he wanted to be just like my dad: work hard, strive to be the best, and earn people's respect.

I knew that Reider was having a workout with WWE in Tampa soon. I was so excited for him. I think there was a part of him that wished my parents got back together. It was also difficult for him to see the media coverage of our parents' divorce. We spent our lives in Charlotte. Our parents were a part of the community. When things received media coverage and that coverage included things that were not true, it hurt.

There was an incredible energy going to the Citrus Bowl. I kept thinking what this week meant to my dad and the thousands of people who traveled from all over the world to be a part of this historic day. Being backstage with my siblings reminded me of all the years we attended our dad's shows together. From that moment where we were on camera in the locker room at Starrcade '93 to WrestleMania XXIV in 2008, we've all traveled our own paths.

One trip we took together that day was something I was nervous about. My mouth dropped when the four of us—Megan, David, Reider, and me—went onstage to greet the crowd during the Hall of Fame introductions during WrestleMania. Never in a million years did I ever consider we would do that.

When we were told it was time to go, my heart began to race. My legs trembled as we got closer to the entryway. I couldn't believe it. My lips quivered, and I couldn't get them to stop. I was about to go onstage and be in front of more than seventy-four thousand people. I thought I was there to see my dad get inducted into the WWE Hall of Fame and have his last match—how was I now part of WrestleMania?

How the heck did he do that for a living for thirty-five years? I was overwrought with anxiety. *What will the crowd be looking at? What will they be thinking about?* And all I did was stand there with my siblings and wave. I never thought I'd be on a stage looking at so many people. I couldn't tell where the crowd ended; it seemed like it just kept going.

When it was time to watch the match, we took our seats. As always, our family sat at ringside when my father performed. Being on the floor level at the Citrus Bowl and seeing the enormity of the open stadium from a different perspective was unreal.

I got chills when my dad's music played. When I heard the huge crowd "WOOOOO!!" in tribute to him, I became filled with the same sense of pride that I'd known all my life. The moment he stopped walking, lifted his arms, and did his trademark rotation as fireworks shone was majestic.

As I looked around, the people in the audience looked like they felt the same way; everyone was standing, crying, and holding their Flair-themed signs or the symbol for the Four Horsemen. I was overwhelmed by the adulation for him. People felt that they grew up with my dad, and he was part of their households because he was on TV for so many years.

How could one of the greatest villains end up revered to the point where all the seventy-four-thousand-plus in attendance wanted to see him win and his career go on—and against an icon like Shawn Michaels? Only my dad. It was at that moment I understood everything my father meant to the fans around the world and why he meant so much to his peers.

My siblings and I were so proud to stand there together as one and cheer him on. One of my favorite things was watching my dad skim the crowd from the ring to see where we were sitting. He always blew us a kiss before the match started.

Every second of the match felt like it went by in slow motion. The crowd intently watched and reacted to every move he and Shawn made. I couldn't believe he jumped off the top rope onto Shawn. When I saw him get backdropped over the top rope, I was worried. And Shawn Michaels's moonsaults were phenomenal. I loved hearing the crowd roar when my dad put Shawn in the figure-four leg lock. I couldn't wait for the finish. What was his final three count going to look like? After thirty-five years, everything came down to those final minutes. How hard was this for him?

I knew my brother was watching the match in a different way. Reider idolized our dad and wanted to be him. He was also a huge Shawn Michaels fan. I knew he was watching the match move for move, hold for hold, and trying to figure out why things were being done or not done at certain times and the meaning behind everything. If Reider had ever wanted to lace up a pair of boots and get in that ring, this was the night. It was my brother's dream and ultimate goal to carry on the Flair name.

When my dad got up from the mat and put his fists up, I waited for what was next. Shawn hit him with his signature kick, and the referee, Charles Robinson, counted . . . one . . . two . . . three. My siblings and I couldn't hold in our emotions anymore. Tears streamed down our faces. We were so proud of our father. We were so happy for him and moved at how his life and career were celebrated. We were happy that he had the opportunity to move on to the next chapter of his life while still being in involved in WWE. When he came out of the ring and hugged each of us, I know none of us wanted to let him go, but we had to. He needed to bid farewell to his legions of adoring fans.

We also cried because we were sad for him. Being identified as a wrestler and a champion and performing in the ring were everything to my father. It was the profession that kept him away from his family for days, weeks, and, when Megan and David were kids, months. To know that all of it just came to an end was an overpowering experience.

Our family had come together, something that we had not done in a long time, and celebrated my father's career. It was rare that the four of us were at one of his matches. It was a wonderful night.

When my dad called us the next morning about going to *Raw*, I knew it was going to be special for him. It was always a little intimidating being backstage. No matter how old we were, my dad introduced us to everyone we saw. He always wanted people to meet his kids. When we got to the building, we were told that WWE planned a closing segment to the show around a special tribute for him. What they didn't tell him was the magnitude of the segment and that we'd be coming out to the ring also.

In a matter of twenty-four hours, I was on WWE programming twice in front of a live audience: once onstage at WrestleMania in front of more than seventy-four thousand people and a worldwide pay-per-view audience, and second on *Monday Night Raw*, also in front of a live audience and broadcast on live television! I was petrified, and I thought, *I knew I should've brought a third dress!*

Watching his speech from the monitor backstage was a special moment. When I saw him hug Uncle Arn in the ring, it brought me right back to the days of hugging them on our deck, the backyard explorations during Easter egg hunts, and vacations with both our families.

When Batista came to the ring, I thought of how much fun we had with him at my dad and Tiffany's wedding. I'll always have a sentimental feeling about Ricky Steamboat and the time we spent with his family as children. I heard so many great stories about my dad and Harley Race and knew that Reider trained at his wrestling school. My dad was closely linked to Greg Valentine and his dad, Johnny, early in his career. Seeing Dean Malenko backstage before he went to the ring reminded me of all the great times Reider and I had with him when we were kids in WCW. And my dad became good friends with Chris Jericho and John Cena during this time in WWE. And yes, what my dad said at the Hall of Fame was true—Megan and I did think Chris looked like Jon Bon Jovi, but we never thought my dad would say that!

When it was our turn to walk through the curtain, once again, my legs trembled and I had goose bumps. To walk to the ring on *Raw* in some ways was more terrifying because the night before, we walked to a point on the stage and waved to the crowd. On *Raw*, we walked down the ramp and into the ring. I asked myself, *How is this happening two nights in a row?*

And then Shawn Michaels came out, followed by the entire WWE locker room. I felt like my dad was not just my hero, he was everyone else's too.

We knew to exit the ring once we heard the Undertaker's music. To be so close to the ring during that entrance was an indescribable experience. I know my brother David worked with Undertaker and could speak to that experience firsthand. For Reider, I considered this to be another moment that made his drive to become a wrestler and carry on the Flair name even stronger.

I couldn't believe that Mr. McMahon also came out to honor our father. I knew he was always very supportive of my dad and treated him extremely well. As the show came to an end, which I found out later, it ended for people on TV before the Undertaker came out. Seeing my dad smiling in the ring with his children was the perfect way to end the night.

As we prepared to return to our own lives on Tuesday morning, I felt such love from and for my dad. I believed that WrestleMania weekend reunited him with me and my siblings, and me with them. We were always so close. All my memories are of us doing things together and always being there for each other. For example, after my sister, Megan, graduated from college, she moved from Minnesota to Charlotte to be closer to Reider and me. She came to all our sports functions and special events. When I was in high school, if I wasn't home, you could find me at Megan's with her family.

Thanks to my dad and siblings, for that weekend in Orlando, I returned to who I was.

Over the past few years, I've said a lot of hurtful things to my dad. I was hurt, I was angry, and I was immature. I felt lost without my family and didn't know how to deal with the uncertainty of what life would be like without all of us being together.

My dad always forgave me after I said those things. That weekend, it was time that I forgave him. We had to rebuild our relationship. This trip was an incredible way to start us on our path. Seeing how happy he was with us from the moment we arrived in Orlando to the time we said goodbye in the hotel, that process began and I didn't even realize it. The hug we shared in the hotel lobby before we went our separate ways was one of the strongest we'd had in a long time. Wrestling kept him away from his family more than he wanted, but it was wrestling that brought us back together.

People commented to me during the weekend how much they enjoyed meeting and speaking with Riki. I couldn't understand why he couldn't be that way all the time and, even more so, why he could be that way with everyone except for me. Why was there this level of hostility toward me?

One of the things I looked forward to that fall was my dad visiting us in Chapel Hill. Riki's sister was also in town that weekend. I always tried to have a good relationship with her. For some reason, I wanted her approval. She did everything but give it. She kept in touch with his ex-girlfriends and always brought them up in conversation. She'd make a point to say how "perfect" a certain girl was and went to great lengths to make me feel like an outsider. I found her to be moody and manipulative.

When my dad came into town, I thought it would be nice for Riki's sister to join us at dinner. After we came back to our apartment, the fun mood from the restaurant suddenly changed.

Riki's substance abuse worsened in previous months, and it was to the point where it was beyond doing things at parties. After everyone went to bed, he wanted to call someone to get things that would "keep the night going."

We started arguing because he knew I did not want anything like that in the apartment. My dad had zero tolerance for drugs. The more I insisted, the more Riki persisted, and we were in the midst of another heated exchange.

My dad woke up and came into the room. He tried to calm things down. He and Riki had words, and I thought that was going to be it. All of a sudden, Riki threw punches at my dad. I became hysterical. The neighbors called the police. When the police arrived, I was in a frantic state of mind. I was not drunk. In the emotion of what had just occurred, I was not thinking clearly. I couldn't believe what I had just seen. I was also worried because I was afraid that if Riki had something illegal in the apartment and the police found it, we could be in serious trouble, on top of the fact that my dad would then know what went on. All this happening at once made me feel like the ceiling was slowly caving in on me.

When the officer asked me to put my hands behind my back, I was hysterical and did not do what I was asked. I told the officer to get his hands off me. I know I shouldn't have done that. I know how it looked. The reality was I wasn't purposely disobeying his request; I was showing that as a twenty-two-year-old, I couldn't handle what was going on and I made a mistake. I wanted to make sure that Riki and my dad did not get into trouble. I also was worried about how Riki would treat me the next day and what myriad of mysterious factors would play a part in that.[*]

The story was reported in the media, and it turned into something it wasn't. Since this was the only time I had gotten into any type of trouble, there was a fine and community service.

These scenarios grew worse and worse. Issues with members of my family became more prevalent because now, this showed there was "something" to what people may have feared. If there was an argument between

---

[*] Ric: "This was the first time I had any indication that something was seriously wrong with my daughter's relationship with her boyfriend. I never liked Riki. He had no drive, no initiative, and my daughter did everything. I learned to accept that this was who she wanted to be with. After that night, I was deeply troubled, but I believed her when she said that something like this had never happened before. I wish I hadn't."

Riki and one of my siblings or my parents, I took Riki's side or ignored the situation, and I avoided conversations with anyone after the occurrence.

By this point, the trend was that after something happened, things would calm down. And when things were going well, I loved Riki, and I thought it signified a turning point in our relationship, especially with what happened at Christmastime.

We were a few weeks removed from Reider's in-ring debut at an independent wrestling event in Charlotte. He and my brother David worked as a tag team. My dad was in their corner. It was a special night. We all sat in the front row, and my dad addressed the crowd. We were so proud of Reider and David. Riki was there too. After the incident at our apartment, he apologized to my dad, who focused on moving on.

My entire family was set to go to my dad's house for Christmas Eve dinner. Before Riki and I went there, we were at my Piper Glen house with my mom. Riki asked me to come talk to him in my bedroom.

I walked in and saw a huge wrapped gift box and a decorative present bag next to it. He told me to open the bag first. I pulled out a blue bathrobe with my favorite face mask. He said this was for relaxation. I put the robe on and enjoyed the moment with him. I opened the box to another box to another box to another box to the tiniest box and saw "Fink's." If you lived in Charlotte, especially if you were a member of the Fliehr family, you knew that Fink's was a jewelry store my dad had gone to for years for all the women in the family!

When I opened the box, Riki got down on one knee and proposed. The ring's diamond was from an old setting my mother had from a "Past, Present, Future" necklace my dad gave her. It gleamed with a timeless beauty. I thought this could be it. This could be things turning around, and the symbolism of asking for my hand in marriage with a rare piece of jewelry from my mother's collection was all I needed to say, "Yes."

I ran downstairs to my mom. She was smiling from ear to ear. She was so proud to see me wearing her diamond. I didn't sense she was proud that I accepted it from Riki, but she didn't know, like anyone else, for sure, about the darker side of our relationship. She was happy that I was happy.

We had Christmas Eve dinner at my dad's house. By this point, his relationship with Tiffany was over, and he was seeing a woman named Jackie. Jackie and my mom got along, so my mom being there for Christmas Eve dinner was a nice surprise, especially given the added reason to celebrate. We had the traditional Fliehr family Christmas Eve dinner: shrimp cocktail, salad, filet mignon, and baked potato.

My mom and dad made the occasion extra special with getting a cake and serving champagne.

Whether my dad liked the idea or not, he was happy for me. We all had a wonderful time together with two people who would become new members of the Fliehr family.

When Riki proposed, I had a feeling it was coming, but I wasn't exactly sure how he was going to do it. In looking back that day, I should've known something was up when my mom said out of the blue, "You should get your nails done today, honey. Why don't you get a French manicure?"

I thought the good times we had meant "good" and that I was in love. Riki and I had talked about getting married. I was a full-time student at the time. He was finishing his degree at UNC–Chapel Hill and worked part-time jobs. We were not in any stable situation, financial or otherwise, to get engaged. But we did.

I don't know how happy my family was that I said yes to marrying Riki, but they were happy that I was happy. As I looked ahead to planning a wedding, I thought that the bad times were behind us and it was time for my "happily ever after."

13

I THOUGHT IT WAS JUST DINNER

I had nothing to lose but my life.

June 2010

Riki graduated from college a semester before I did. During my senior year, we lived in an apartment in Raleigh. Riki worked six days a week at the animal hospital down the road from our place. Most of his time during the day consisted of cleaning the animal crates and taking care of the animals.

My remaining classes at NC State were split between taking them on campus and online. I wish that online had been possible when we lived in Chapel Hill so I could have saved that commute time. A part of me loved the flexibility of splitting up my classes. At the same time, taking classes online added to my isolation. I didn't leave the apartment unless it was for school or to go running, go grocery shopping, or take Riki somewhere. I never hung out with friends or did things just for fun. Over the last two years, running became an escape for me. Rain or shine, I ran every day to songs by Lady Gaga and Kings of Leon that shuffled on my iPod.

I didn't realize it at the time, but everything I did had a purpose. I cleaned the apartment, did the laundry, walked and fed the dogs. Riki's hospital scrubs were washed and folded on the seam every night. I woke up with him at 5:00 a.m. and made him breakfast even though I didn't have to be up for anything myself. We still had our dogs from when we met: Riki's bloodhound, Yonder, and my Cavalier King Charles, Louis. We got a third one together: a chocolate Labrador named Captain Junuh. They were like my children.

When I think about it now, Riki and I lived like we were fifty-year-olds who'd been married for thirty years. I acted like a 1950s TV housewife except that I was in my early twenties in the 2000s. I had my whole life ahead of me. I became a servant to my fiancé. There was never anything done with me in mind. My needs were never a concern. How did I end up in this environment filled with physical, emotional, and verbal abuse? Why did I think that was okay? I was in such need of help.

A highlight of my senior year was when my mom, Reider, Megan, and her daughter, Morgan, stayed with us for Thanksgiving. Reider's battle with addiction became more known the year before when he was pulled over and drugs were found in his car. My parents sent him to rehab. He wanted to get better. When my brother was doing well, he looked great, sounded great, and was completely focused on pursuing his dream of a wrestling career. Our family, like many with a loved one battling addiction, learned that the challenge escalated when attempted recovery turned to relapse. Often when an addict relapses, it raises the level of substance abuse to a more severe level than before.

I went to the grocery store to get everything for our holiday dinner. I passed a box of Keebler Club crackers in one of the aisles. When I saw the green box, it reminded me of when I was a kid and helped Grandmommy crumble up the crackers as part of her casserole recipe. I stumbled on things like that every now and then. It reminded me of how my life used to be so different.

At home, when I looked at myself in the mirror, I felt like I wasn't there. I was lost without my family, without my friends, without sports. Where was I? Who had I become? I couldn't wait to see everyone, especially my brother.

Things between Riki and me had been relatively calm in the couple of months that led up to our wedding. I was focused on graduating from NC State and looked ahead to our May 24 wedding day, but I was still sure that I was to blame for the violence that defined my life. During our relationship, I went through periods when I believed that my fiancé was seeing another woman. In the beginning of 2010, the thought that Riki was cheating on me triggered our most frightening confrontation.

It was Sunday night. I was watching the Grammy Awards in the living room. Riki was nodding off in bed watching TV. I took his phone from the charger and brought it into the living room to go through his text messages and emails—searching for evidence—to prove that my suspicions of his infidelity were true. That night, I was determined to find out. One would think I already had every reason to leave. I was always looking for something. Maybe I wanted to uncover some kind of proof and it could be my way out. Then I couldn't be blamed for anything. If I did discover something, though, what would I do?

I sat on the couch and scrolled through the text messages on his phone. I tapped Inbox on his email. I scrolled. I tapped Sent and scrolled. Then I went to his deleted messages—then I went through that folder again—there it was. It was a message thread with an ex-girlfriend. I looked at the date of the message and put the pieces together. My heart raced as I connected the dots and realized that these messages were sent on his birthday—after we went out. When we got home that night, I went to sleep. Riki stayed up. I wondered, *Did this girl come to the apartment? Did he go out and meet her somewhere while I was asleep? What happened that night?* No matter how much Riki insisted that I was delusional for thinking like that, I always believed there was someone else. I just didn't know how steady it was and if there was more than one girl.

I walked into the bedroom and shook his shoulder. When he woke up, I showed him the phone and asked, "What is this?" Right away, he started shouting at me. He launched himself out of bed and then did something I never imagined, even during my most disturbing thoughts of what was going to happen during our next fight. He pulled out the gun he kept in our bedroom that had been given to him by a childhood friend.

I ran as fast as I could. I made it out the front door and into my truck.

Thankfully, I had my car keys with me. I locked the doors and started the engine. The radio came on, and I turned it off right away. My eyes were filled with tears. I couldn't see past the steering wheel. It was difficult to breathe. Was Riki going to come after me? Was he going to shoot me in my vehicle? Was this how my life was going to end? I didn't know what to do. Where could I go? My first instinct was to call Brittany. But that night, North Carolina was hit with one of those severe ice storms that tore its way through the area about every five years. That wasn't an option.

Hours later, I went back into the apartment. I felt a chill in my body as I walked through the door. I curled up on the couch and lay there in the dark, trying to make sense of it all. The fear of what would happen once the sun rose kept me awake. I couldn't wonder anymore. I eventually fell asleep.

The next morning, Riki told me that our relationship was over. He continued to insist that my actions set him off and made him do something this terrible. According to Riki, all this was my fault. My heart sank. I felt like the ground underneath me had crumbled and my world had ended. By searching through his phone, I had found concrete evidence of his infidelity. Of that I was certain. Now I was listening to him rant and rave, saying that I had driven him to this kind of vicious behavior.

That morning, the violence continued. I remember being pushed and feeling my arms above my elbows being squeezed. The episode ended when I apologized and begged him not to end our relationship. During this period, everyone in my family knew that Reider battled addiction. At one point, we had a family intervention. He was determined to get better. What no one knew, with the exception one or two people, was that I was just as sick. In a different way, I was surrounded by darkness with no light in sight.

Brittany called Riki that evening and asked him if she needed to pick me up. He said, "No, everything is okay." Later that week, we left for Hilton Head to celebrate my sister's wedding and to visit Riki's mother, who lived there. I felt sick from everything that had happened, and faced with so much day-to-day uncertainty, I didn't eat for that entire week. That trip was just another example of how people were fooled into thinking everything was fine. Outside appearances seemed normal. No one knew that I continued to sink deeper into my own hell with no way out.

After Megan's wedding, the gun incident was forgotten. That spring was dedicated to my graduating from NC State, finalizing wedding plans, and moving back to Charlotte. I was driven to forge ahead and put the pieces of this twisted puzzle together at any cost.

I spent my days on the computer, picking out every detail for our wedding. For some reason, I was determined to continue this charade— that I was leading the life I always wanted, that everything was wonderful, and that, above all else, I knew what was right for me. I wasn't going to fail. I failed at volleyball, and maybe I was trying to tell the world that I was going to change Riki and that he was going to be committed to me. I was going to pin down the charismatic playboy. I was going to be his everything. He was going to settle down with me. Why was this so important? Why did I feel that there was some prize for accomplishing this? I'm also not sure why I thought things were going to improve with Riki, especially given our history. The more time went on, the worse the abuse became. I chose to ignore that fact.

Graduating from college nine days before my wedding was sheer hysteria. I remember graduation at NC State like I just returned my cap and gown. It was another rare occasion when my family was together: my parents, Reider, Megan, her husband, and their daughter, Morgan. The night before, we went down the road from my apartment to my favorite Chinese restaurant. My sister and I both wore yellow dresses, and Morgan was attached to Reider the entire night.

The dress I wore to graduation was in NC State Wolfpack red. My family was proud of me. The person who was the proudest was my brother. The whole weekend, Reider told me how happy he was for me and how much he loved me. While we didn't talk about it, I felt that Reider secretly wanted the same thing for himself. Or maybe I wanted that for him? My brother was so intelligent and personable. I always envisioned him shining in a college setting. I wish he could've enjoyed the full college experience. It was difficult for him, because sometimes people who were supposed to be his friends criticized him for not taking that road. But Reider chose a career path that he felt required a different type of education. He wanted to dedicate himself to learning the sport and art of professional wrestling. Despite his battle with addiction, my brother was steadfast in getting better and achieving his dream: to be a WWE Superstar.

Once the music played and the class of 2010 filled the auditorium, I was overcome with a sense of pride. It was a feeling I hadn't experienced in a long while. And this time, unlike my high school graduation, my family's presence made it truly special. I remember my name being called and walking to the stage. Earning that diploma was an important accomplishment. I took pictures in my cap and gown with everyone outside the auditorium. I can still feel Reider's arm around me as we looked at each other and smiled before my mom took pictures of us.

As graduation came to an end, I had my to-do list for the wedding running in the back of my mind. It was like a ticker with sports scores going in a continuous loop on the bottom of a TV screen. After a year-and-a-half engagement, my wedding was just days away.

I came home to Charlotte the week after graduation for the big day. Riki and I stayed with the three dogs at his mom's house. I went back and forth between her house and my mom's. It seemed like just as I was about to sit down for the first time, there was something else to pull together or drop off. I also went to see friends and family who were in town for the big day.

When it came to picking things out for the wedding, I wasn't worried about cost. I guess that's what happens when you're not paying for it. My mom and I went to try on my wedding dress for the final time at Nitsa's at Phillips Place. Once I saw the dress from the designer Amsale, I had to have it. It was the most beautiful dress I've ever worn. It was sweetheart cut, all lace. No matter what it cost or what it was going to take, my mom was going to get me that dress. I can remember her helping the lady pick out the most beautiful brooch for the center of the dress. The veil looked like something made for a princess. The earrings we chose were just as elegant. My mom said I looked absolutely stunning. I was overwhelmed with the dress and how much I loved it. My mom had a lot of fun helping me with everything.

The flowers I picked out were also important to me. I wanted exquisite pastel flowers with a Southern elegance. They had to be regal and majestic too, and that's what I got. When I think back to my wedding day, regardless of how things turned out, I'll always be proud of those flowers. My mom and I also enjoyed selecting the wedding cake. I wanted a classic, off-white, three-tier cake.

The night before the rehearsal dinner, we all went to McCormick & Schmick's for dinner. I didn't eat much, because I was worried about how I was going to look in my dress. I got fitted for it in the fall of 2009. The next night, my parents hosted the rehearsal dinner at Brio. The entire dinner was a collection of all my favorite Italian dishes. There were centerpieces made of peacock feathers on every table.

I went from table to table seeing my relatives and Riki's side of the family. At no point did I take a moment for myself, and at no point did Riki say, "Can I get you something? Would you like something to eat or drink?" As I write this, I should've realized that I didn't have a handle on what was important, nor did I fully grasp everything my parents had done for me. I was basically putting on a show.

Was it selfish of me to ask my parents to pay for all this? My stomach turned when I stopped to think about the meaning of everything. I should never have been in a relationship with this person. I felt that this was the expected next step because Riki and I had been together so long. Then there was the external perception, based on appearance, that we were the perfect couple. It was all smoke, mirrors, and illusions, enhanced by designer clothes.

Even if I were in a healthy relationship, this was not the time to get married: neither of us had jobs lined up; we did not have a place to live; and without the money my father gave us as a wedding gift, the only thing we hung our hat on was that we were moving back to Charlotte. It didn't matter. I was getting married. That was it.

Why was I so consumed with pleasing Riki and everyone else around me? Why was it always about other people's perceptions and expectations? Why didn't I listen to Zahn? Why was I hell-bent on pretending to be something I wasn't? And the question I couldn't stop asking myself:

What was I going to do with my life now that I'd graduated from college?

I graduated from NC State with a degree in interpersonal and public communications. What was I going to do with that? My dad sent me to a contact at ESPN to see if they had any opportunities. Any internship or entry-level, full-time position required moving to Bristol, Connecticut. I appreciated the thought, but that didn't interest me. Even in the achievement of graduating from a school with the reputation of NC State, I didn't see myself as anything more than Riki's fiancé. How could that be, given all I did to get to NC State and everything it took to see it through and graduate with a degree?

Riki was unsure about what he was going to do. He graduated from UNC–Chapel Hill, which looked amazing on paper and sounded even more impressive in conversation, but what was he going to do with that? All that took a backseat. The big day had arrived.

On the day of the wedding, I stopped in my tracks when I saw the wreaths hanging outside Myers Park United Methodist Church. They were absolutely stunning. I handpicked every detail from the church to the reception venue, the invitations, the bouquets, down to the gardenias the men wore on the lapels on their tuxedos.

I remember kissing my mom, dad, and grandmommy in the back room of the church before they walked me to the entrance.

I can still see all the bridesmaids, groomsmen, and my parents at the front of the church. One of my favorite memories is high-fiving my two nieces and my little cousin Katie.

I became the most headstrong I ever was in painting this false portrait of true love and the most creative in convincing myself of why this wedding should happen. I lived a lie but felt I had gone too far to turn back.

My dad was ready to walk me down the aisle. The music began, and I heard everyone get up from their seats at the same time. Deep down, I knew my father was not supposed to walk me down this aisle and give me away to someone like Riki. I felt beautiful but not real. It was like I was playing a role. It didn't feel like my wedding day. How could it? At that point, I thought about my terrifying relationship, but I wanted to have a fancy wedding. I wanted the appearance of glamour and perfection. On the inside, I was torn and broken. What people didn't realize was on that day they saw a girl who was lost.

A clear moment from the reception was the first dance with my dad. The song "Butterfly Kisses" was my dad's favorite song as long as I could remember.*

That night, my parents had something special planned for Riki and me. A limo took us from the Morehead Inn, where the reception had been, to another hotel where a lot of our friends were staying. My mom had these big white robes made for Riki and me with "Mr. and Mrs. Johnson" sewn on them in red cursive. I wore mine over to my mom's the next morning as I said goodbye and thank you to my relatives before they left.

And just like that, it was over. College graduation, my wedding, and honeymoon were now referred to in the past tense. One thing we did get arranged was where we were going to live, at least temporarily.

As I set up bowls for the dogs in the kitchen, reality set in. We had a few more boxes to unpack. Riki's mom bought a house in Charlotte with inheritance money from Riki's father. She was moving and said we could live in her old house, which was fully furnished. We didn't have all the details figured out, but the plan was to start working and pay his mom rent every month to cover the living expenses. Being back in Charlotte was going to be the best thing for me.

While the idea of living in his mother's vacant house sounded good in theory, moving into the house and getting situated wasn't as easy as it sounded. Riki's siblings were both in college. They came and went through the house as they pleased. I understood that; it belonged to their mother. She was very gracious, supportive, and helpful during our relationship,

---

*Ric: "This was a difficult time for me as a parent. I took one day at a time with Reid. With Ashley, I didn't want her dating Riki, let alone marrying him. A part of me hoped she would've ended things while they were engaged. She didn't need to be with someone, but I thought maybe she'd meet someone at school. But from what I saw, whether I liked it or not, my daughter was happy. I wasn't going to disown her or not be involved in her wedding."

but still, I felt like I was in a home that wasn't mine. My name wasn't on the deed. I didn't like this setup, but at the time, I had no choice.

I missed the feeling of being in my own place, picking colors I liked and decorating, creating a home that I could say was my own. I wanted that with the man I was going to start building my life with. But there were three women that I knew of in his life: his mom, his sister, and me. His mother depended on him a great deal. I know that Riki continued to feel an increasing pressure to be the parental figure for his brother and sister.

When I put our dishes away in the kitchen cabinet, I asked myself again, *Why did I do this?* Not that this should matter, but it's not like everyone I knew was getting married and having kids, and I was thirty and single. The more I thought about it, the more this marriage didn't make sense.

Those last two months were another example of when things were good, they were good enough for me to wonder, *Maybe this is the turning point?* In my damaged mind, I thought getting married was going to make our relationship better. I would soon learn that, like our living arrangement, this was temporary and that things were going to escalate and become more terrifying than I could have ever imagined.

When I thought about finding a job, I thought about doing something I did practically my whole life: physical fitness. I thought that with all my years of working with a personal trainer and my athletic background, becoming a trainer could be the way to go. Before I graduated from NC State, I ordered all the required material to become certified as an ACE personal trainer.

Once I passed the exam, I contacted a trainer who had worked at my dad's gym years earlier. He now owned two private studios in perfect locations: the South Park and Ballantyne sections of Charlotte. I told him that I had graduated from NC State and had my ACE. I interviewed with him, and a few days later, I started work.

The first two weeks, I took the term *shadowing* to new heights. I was at my boss's side learning the ins and outs of what I needed to do as an employee and what I needed to do to develop a clientele. This was an exciting career opportunity. It was great to be in a gym again every day. Right away, I fell in love with my job. I poured every hour of the day into my work. I started to build a clientele. Personal training packages were expensive. Most of my clients consisted of established professionals who ranged in age from their late thirties to their sixties. They considered fitness an investment. They wanted to be held accountable when it came to going to the gym and taking care of themselves. Soon those clients recommended me to their friends and work colleagues. My calendar filled up fast—it was fantastic!

I found this work rewarding because I could see the positive results my clients achieved from our work together. I loved motivating people and having a positive impact on their lives. I made good money too.

Over the next two years, I developed close friendships with many of them, and I opened up to some of them about my personal life and my relationship with Riki. I began to emerge from my isolation. I started to see myself as a real person again. I could feel myself growing as an individual. I started to contact my family more often.

I was happy that my clients learned so much from me. They'll never know how much I learned from them. I continued to build my personal training business out of this studio. Not one minute of it felt like work. Plus, my job at Ciarla Fitness was going to set Riki and me up financially.

Between the friends Riki made at Providence Day and UNC, he had a lot of connections. He reached out to a friend we knew from high school about a possible job in sales.

Soon after we moved into his mom's house, the "good times" we enjoyed the previous few months were gone.

Riki and I had been fighting through text messages, and he said he wanted a divorce. He took his manipulative theatrics to a new high and emailed me divorce information. When he got home, I tried to sort out what was going on. I don't know what the argument stemmed from. I remember it was in the afternoon because of the way the sun shone through the front windows.

We were in the kitchen arguing, and he threw a plate at me. My heart pounded. I ran behind the kitchen counter. I put the table between us hoping that would give me time to get out of the room and let things calm down. Riki picked up a chair at the other end and launched it at me with both hands. He missed. He picked up another and threw it the same way. I bolted out of the way. That chair broke when it hit the wall. I ran for the staircase. He caught up to me. I was on my back and felt him over me. That's when I knew it wasn't over.

On instinct, I put my forearms over my face. Riki started swinging at me like we were in a street fight. Over his screams, I could hear his fists hit my arms. I managed to block most of the punches, but one shot got me in the ribs. I began to gasp for air, but he didn't stop. I finally bucked him off and made it to the upstairs bathroom. I locked the door and tried to regulate my breathing. I can't recall the moments that followed. The next thing I remember is running to the car and leaving. I tried to focus on driving. I tried to fend off a full-blown panic attack. I should've gone to the emergency room. At that moment, I was stripped of all my emotions. I was empty.

Later that night, I returned to the house. My side hurt so badly that I could barely sit up. It was excruciating. I had to lean on my other side to move from a seated or reclining position. I felt like everything inside me was torn. I went to the doctor and got an X-ray. The doctor told me that I had torn cartilage between my ribs and that my ribs were bruised. He prescribed anti-inflammatories. I could barely move for two weeks.

I hid this episode from everyone in my life. I just let my ribs heal and made it through the rest of the summer.

Around that time, I spoke with Reider about living with us. I thought I could set him on a career path so he could earn money and pursue wrestling on the independent circuit. Like me, my brother had worked with physical trainers most of his life. With Reider's athletic background, his knowledge of nutrition and fitness, and his personality, I thought he would be a fantastic personal trainer. I spoke to the owner of Ciarla Fitness about hiring him to work at the SouthPark studio. My boss was all for it.

From my brother's first day of work, he was off to a great start. He quickly built a clientele because of his outgoing, friendly personality and his love of helping people. Reider was a great motivator. His knowledge of training naturally came through every time he spoke about fitness. He excelled when it came to working with people. After a few weeks, my boss told me how many compliments he had received about Reider from the staff and the clients.

At this point, Reider had been in a couple of rehab facilities. One of the other reasons I wanted him to live with me was that I thought if he felt good about the work he was doing and had the ability to continue wrestling, he'd keep moving in a positive direction. As his work at Ciarla continued to be well received, I thought he was on his path to beating addiction and that he'd never look back. Until Riki said something to me during one of our arguments.

Riki told me that my brother was not clean. "Things" were going on in the house. At first I didn't believe him because, one, my brother was doing so well and looked like he was in a strong place mentally and physically, and two, I thought that Riki wanted to spite me and find another way to hurt me. After some time went by, I realized that Riki had told the truth. Then I made another discovery. While I was at work, Riki and my brother were using together behind my back. Reider didn't like Riki. While he wasn't aware of all the details, he knew that Riki had been abusive toward me in the past. For them to be using drugs together meant that Reider was still battling his illness and needed the kind of help I couldn't provide.*

I never felt sicker and more conflicted in my life. I was torn. Should I get mad at my brother? Should I end my marriage? Who was at fault? Who should I be upset with?

I knew that my husband still used, but he made it seem like it was under this guise of "recreation" and "every once in a while." Since Reider didn't like Riki, I didn't think my brother would spend a lot of time with him. I wished I were strong enough to kick Riki to the curb and to do what

---

*Ric: "Our family became educated on addiction. This was a culture I still didn't fully understand. When Reid was in rehab, he would do very well. When he'd relapse, it would be worse than before. He was determined to get better, and you could see the progress he made when he'd get himself back on track. We were all behind him. Ashley wanted to help her brother any way she could. I didn't know about the range of problems in her marriage. I just knew that Reid relapsed and he needed to return to treatment."

was right for my little brother. I learned later that I was an enabler who suffered from crippling codependency. It was a never-ending, sick cycle that I couldn't make complete sense of or escape from. All I could do was get angry at them. My brother moved out.

I prayed for Reider. I prayed that he'd find the courage and control that I knew he had to get better again. I prayed that he would strengthen his resolve and return to the path I knew he—along with our family—wanted him to remain on.

At that moment, I immersed myself deeper in my work. I spent more time at the studio helping my clients. They became an outlet for me. I asked them things like, "What should I do? How do I handle this? What's best?" They probably saw a young woman who was lost, in a toxic relationship, too young to be dealing with that kind of trauma and adversity. They were right.

The situation with my brother continued to weigh on me. Every day, another piece of my heart broke over what had happened. What had I done? Where would he go? What was going to happen? I knew Riki wasn't good for me. Why did I keep this going? I should've known better than to have Reider live with us. I really thought that if my brother was on this path, it would put him on the road he dreamed of. And because he wanted his own place, it was better than his living with either of my parents. My sense of sorrow and conflict consumed me. I felt like I couldn't escape the adage "Damned if you do, and damned if you don't." I think about that girl now. I didn't know if I was going to make it. I didn't know how much more I could endure.

While my life behind closed doors kept deteriorating further, my professional life at Ciarla was thriving. Heading into the holidays, I told Riki I wanted us to move out of his mother's home and get our own place. Through Ciarla, I met the owner of a large security company in Charlotte, and told him that my husband graduated from UNC–Chapel Hill and was looking for work.

By the beginning of 2011, Riki was a full-time employee of my client's security company, and a top salesperson selling alarm systems. We both had steady incomes and rented a house in Charlotte. I was proud that I was supporting myself, that Riki was doing well at work, and that we did this all on our own. The more successful I became at Ciarla, the more clients I wanted to take on. I worked fifty to sixty hours a week, seven days a week. My calendar was happily covered in ink. My first appointment was at 5:00 a.m. I would take my last session as late as the studio stayed open, usually around 10:00 p.m. To the outsider, I was ambitious, driven, and passionate about empowering my clients through physical fitness—and I was. But there was another reason.

I was running every day. I was running from what happened with my brother. I was running from the reality of a marriage I shouldn't have been in. My work was so rewarding that it helped me disconnect from my personal life. I saw smiles on people's faces. I felt I made a difference in their lives, but there was something going on with my husband that could no longer be ignored.

Riki was fired from his job. At that moment, it was clear that his use of substances was beyond recreational and that it was consuming him. That should have served as another wake-up call.

I remember sitting in the office at Ciarla Fitness. My fingers frantically typed on the keyboard as I searched for rehab centers. I found one in Jacksonville, Florida. I called my dad and asked him to help me financially. Despite his personal feelings about Riki, my dad didn't hesitate to help. I assured Riki that I was going to wait for him and be there every step of the way.

While Riki was in treatment, I developed anxiety. No matter how much I worked, the days dragged. I couldn't sleep at night. A woman at the studio checked on me every day, because she said I lost all the color in my skin. I drove to work every morning for my 5:00 a.m. appointment. I felt I had nothing left. I was hopeless and confused. A part of me was relieved that Riki was gone. The other part of me wanted to believe he was going to change and that this would be the turning point I desperately needed. I was grateful for my dad's help, but that also meant the issue was now out in the open and that he'd check on things, like any parent would. At one point, he was helping my brother and my husband while trying to take care of himself during his marriage to Jackie. We all believed it was a mistake for him to be with her.

My other concern about Riki was financial. Would he be able to find another job when he got home? Would I have to continue to support us both? What would life be like when he came home? We would have to make changes: our social circle, attending family functions and events, going out to dinner—everything would need to be adjusted. I took off from work to go to family week at the rehab facility in Jacksonville. This wasn't my first time going to see someone in rehab.

I pulled into the facility, and even though it was against the rules, Riki ran to the car. I smiled through the window and saw him later in the day. That afternoon, we had the "family recall session." This gave me the opportunity to express how so many things in our relationship had hurt me. Even though I verbalized my pain, I think because so much had happened, at this point, I was just numb.

I went home and waited for Riki to successfully complete treatment. This was the midpoint to his supposed road to recovery. He spent the following months in weekly Alcoholics Anonymous meetings. This was also an anxiety-filled process for me. I learned that part of the AA treatment is to reach out to people you've wronged and attempt to make amends with them. I was skeptical about his ability to accomplish this and whether or not he was making a genuine effort to get better.

What I should've anticipated during Riki's path to clean and sober living was that there would be one person he never attempted to make amends with: me. Throughout this whole ordeal and to intensify the situation, no one in his family took any interest in what was going on or offered any assistance. None of them visited him in rehab. I was on my own. His mother was good to me. I know she loved me, but in the end, I was not her child. After the wedding, I tried telling her about Riki's substance abuse and anger problems. I was ignored. Even at this point, when he left Charlotte to go to a rehab facility in Florida, she was still in denial. Nothing was going to get in the way of her children's happiness. Even if Riki succumbed to substance abuse and everyone knew that he became violent when he got angry, she blatantly ignored whatever she didn't want to see. I became Riki's mother and caretaker. Everything fell on my shoulders.

Another client of mine at Ciarla had an executive position with a big inventory supply company in Charlotte. Once again, Riki's degree from UNC and his ability to present himself well during the interview process helped him secure a job. The potential for growth in this job was limitless.

I was so troubled at this point that we even spoke about starting a family. I thought the joy of having a baby would make things better between us. Riki wanted to have a child. After being unsuccessful at conceiving for a few months, Riki became hostile. He blamed me for being "too skinny" and "overexercising." What I should've said was that I didn't know that working in a veterinary clinic for six months cleaning animal waste gave him a medical background in fertility and the human reproductive system. At his insistence, I went to the doctor. My doctors found that everything with me was normal.

While Riki ignored my countless suggestions that he see a doctor, once my physician suggested he make an appointment, he agreed. After all Riki's insults and baseless claims, it turned out that he had a blockage that prevented him from reproducing. Surgery was the only remedy.

Given Riki's past difficulty with substances, I was concerned about the postsurgery medication. I insisted on non-narcotic prescriptions. This sparked a major argument, and before I knew it, we were back at square one. My husband, who recently completed rehab and was doing well at the second job I got for him, told me I was crazy and controlling, all because I was concerned about prescription pain medication. The days were unbearable.

Every night after work, I'd fall asleep watching TV. Like clockwork, the minute I sat down, I passed out. Riki became annoyed at that and said he didn't understand why I was always tired. One particular night, Riki shared the news with me that he was getting a new tattoo. I was shocked that he felt this was a priority. I didn't spend any money beyond what was needed, and he had just started to earn an income. He already had a sketch of the tattoo. I had no idea where the design came from. Riki argued that we had nothing in common and that he was unhappy. This was a recurring theme in our narrative.

I paid closer attention to his behavior. It was odd. Riki started listening to different music and watching different TV shows, and he even started using different language when he spoke. He also made it a point to bring home a dessert made for him from a random coworker. Nothing added up, except that I had seen this movie before.

Finally, I found a picture in his phone of a girl he worked with that dated back to New Year's. She sent him a selfie. I didn't know how much more I could handle.

I showed him the picture. We got into an argument in the living room, and I saw a level of rage I hadn't seen in Riki's eyes in a long time. It was like a monster had been dormant, and that night it reemerged from a cold, dark place somewhere inside him. It escalated. Riki charged at me. I was on the hardwood floor, on my back beside the fireplace. Riki started swinging at me. I kept blocking the punches. He kept swinging. One got past me. Riki punched me right in the head. Everything stopped. I had never been hit like that before. The pain was excruciating. I stayed on the floor. When I got up, Riki was gone. I didn't know where he went. I called one of my childhood friends' moms and told her I needed her right away. I panicked. I was hyperventilating, and I threw up. At that moment, I was completely overwhelmed.

I drove to her house. I couldn't wipe the tears away from my eyes fast enough. I felt the pain on top of my head getting worse. When I got there, she tried to calm me down and begged me to go to the hospital. After an hour, she convinced me and drove me to the emergency room. My head became lopsided. She insisted on staying with me. The ER staff immediately took me for tests. I can't remember which ones. I remember the tech helped me lie on the bed. I almost went deaf to voices around me.

The results came back negative, meaning everything was fine. I remember the doctor questioning me. I didn't tell the truth. I said I hit my head on the fireplace. I was scared about what would happen if anyone found out what really occurred. My friend's mom told me I was in a safe place. I told the nurse what happened. I didn't press charges. For some reason,

I was concerned about Riki's well-being. My illness had reached its most damaging point. It was like I was an ice sculpture and this relationship continued to chip away at who I was. I began to lose the will to live.

My friend's mom repeatedly begged me to call the police. I could tell by the look in her eyes and the tone of her voice that she was frightened for me. I didn't call them. I stayed up all night in her guest room. What would happen if my parents found out about this? Was this rock bottom? Somehow, it wasn't.

I did the best thing I have ever done. I went to the church I had been going to and saw a woman who offered free counseling. I opened up to her, and she explained the kind of situation I had been experiencing for so many years. She educated me about my emotions and explained that Riki was my drug. I was codependent. I lived through his behavior and emotions. I'll never be able to describe how she helped me over the course of those few, one-hour sessions. I wish I could let her know how much of an impact she had on my life.

I continued to focus on building my business as a personal trainer. I reached a point where my projected income could have reached close to six figures. Riki also did well at work. It seemed like a good time to look into buying a house of our own. Or so I thought.

Riki got fired from his job. From what I was told, he allegedly used the company car for personal trips during paid business hours. His mileage and gas, based on work-related appointments, did not add up correctly. I didn't know all the facts.

I wasn't sure about what to do financially, and I didn't know how much more of this marriage I could take. Just as we were in the process of buying a home, dealing with calls from so many different people, and trying to keep things together . . . well, it wasn't easy. I knew that once again the pressure to keep everything afloat at home would fall on me. When the phone rang for what seemed to be the hundredth time, and it was my dad, I was really happy to hear his voice. When he told me the reason for his call, I was overjoyed. This interruption in the nightmarish life I was leading was like a gift from heaven.

For the last two years, my dad was under contract to a wrestling company called TNA. My brother David worked there in 2003 and did a story line on TV with Dusty Rhodes. I knew my dad still kept in touch with his friends from WWE, but he did not work with them, so when he told me he was being inducted into the WWE Hall of Fame again I was suprised. One, because he was under contract to another company, and two, he was being inducted for his work in a group that revolutionized wrestling but did so during his time in the NWA and WCW: the Four Horsemen.

He said that WrestleMania was going to be in Miami, Florida. He also told me that Reider and I were going with him. I was so proud of my dad. To be the first Superstar inducted while he was still active on the WWE roster in 2008 was such an honor for him and our family. This time, to be the only two-time WWE Hall of Fame inductee seemed fitting for someone who had dedicated his life to this profession. It was four years since his first induction and three years since I was at a WWE Hall of Fame ceremony. This trip represented so many things for our family. It also represented the first time in several years that I'd be going on a trip without Riki. It would just be Reider and my dad, like the old days. I couldn't wait to get there.

The atmosphere at the American Airlines Arena served as a reminder of the excitement of WrestleMania weekend and the prestige of the WWE Hall of Fame.

When Reider and I saw Dusty take the stage, we knew the Horsemen's induction speech was going to be one to remember. My brother watched intently. When Dusty proclaimed that "the Four Horsemen rode that lightning bolt in the business called professional wrestling," my brother smiled ear to ear. When the Dream mentioned that my dad's induction marked the first time a legend had been inducted twice into the WWE Hall of Fame, and that "Ric Flair is a national treasure," my eyes began to tear. I thought back to being a little girl and walking around WCW's offices in Atlanta with my dad and seeing Dusty in the hallway.

Reider and I beamed with pride when our dad took the Hall of Fame stage. That feeling only intensified, because Dad shared that stage with Uncle Arn. They received a standing ovation.

Even though I was a little embarrassed when my dad asked Reider and me to stand up twice during his induction speech, I knew it was because he loved us very much and was so proud of us. By the end of the ceremony, I felt more like myself than I had in a long time.

My dad and brother were going to dinner with a WWE talent executive named John Laurinaitis. I was joining them, and it couldn't have come at a better time—I was starving! John had known my dad and our family for more than twenty-five years. The purpose of the dinner was to talk about how my brother could earn a WWE tryout.

At the restaurant, Reider told John about his training, and he talked about wanting to work on more independent shows outside of the Carolinas. I was at the table but not part of the conversation. I could tell that my brother was listening intently to what was being said. John told Reider that he needed to gain more experience so that WWE could see more of his work. After that, they'd take a look at everything and talk about returning for a tryout.

Then John looked at me and said, "So why aren't you doing this?"

At first, I thought he was talking to someone else. When I realized that was directed at me, I didn't know what to say. I thought he was joking or that he just wanted to be polite and bring me into the conversation. As he continued to talk, I thought, *Me?*

John knew my background in athletics and that I'd played volleyball during college, but I didn't expect him to extend an offer for me to go to WWE's FCW training facility in Tampa, Florida. I felt it took a vivid imagination to see me as a WWE Diva. I remember walking past Michelle McCool in the makeup chair backstage at WrestleMania XXIV. She was also an NCAA athlete. But when I saw Michelle getting ready for the show, it was like I saw a movie star preparing to walk the red carpet.

John continued to describe the training program, while Reider said, "C'mon, we could do this together."

My dad looked at me and said, "I know you can do this, but you can't half ass it."*

I didn't know what to do. I never thought of wrestling as a career. Move to Tampa? I was in the process of buying a home in Charlotte. What about my clients? I'd built this personal training business and was making great money. Then I thought—in a different way—about what this could mean.

I knew that if I didn't do something with my life—and soon—I'd lose the little I had left. I knew I couldn't keep this marriage with Riki going much longer. I just wouldn't make it. I didn't know what I would do once I got to Tampa. Would I try to become a member of the ring crew, a ring announcer, a backstage interviewer, a commentator?

This was another moment where appearances were deceiving. As the daughter of Ric Flair, most people thought I knew about the sports-entertainment industry. No. I knew about my dad's career. I knew that I loved watching him perform, and I knew certain people from the business on a personal level. Reider was different. This was what he wanted to do from day one. He could recite specific interviews from our dad's career. He could describe matches with dates, the venues, and outcomes. What could I do in WWE?

All I knew was that this could be my chance. In the back of my mind and in my most private thoughts, it was the chance I had been waiting for. The opportunity that in my most heartfelt prayers I had asked God for. The chance that could save my life.

I thought that if I did this, it would ensure that Reider could pursue his dream. The one thing he always wanted to do with his life could now be the thing that saved it, and I could be part of it. I could be with him every step of the way, like what his living with me in Charlotte was sup-

---

*Ric: "I never doubted that Ashley could do this from an athletic point of view. Are you kidding? I wanted to make sure she understood the unrelenting commitment, singular focus, and sacrifice this business requires in order to be a success. And that it would be even harder because of her last name, which I knew she was aware of, but as her father, I wanted to reiterate that."

posed to be. He looked so excited at the possibility that this could happen. I did the only thing there was left to do. I said, "Yes."

About a week later, I called Triple H. I always knew Hunter as someone my dad trusted, someone he confided in a great deal. Triple H has been close to our family since I was in high school. I was not nervous about speaking with him; I was nervous about the subject of our conversation.

I told Hunter about my dinner with John Laurinaitis in Miami. He was supportive, but he asked me questions and wanted to make sure I knew what to expect.* One of the things he said was that a door was opening for me, but that didn't mean that it was going to open for my brother at the same time. I understood that. He explained that he was in the midst of a complete overhaul of WWE's talent development program. He said I'd relocate to Tampa to begin training but that soon after, everything would move to Orlando and something called the WWE Performance Center.

He said I'd receive a call from someone on his team named Canyon, and he'd go over the details with me. As we finished our conversation, I let Hunter know that I realized the importance of this opportunity, how much it meant to me, and that I'd show him how hard I was going to work. There was no turning back.

A few days later, I spoke with Canyon. He explained that I was the first talent he was going to hire. Canyon told me the date I needed to report, what I could expect on the first day, and how I'd receive help finding a place to live. He also said not to expect any handouts or special treatment because of who my dad was. I understood that. He didn't say it in a rude way. I knew about kids with relatives in the business, their sense of entitlement, and how they carried themselves. I was disappointed that someone had the same idea about me based on one brief phone call.

---

*Paul Levesque: "I was shocked when Ashley called me and said she wanted to get into the business. I wondered where this was coming from, because she'd never shown an interest in it. She needed to know that she'd be starting at the very bottom. You're away from your family. Marriages don't last. And if she thought being compared to her dad was bad, that would only be the beginning. I told her if she made it through the Performance Center, any success she'd achieve would be attributed to her dad. After all that, she still wanted a shot."

I had an entire industry to learn. I knew that it was so multifaceted that the more I learned, the more I'd need to learn. Every second of the day, I thought about the journey I was going to take. I was confident in one thing: when it came to cardiovascular training, they'd be lucky if any of the girls there could keep up with me.

I wrapped up my work at Ciarla Fitness and said my emotional good-byes to my boss, colleagues, and clients. They became my friends and gave me the courage to consider doing this. For the first time, I would not live in North Carolina. Tampa was about an eight-and-a-half-hour drive from Charlotte and about an hour and a half by plane. I was leaving my family behind. Riki was going to drive us down there. He'd make the move once I was settled in and look for work.

Before I packed my U-Haul and hit the road to the Sunshine State, there was something I needed to do: hit the ring.

My dad and Reider took me to HighSpots training facility in Charlotte. That's where my brother and Richie Steamboat trained under George South. Former WCW superstar Lodi would be there working out with us. I remember the walls of the facility lined with wrestling action figures in their packaging.

This was a two-day crash course for me to become familiar with the fundamentals, but first, in classic Flair fashion, my dad emphasized cardio-vascular conditioning. After all the years of hearing him tell stories about Verne Gagne's training sessions that began every day with five hundred free squats, it was my turn. Before I set foot in the ring, that's what I did—and he did them with me. My dad did them for the first time in a barn in Minnesota. I did them in a warehouse in North Carolina. What was funny was that my dad did five hundred free squats and then picked up his coffee and drank it like it was no big deal.

I remember doing forward rolls diagonally across the ring from corner to corner in sets of ten. My dad and Reider counted off for me. I can still hear my brother clapping and saying, "Good. Good job. Keep going, Ash. You're halfway there. Let's go. Good." I got to the seventh one, and my dad said, "Nope. That was terrible. Start again. Start over from six." I went back in the corner and started again. My dad said, "Okay, eight. That was good. Nine. Ten. Good, that's how you finish." After that, he and Reider showed me how to run the ropes and lock up with my opponent in the ring.

The second day, I began the session with another five hundred free squats and more conditioning drills. I worked on learning how to balance on the top rope and flip from it. In wrestling, it's called a moonsault. It took me a few tries to get comfortable with being on the top rope and having my back to the ring. The first couple of attempts, I flipped off the top rope and fell! The next time, I flipped off the top rope and landed on my feet in the center of the ring—I nailed it! I had a long way to go. It felt good to get that technique down.

After that, I practiced doing what I learned was called a double hand-spring elbow. I was hesitant because I didn't want to land in the corner on Lodi with all my momentum. Before I went for it, my dad said, "Don't worry, you won't hurt Lodi. I'll take his spot." And Lodi said, "Don't worry, you won't hurt me. C'mon." I did the two flips across the ring and landed the move on him in the corner. He was fine. I knew that once I got to FCW, I'd be able to learn how to use my gymnastics and cheerleading balance skills.

I arrived in Tampa a couple of days before I was due to report. I was scared to death driving to the training facility. I tried to anticipate what this journey had in store for me. I knew I had to work hard, treat everyone well, and earn people's respect. I pulled into the parking lot and walked to the door. I did the only things left to do: open it, walk through, and be ready for anything. This was it.

14

A WHOLE NEW WORLD

I had to learn a new sport, a new business, and a new culture.

March 2013

Walking into FCW for the first time that July was like being the new kid in school, but with a twist—I didn't know anyone, though it felt like everyone knew me.

Despite the hope that my identity would be kept secret, by the time I arrived in Tampa, everyone knew I was Ric Flair's daughter. I didn't realize that when I signed my WWE developmental contract, sports-entertainment media outlets would post that as a story. I didn't know sports entertainment had media outlets. Anyone who didn't see those posts figured it out too. Introducing myself to the few people who didn't recognize me by my first name only served as temporary relief.

I had a high mountain to climb. I had to prove that I belonged. I had to earn people's respect. Three things made that more challenging: I was Ric Flair's daughter; I was the only person there who did not have a tryout; and I didn't have any wrestling experience. Everyone knew that. But they didn't know I had confidence in one thing: my conditioning.

One of my vividest memories about my first day at FCW was doing conditioning drills. I remembered what Canyon told me about not expecting a handout. When it was time to fall in line for the drills, I was determined to show that, yes, Ric Flair is my dad, I had a lot to learn, but I wouldn't be outlasted when it came to conditioning.

Men and women did these drills together. Everyone was in good shape. I could hear the whistle being blown to start, stop, drop to the mat, and pop back up, the sound of a voice counting us down. One by one, I saw people around me go to the side of the room. The number dwindled until, finally, I was the last person standing.

I wanted everyone—the trainers and trainees—to know that while this was a new area for me, I was a well-conditioned athlete who took this seriously. I was not the stereotypical generational kid who thought she could coast because of her last name. I had a long way to go to prove that. I felt that outlasting everyone in those drills was an important first step.

During my first few weeks in Tampa, it seemed like the more questions I asked, the more questions I needed to have answered. One thing I knew right from the start was that I loved what I was doing! I drove out of FCW's parking lot one night and asked myself, *Why did I wait so long to do this?*

As recruits came in, people recognized one another from company tryouts or crossing paths with each other on the independent wrestling circuit. WWE talent scouts traveled the world and invited people to try out, or they signed talent to come to Tampa to train. One day, I looked around and thought, *Besides some of the trainers, I'm the only one here who's appeared on WCW TV.*

When I started in FCW, I immediately enjoyed living in the warm Florida sun every day, even in the notoriously hot summer. Inside the training facility, it was like winter. All I got were a lot of cold shoulders. It was like I had the plague. When I started, with the exceptions of my trainers, almost no one spoke to me.*

---

*Ric: "When I started out, Verne asked if I wanted to go to Japan for three weeks. I said, 'Yeah, who am I going with?' He said Rhodes, Murdoch, Buddy Wolfe, Skandor Akbar, and Nelson Royal. I was so excited. We flew to Dallas and spent a week with Dusty's family. All the guys had short haircuts and told me I had to get my hair cut. We went to the barbershop in the airport, and they cut off all my hair! In Japan, I carried their bags for three weeks—every train station, every hotel—every day. No one spoke to me that first week. We'd ride the trains, and Dusty just sat across from me. Nothing."

As an athlete, I was comfortable getting to know people through training sessions, practices, and playing in games, but this was different. One of the things I realized after my first couple of days in FCW was that there was a wrestling culture that I needed to learn.

There was an etiquette that had to be followed every day. This was to show your respect for the people you trained with, respect for the people who were training you, and respect for the business.

Things that will always stick out in my mind include showing up to the facility an hour before start time to prepare for that day's session; once you're there and before you start, you must shake everyone's hand. You repeated that when you left for the day. At live events, everyone helped set up the ring; during the show, everyone watched what was happening in the ring on the monitor backstage; you had to watch the matches before yours. Everyone stayed until the end of the show and helped take the ring down. I felt like every step I took, I made a mistake.

My education continued. You had to know everyone's ring name, what their finishing move was called, and what the move actually was.

There was a vocabulary I needed to learn—certain words that wrestlers used with one another that, to the common person, have a different meaning. When spoken fluently in a conversation, it's like its own language, and downloads of Berlitz courses to listen to in the car or on my iPod while I ran were not available for purchase.

I'm sure there were people at the training facility who thought, *She must know all of this already. She's Ric Flair's daughter. She's been around this business her whole life. She knows people like Arn Anderson, Dusty Rhodes, Ricky Steamboat, and Triple H.* Nope. Not even close. Yes, I knew those people on a personal basis. That had nothing to do with the work I was doing.

As a child and a young adult, people didn't talk to us using terminology that the wrestlers used. I never heard those terms backstage and never heard them from my dad. If I saw someone with him, I shook his or her hand, because that's how my parents raised us. While making my way through a larger-than-life cast of characters, I had no idea that there was an entire culture based on what they did, how they did it, and what they said. I just said, "Hello."

Something else I learned right away was that trainees had jobs outside of training. I took tickets when fans entered FCW shows, I sold programs, and I got my degree in guerilla marketing when I worked on a "street team."

Street teams drove to different towns in Florida and put posters in business windows and on telephone poles to advertise FCW live events. The first thing we did on our day off was go to the print shop and pick up a thousand posters.

Since I was a newer trainee, let's just say we didn't drive around Tampa. We'd go to Miami, which was almost a 600-mile round trip; Fort Pierce, which was a little more than 300 miles; Immokalee was almost 320 miles total; and Jacksonville, just about 400 miles there and back. Another rule I learned was that you never fall asleep in your car pool when someone else was driving.

Street team was a long day, but it was what you made of it. I thought it was fun. You're in a car, listening to music, and putting posters up. And I knew it was all part of paying dues. It was a lot better than some of the stories my dad told us when we were kids.*

There were different classes throughout the day. The girls and the guys trained together. Sometimes there were thirty of us in a class. We'd get seven or eight minutes in the ring. I'd start shaking every time trainer Norman Smiley called me to get in the ring with him. I was very nervous

---

*Ric: "On that same trip to Japan, we were eating lunch together. The guys just started making small talk with me. We were eating hamburgers and french fries. Murdoch had a tray full of fries. I saw Dusty reach and get one, and then Nelson Royal did the same. I reached over to grab a french fry from Dick's plate. He took his fork and stabbed it all the way through my hand—into the table—like in the movies. He said to me, 'Rookie mistake, kid.' And then he pulled the fork out of my hand. I was shocked. I went to Nelson's room and had tears in my eyes. Nelson was the only guy who had any compassion for me."

in front of everyone. I had stage fright at the thought of people watching me while I was trying to learn what I was supposed to do.*

I never had an issue playing sports in front of an audience. There would be thousands of people in a gym during national tournaments, and reporters and photographers covering our games. But this was different.

It was hard for me to abandon my instincts as a gymnast who was taught to be graceful. It took me months to feel comfortable running the ropes and not look so methodical doing it. Getting rope burn on my back was definitely not fun. I was obsessed with my technique. Was it good enough? Was my form where it needed to be? It was difficult for me to let go and be free-flowing with my movements. I was with people who may have been new to WWE, but they knew their way around a ring.

The women who were training were Paige, Emma, Summer Rae, Vickie and Eddie Guerrero's daughter Shaul, Audrey Marie, Ivelisse, Anya, Buggy Nova, and Alicia Fox's sister, Christina.

On the male side, trainees included Richie Steamboat, Seth Rollins, Cesaro, Dean Ambrose, and Leakee, who became Roman Reigns.

Almost everyone had experience wrestling on the independent scene. For the women, Paige and Emma were standouts. For the guys, Richie Steamboat and Seth Rollins were touted for their matches at FCW live events and on the FCW TV program that aired in Tampa every week.

I knew that many of the trainees were annoyed because I didn't have a tryout match, and I hadn't been selected by one of the trainers. I understood that. In the college and professional sports world, I would be considered a walk-on. It didn't work that way here.

Some of the first people who befriended me were Anya (we had our physical on the same day), Emma, Dolph Ziggler's brother Briley Pierce,

---

*Norman Smiley: "I worked with Ashley's brother David. I could tell right away that Ashley was an excellent athlete who was very well coordinated. She was very coachable. She learned things quickly and then applied it to whatever we were doing. I thought sometimes she was a little too hard on herself. In those early days, I told her to relax and to be patient, that learning a new art takes time. She was so determined."

Mike Dalton, and Mojo Rawley. I remember talking to them about my ring name.

I didn't know what I wanted my ring name to be. I wrote down names that sounded like they were from a soap opera: Ella Reid, Charlotte, Ryan. I chose Elizabeth because it's my mom's name and my middle name. When that was turned down, I didn't consider the reason for rejection as a possibility—Miss Elizabeth. It was decided that I was going to be Charlotte. Now that I had a name, where was I going to be from?

For a while, I was Charlotte from Charlotte. Was that a joke? It was announced as Charlotte, North Carolina—not from the Queen City like it is today. It reminded me of the scene in *Austin Powers* when Austin's at the blackjack table and says to Number Two, "Allow myself to introduce . . . myself." I don't think anyone really put a lot of time into it.

I thought I had built a good rapport with the trainers. They always treated me well. There was a brief period when I felt a little lost because I wasn't anyone's signee. No one stamped their name on me after seeing me perform in the ring. No one invited me to a tryout after watching footage of me. I understood that. It's the scout's job to find, hire, and develop talent, to get them ready for the next level: the WWE main roster. I had to work harder to be noticed, although with the new job assignment for FCW shows, being noticed would no longer be a concern.

When I was told I was going to be a ring announcer, I thought someone was playing a joke on me. I thought, *Well, this is one way to deal with stage fright.*

I was terrified when I was told I'd start out in front of the camera, in front of an audience, and stand in the middle of the ring as the ring announcer for FCW. The crowds usually totaled thirty to fifty people. They were very loyal fans, and they knew I was Ric Flair's daughter. Usually at least once a show I'd hear "WOOOOO!" from the crowd. I was so nervous. I got compliments on my ring announcing, but I thought I was terrible. It's tougher than it looks.

I started to make a life for myself in Florida. The developmental program moved from Tampa to Orlando. Riki drove down for a few weekends to visit me. Overall, I became less focused on catering to Riki. I still sent text messages and called when we were apart, but it was not with the same sense of urgency or frequency.

After a few months of living apart, Riki decided to change the plan: he was not moving to Florida. Instead, he chose to move to Mississippi so he could be closer to his family. Part of me was upset about this. He was my husband. Even though I hadn't felt like I was in a loving relationship for a very long time, a small part of me still wanted it to work.

That fall, Riki's brother played in a college football game in Dallas. I told him I didn't want us to go. I was concerned that his being in that type of environment would trigger a drug and alcohol relapse. Riki prided himself on being defiant. He insisted on going to the game. I pleaded with his mother to speak with him. She told me that I needed to let her son do what he wanted to do. Same old song: denial. Given Riki's history, I couldn't believe that she could still could not bring herself to acknowledge this problem. I wasn't working at FCW, so I went with him.

From the moment we were at the stadium, he started drinking and became belligerent. We went to a fast food restaurant after the game and Riki caused a scene while we were inside, and then took a taxi back to the hotel. In the hotel room, he became hostile and destructive, and he started breaking things. I was in the hallway with his mother and said, "Now do you see? This is what I've been dealing with."

I realized that even though I left Charlotte, I hadn't escaped. At that moment, in the hallway, something clicked. I'd had enough. It was time for me to leave this dark period of my life behind for good. I got on a plane and flew back to Tampa. When we talked on the phone, I said something to Riki I should've told him a long time ago. It's one of the most important things I ever said in my life: "I want a divorce." I wanted to be free from this darkness. I wanted my life back. I was stronger than I realized.

When I look back on my relationship with Riki, it was a toxic relationship that could even have turned fatal. The world revolved around him. Angering him was the worst thing I could do. Even if I knew I was right about something or had the right to ask a question. Even if I wanted to express my feelings—body language turned into words, words turned into rage, and rage turned into violence. It was like I was married to someone who was possessed.

When people are in abusive relationships, they need to be able to recognize warning signs. They need to be able to listen to the people around them who are concerned for their safety and well-being. Screaming at someone or emotionally and physically harming someone is not love. That person must find a way out of the relationship before it's too late. The abuse doesn't go away; it only escalates with time.

I felt like a weight had been lifted off my shoulders, like I could actually focus on me. I could focus on being healthy in every aspect of my life and pursue this new career with a clear mind.

Thinking of my first match brings back so many memories. It was in October. I worked with Emma. If I thought I was nervous when Norman Smiley called me into the ring, this was a nightmare. I was trying to follow what was happening. During this time, my trainers gave me strict instructions not to do any of my dad's moves or mannerisms: no chops, no knee drop, no standing vertical suplex, no figure-four leg lock, and most of all, absolutely no "WOOOOO!"

From day one, Emma was really talented as a performer in the ring. She could work with many different types of opponents, including someone like me, who was learning every minute of the day. Emma did everything for me in that match; she carried me through. I'll always be grateful to her for that. After our match, some of the guys came up to me and said, "Wow, that was pretty good for your first match." All I said then was the same thing that I can write now: "Thank you, Emma."

When I went back to training, I met someone I had only heard about by name and reputation, a new trainer WWE had hired: Sara Amato.

Coach Sara was an amazing wrestler during her career. She was trained by Daniel Bryan and performed all over the world as Sara Del Rey. She was so strong in the ring that she was known as "Death Rey." Sara's one of the few women in history who was voted on the *PWI 500*—a list from

Pro Wrestling Illustrated magazine of their top five hundred wrestlers in the world. I knew about her and her reputation as an incredible performer. I was learning new things every day. I knew enough to realize that WWE hiring Sara Amato made a major statement about where female training and in-ring competition were headed.*

To close out the year, I found myself in a match I never envisioned participating in—a Divas Christmas Battle Royal. All the women wore Christmas-themed outfits. I didn't last long, but any experience I could get in the ring, in front of an audience, was good for me.

I didn't expect to find myself in a relationship. I met Tom during his time as a trainee in the developmental program. We were friends and saw one another in groups of FCW people when we were all hanging out. We were both coming from recent relationships. Since we were friends, we agreed to take things slowly, which made sense.

I felt comfortable with Tom because I had seen what he was like while we were both training. I saw how genuinely nice he was to everyone and how well liked he was. I also noticed how well he treated me.

He had been released from his WWE developmental contract when we decided to try dating. He didn't want to have any downtime, so he started getting himself booked on independent wrestling shows. I continued my progress in WWE developmental.

My family wanted me to come home for the holidays. I missed them very much, but I decided to stay in Florida. For the first time in a long time, I was in a good place. I was happy.

Reider was in a good place too. He kept up his wrestling training and

---

*Mike Johnson, PWInsider.com: "WWE made a huge statement when they hired Sara Amato. She was an extremely talented pro wrestler during her career. That experience enabled her to step inside the ropes with the girls and help guide and direct them with a woman's perspective. Sara also knows how to make talent stand out, and because of her experience, she could prepare trainees physically and mentally for what was ahead. She's one of the most important hires for WWE in recent history."

had an opportunity to train in Japan. My dad was going there to work for All Japan Pro Wrestling. Reider was going to train in the All Japan dojo.

I was thrilled for him. When I started in developmental, I was worried that he might not be able to beat addiction. He worked so hard to get better, and he never lost hope.

Reider and I were a lot alike. We loved sports, loved movies, and were very devoted to our family. We were also as close as two people could be, but we also had qualities that made us different from each other.

There was a part of my personality that enabled me to block out critics and use that negativity as motivation to silence them. My brother did that too, but I think sometimes he let criticism bother him personally. It was difficult to be criticized when he was just learning to wrestle and when people said that he wasn't as good as our dad or that he'd never be our dad. No one claimed he was going to be any of those things. Wrestling was what he always wanted to do. He wanted to train and gain experience by working in matches.

I didn't know what it was like living in our dad's shadow like he or my brother David did. No one expected me to get into wrestling. I think there was a part of Reider that hoped my parents would get back together. I was happy that he'd have the opportunity to learn in Japan, a positive environment.

While Reider and my dad traveled to Japan to begin 2013, I kept learning in developmental. I still acted as a ring announcer, and I was performing in more matches during live events. My dad always told me that the best way to learn is to perform in the ring.

I remember when I got to FCW, one of the trainers said in his speech to the class, "Not all of you will make it." I wanted to continue to learn and continue to improve. I was determined to make it.

It was cool to keep in touch with Reider through social media and email. He was in Japan, and I was in Orlando. I saw all the amazing things he was doing and the great places he was going. I loved the pictures of him during cardio sessions of running up a mountain. Reider didn't want to be famous. He didn't want to be known for his last name. He loved wrestling. He wanted to the best at what he did in a profession that had captured his heart and imagination from the time he was a little boy.

When our dad had a blood clot in his leg and couldn't wrestle, Reider filled in for him. My brother was doing so well that he was back in the ring having matches after five days in the All Japan dojo. His stay in Japan was going to be extended, and he was going on his first All Japan tour.

We'd FaceTime too. Reider looked so good. I could tell he was in such a great place mentally, emotionally, and physically. He loved the Japanese culture. He was honored that the people who ran the dojo made him an instructor and asked him to teach young children the fundamentals of wrestling. This was a wonderful turning point.

During one of our FaceTime sessions, he met Tom. My brother said, "If you hurt my sister, I'll kick your ass." Even from the other side of the world, Reider was thinking of me. He was always looking out for me.

I received incredible news at work too. I was selected as one of the trainees to perform in matches at Axxess during WrestleMania 29 week in New Jersey. What made me more excited was that my dad was bringing Reider home to see me perform. It was amazing to think that two years earlier, my brother and I watched our dad become the first-ever two-time inductee to the WWE Hall of Fame. Reider was getting booked on independent shows, and I was a personal trainer who was just asked at dinner why I wasn't in the business. Now Reider was a part of All Japan. I made steady progress with WWE in the NXT developmental system, and I was having a match at Axxess! I couldn't wait to see my dad and my brother at WrestleMania.

I knew Reider got back to Charlotte after the long flight from Tokyo. He was excited about seeing my parents and his girlfriend, Whitney, when he was home. Reider and I talked a few times on the phone. He was also looking forward to keeping up his training regimen. Everyone missed him so much. More than that, we were so happy for him—and so proud!

I was home packing. I had an outdoor show the next day at the Miami-Dade fair, which would be my final performance before flying to WrestleMania. I was set to travel the next day with Emma and Mojo Rawley. Tom and I were talking about WrestleMania and my match; I was scheduled to have a match with Paige. I couldn't wait to work with her. She was so talented in the ring and on the microphone. She was naturally beautiful and had a different type of sex appeal. She was a Diva but could go in the ring with anyone, male or female. I so looked forward to the opportunity to work with her. I was packing my ring gear, an outfit just in case I'd be going to the Hall of Fame at Madison Square Garden, and, of course, getting some clothes together for dinner, because I knew my dad was going to take us out. Tom was so happy for me. We continued our conversation as I walked around and packed.

My phone kept ringing. I ignored it and kept talking to Tom. It rang again. We continued our conversation. It rang again.

Tom said, "Your phone keeps ringing. Can you answer it, please?"

I told him, "I'll call them back."

Then my phone signaled that I had a text message. I picked up my phone. It was my dad. It said, "EMERGENCY." An empty feeling and a terrible pain ran through my body. I knew.

PART III

LIFE WILL NEVER BE THE SAME

15

SWEET CHILD OF MINE

Reid was doing so well. I was so proud of him.

March 2013

opened the door to the hotel room. Reid was in bed. He didn't respond when I called his name. I knew by looking at him that something was seriously wrong. I ran to the phone, called the front desk, and asked them to call 9-1-1. Then I called 9-1-1. I pleaded with the operator to send an ambulance to the hotel right away. I told him that I was calling from room 617. We needed help as soon as possible. My son was unconscious.

I just wanted to help Reid. I felt powerless. I didn't know what to do. The ambulance arrived within five minutes, and the EMTs tried everything they could to resuscitate him. After their final efforts failed, I was told something I never thought I'd hear. My son, my youngest child, who was just twenty-five years old, was gone. And I couldn't get him back.

I kept calling his mother but couldn't get through to her. The next person I called was Paul. He tried to calm me down and told me he'd do whatever we needed. I hoped Beth would call me back. After I told Paul what happened, I called Ashley. I couldn't reach her either. Her phone just kept ringing and ringing. I kept calling and calling.

I sent Ashley a text message—"EMERGENCY"—and she called me back.* I was really concerned about how she would take this news. I felt the same way when I tried contacting Beth. Yes, we were divorced, and yes, our relationship after that had experienced its ups and downs, but we had children together. We were parents together. Reid was our son. We will always share that connection.

How in God's name did this happen? Reid was with me at dinner, and everything was fine. We went back to the hotel bar to watch the game. He was still drinking water. I went to bed and told him I'd see him in the morning. We couldn't wait to get on the road for our appearances and to see his sister perform as part of WrestleMania weekend.

I was also worried about Megan and David. All four of my kids were close. When Ashley and Reid were younger, Megan and David watched over them like they were their own kids. Megan and David had families of their own, and those children loved Reid. He was such a sweet, wonderful guy with a heart of gold. How would they deal with it?

We had to face unspeakable tragedy and plan Reid's funeral. His favorite band was Guns N' Roses. At the viewing, David put every one of the group's CDs into Reid's casket. I put my WWE Hall of Fame ring on Reid's finger so he could always have it.

At the funeral,† our family was supported by so many relatives and friends. Reid was beloved among everyone. I prayed that he knew how

---

*Ashley: "When I saw the text message from my dad, I knew what it meant. My heart broke instantly. This was our family's worst nightmare. I called my mom. I told her what no parent should have to hear, that her child passed away. I heard my mom's heart break over the phone. I just wanted to get home to Charlotte to be with my family. Tom drove me there straight from Tampa."

†Ashley: "I called Aunt Erin and my mom's best friend, Susan Beck, and asked them to go to my mom's house. I didn't say one word during the drive to Charlotte. I broke down when we got to Megan's house. I couldn't hold in my pain anymore. It was like all my years of worry and fear just came out. Reider had finally turned the corner. And now, somehow, my best friend was gone. It wasn't fair. I was numb at the funeral. Seeing so

much we all loved him. People came from all over the country to be there for us and to celebrate Reid's life.

I was so grateful for Wendy. She loved Reid like a son. Wendy didn't leave my side during Reid's funeral, and Melinda went into attorney mode and handled all business and financial matters. They helped my family any way they could.

I thanked God every minute for bringing Wendy into my life. Wendy was with me when I found Reid in the hotel room. If it weren't for her, I wouldn't have been able to act so quickly in calling 9-1-1, and I wouldn't have been able to make it through the funeral.

I kept replaying our last evening together back in my mind and questioning everything. Why did I bring him home? Why didn't I just let him stay in Japan? He was doing so well there. I wanted him to be able to come back here and feel good about all his hard work, how well he was doing. I wanted him to feel pride in his accomplishments and enjoy sharing that with the people who loved him.

Did I push him too hard as an athlete? Did I let him see too much of the partying lifestyle? Was I too much of a best friend? Should I have brought myself to do what the experts recommended and administer tough love? Would he still be here if I had?

I'll never forgive myself for bringing him home. I'll never recover from not being able to save my son.

How does my family begin to recover from heartbreak like this? How do we pick up the pieces? How do we move on? Where do we go from here?

---

many people from different times of my life was like seeing the pages of a photo album turn. I spoke at the funeral. I didn't know what I was going to say before I went up to the microphone. I wanted people to know about how wonderful of a person my brother was, how sweet, funny, loyal, and protective of his family he was. I wanted to let everyone know how much he loved being in Japan and how happy he was there. I wanted to let people know there was no better friend someone could have than Reider. And then it just came out of me. I recited the words from his favorite wrestling interview from Dusty Rhodes: 'I have wined and dined with kings and queens, and I've slept in alleys and dined on pork and beans.'"

PART IV

REUNITED

16

BUILDING THE FUTURE: WE ARE NXT

*If the match for the NXT Women's Championship was with
anyone else other than Nattie, it wouldn't mean as much.*

One week later . . .

was back in Florida. I couldn't process what happened. My brother, my
best friend, was gone. He had his whole life ahead of him. Reider was
doing the best he'd ever done. He was the happiest he had ever been.
Suddenly, it was over.

In the weeks following Reider's passing, I was consumed by a sadness
I had never felt before. There was something surreal about trying to
understand that I'd never see or speak to my brother again. Any time I
wanted to text him, send him a direct message on social media, schedule
visits with him, or celebrate a moment in our lives . . . that was never going
to happen again. Japan was such a turning point in his life. His future
looked so bright. How could he be gone? He was only twenty-five years old.

Seeing my parents and Megan and David suffer such heartbreak was
something I never imagined. Then I thought about Reider's girlfriend,
Whitney.

My brother was a ladies' man. When the phone rang in our house, it
was usually a girl calling for him. Even when I was a senior at Providence
High School and captain of the volleyball team, I was Reid's sister. He

had many girlfriends. They were all beautiful, wonderful people. Whitney was special.

Whitney was my brother's girlfriend and his best friend.

She was one of us. She was a Fliehr. Whitney helped Reider apply for jobs, drove him to independent wrestling shows, visited him in rehab—she did it all unconditionally. I felt a bond with her. I always knew that my brother was okay when he was with her.

Whitney visited Reider when he was in Japan. That was the happiest my brother had ever been. He wanted to share the best time of his life with her.

Whitney was so proud of him. Everyone in our family hoped that Reider and Whitney would get married one day.

My mind was flooded with memories of running through Providence Plantation, moving to Piper Glen, our pictures every year on the first day of school, my mom's family adventures, sushi at Nakato . . . all the time my brother and I had spent together. How did things change so drastically? My memories almost didn't feel real. It was like they belonged to someone else.

There will always be a piece of me that is missing. My heart will always beat differently when I go back to Charlotte. It will beat differently for the rest of my life.

When Reider died, WWE was there for me in every way. Hunter was there for me every step of the way too. I could take off as long as I wanted; I could go to WrestleMania as a spectator or I could go to perform; paid grief counseling was available. I had never experienced the kind of support system that Hunter and WWE provided for me. I'll always remember that.

I chose not to go to WrestleMania in New Jersey. I didn't want people seeing me perform during an event like Axxess while I was so distraught. But I did decide to go back to work.

My first day back in developmental, Dusty called me into his office. He gave me one of his famous big hugs. He said that what happened to Reider was a tragedy. He let me know that he was there for me. Then Dusty told me something that was very important: I needed to put my big girl pants on and put them on really tight. I was needed here. I needed to get back to work—for me and for my brother.

Dusty always supported me. He always looked out for me. Dusty always believed in me, even if he'd tease me sometimes in front of everyone in promo class for driving around Charlotte in a Land Rover when I was a teenager. He knew that my family had had problems in recent years. I could trust Dusty. He said to me, "There's a point where you have to let it go, baby. You have to keep pushing forward."

Dream loved the Fliehr kids, and we loved him.

Dusty was right. I needed to reinvigorate my spirit to live my brother's dream.

That first week I was back, all the girls were working out in the ring. We were learning how to do a move that uses the momentum from the ropes to get in the ring from the apron. I just couldn't get it. It was especially frustrating because I usually got moves down after a few attempts. I just couldn't get this. On the fifth try, I hit my face on the top rope. That was it—waterworks—I broke down and cried in front of the entire class. All the girls jumped on me and tried to make me feel better.

That spring, the developmental program hosted a huge event in Kissimmee, Florida, to showcase new talent. Hunter, Michael Hayes, executives, producers, and writers all came to see trainees work. Superstars and Divas from WWE's main roster were there. Dolph Ziggler and Briley Pierce were there too. AJ Lee and Big E were on the card, and Sasha and Summer Rae were featured in a tag team match against Emma and Paige.

I wasn't booked on the show to perform in a match. I was the ring announcer.

In one of the meeting sessions we had, Michael Hayes said something profound. He said, "Not everyone here will make it. Who here has what it takes? Who here will be one of the few to be called up to the WWE main roster? Who here is going to grab the fuckin' keys and drive the car?"

I took that sentiment and combined it with my own emotions. It all came out of me during one of Dusty's communication classes. We called it "promo class."

When I first arrived in FCW, the idea of having a class where you worked solely on interviews intimidated me. When your teacher is "the American Dream" Dusty Rhodes, student expectations are even higher. Dusty was the best. At the very least, Dusty was one of the best talkers in wrestling history. My dad used to say Dusty could "talk 'em into the building." That meant that fans would buy a ticket to see Dusty at the next show because they were so captivated by what he'd said in his interview.

I learned from playing sports that sometimes when all-time greats turn to coaching, it doesn't work well. That person may not have the patience to teach people, especially someone like me who was starting from scratch. They might be better as a guest instructor or speaker or someone to give advice, but as a teacher I worked with every day, Dusty's one of the best I ever had. Dream had this innate ability to bring something out of people that was a natural part of who they were and transform that into an integral part of their on-screen personas. He was also great at spotting talent.

When we walked into class, Dusty always had country music playing. To grab our attention, he started every class with a story. He'd say something like, "What's the dirt going around here? Who's got some dirt for me?" Or he would ask us what movies were playing and what we liked and disliked about the movie we mentioned, just to get everyone talking.

Before one of our classes, some of the guys were working out in the ring. I heard them call out some cheer phrases I'd say in practice and give high fives in an overly animated way. Maybe I was being too sensitive, but I thought it was obviously being done in a mocking way.

In every sport I played, I was always a team leader. We always encouraged people on our team. Wrestling is a very individually focused endeavor, but at the same time, you're only as good as the people you work with. I wanted to encourage people in practice. If someone looks good, then we all look good.

Promo class was a great way for us to combine our frustrations in life or work or sometimes both on the microphone with creativity and passion. It took me a long time to become comfortable speaking in front of people.

I took offense to that whole mocking thing and those overanimated high fives. When it was my turn to do an interview segment, or "cut a promo," I used that real emotion and opened up. I used that as an opportunity to explain who I was, where I came from, and why I was doing what I was doing.

I brought up the incident and said, "Maybe I am masking what I feel when I walk through the doors of the Performance Center every morning. The smile on my face and the high fives to my fellow coworkers are much harder to do because of the pain I feel and what I am going through every day. None of you could handle that on your best day. You couldn't walk ten feet in my shoes, let alone a day in my life with what I've been through. I will continue to be me, continue to cheer on my class, because that's who I am and where I come from."

That was a turning point for me. I was able to harness something very real and channel it in a specific way through my character. I didn't see any more of those high fives again.

That summer, I had difficulty balancing work and coping with Reider's passing. I was grateful for Tom. I felt bad for him because he met my family for the first time when he drove me to Charlotte for Reider's funeral. He didn't shy away from that. He helped everyone as much as he could with kind words, a hug, or getting them something to eat or drink. Tom stayed at my side the entire time.

I thought of my brother every second of the day. I was consumed with guilt. Was I there enough for him? Why didn't I go home for the holidays like he wanted me to? Would that have changed anything? Reider tried to reach out to me so many times . . .

I didn't know it until now: all Reider wanted was my approval. He wanted to know I was proud of him. I wish I would've told him that more. I wish I would've posted about him on social media more often so he could have seen how proud I was of him. I felt like I betrayed him. I was happy for the first time in my life, and I was engrossed in what I was doing. I was selfish.

Did Reider know how proud I was of him? Did he know how much I loved him? Did he know how grateful I was that he pushed me to try wrestling? Could he see what I'm doing?

He'd appear in my dreams, and I'd always try to save him, and then I'd wake up in the middle of the night.

I had to stay focused. A major change happened at work: we moved to the brand-new WWE Performance Center in Orlando.

Since I was so new to the sports-entertainment industry and didn't spend that much time in FCW, the significant changes going from Tampa to NXT in Orlando didn't have much of an impact on me.

I knew that the WWE Performance Center was amazing. Nothing from FCW compared to it. Because of my time playing competitive sports and being around professional sports teams, I knew how impressive a place like this was and the type of investment it was from WWE's standpoint.

When I walked through it for the first time, I marveled at what I saw: a full weight training facility, medical rooms, physical rehabilitation rooms, seven rings, an interview studio that we called the mirror room, a video-editing studio, a lecture hall with stadium seating and video screens. In my heart, knowing where I was, I realized, *We're professional athletes now.*

Because of my background in sports, this might've been one of the few times when I felt more comfortable than some of the other trainees.

To me, the WWE Performance Center was what a premier, professional sports team would have as its practice facility.* I knew that expectations were also going to be much higher.† We all did.

There was a professional sports franchise structure to the Performance Center and NXT. I was comfortable with that too. We had a dress code. For company events and appearances, cutoff T-shirts and tops for women that showed cleavage and exposed midriffs were not allowed. Sleeves on a button-down shirt had to stay down—no rolling them up. Coach Suzie, Coach Brubaker, and Coach Bell would be proud!

I trained at the Performance Center Monday, Tuesday, and Wednesday. NXT ran shows Thursday, Friday, and Saturday. We had training sessions before the shows. Setup and teardown was the same as FCW: get to the venue, set up the chairs and guardrails; unload the ring truck; and set up the ring. After the show, we'd tear everything down, drive back to the Performance Center to drop everything off, and be back the next day to do it all again. Sunday was my day off.

My training regimen continued outside of the Performance Center. Tom was not sure about his wrestling future, but he stayed in shape. We trained together every day. Tom got me back to loving weight training again, which was perfect given the work I did every day at the Performance Center.

---

*Paul Levesque: "Historically, our business was very difficult to even try to get into. The previous development systems were not impressive for recruiting. They could've been any independent promotion. When I came on full-time in the office, I wanted to build a new way for WWE to recruit and develop talent. I wanted to create a world-class facility in a great city that would appeal to people who are looking to pursue this as a profession. I tell every recruit the same thing: the expectations of you are higher, because you have so many more tools to start out with than any other generation of performer."

†Ric: "The WWE Performance Center is incredible, and from the moment I saw NXT, I knew it was going to be different from *Raw* and *SmackDown*. I told Ashley what Blackjack Mulligan told me, as a principle, and what he told Reid when they met in Orlando in 2008: in this industry, a performer has four to six minutes every time they're on TV to show what makes them special. Here, she needed to show Paul, everyone at the Performance Center, and everyone in NXT what made her stand out. It was that simple when Jack told me in the '70s, and it's that simple today."

On Sundays, after going to the gym, Tom and I always did something fun. We loved going to the theme parks in Orlando. We'd plan that day as our cheat-meal day. We'd eat all day and watch movies when we got home. Sunday sushi dates were another favorite. We made a life for ourselves in Orlando. It felt good to be with someone who truly cared for me and treated me well. Tom was happy for me and what I was doing. He encouraged me to do things and expand my horizons.

From that spring until the fall, I worked with two women who were standouts in the ring from the first day they were in the developmental program.

Sasha Banks made her name around the Boston-area independents. She wanted to be a WWE Superstar from the time she was a child. Her mom used to force her to turn off the TV. She started training for wrestling as a teenager. Sasha was a phenomenal athlete and excellent in the ring. We were both at WrestleMania XXIV. I was there for my dad; she was there with her cousin Snoop Dogg, who went out to the ring after my dad's match. We were both backstage at the same time. Sasha loved wrestling, and it showed. She idolized Eddie Guerrero. Sasha worked hard in every aspect of her training.

From the first time we locked up during practice, Coach Sara said, "That was a really good lockup." Sasha and I had an instant chemistry. We worked together as opponents in singles matches and were tag team partners. Sasha and I were a generic "good guy" team. We could've been any two girls from anywhere. One time we were in a tag match against Emma and Bayley. The crowd started booing Sasha and me and cheered our opponents, the villains. That was certainly a growing pain.

From the time she was a child in Northern California, Bayley was a huge WWE fan. She started wrestling throughout her home state when she was eighteen. Bayley credited Randy "Macho Man" Savage as the person who influenced her love of wrestling. Bayley was very versatile as a performer and was trained in the Mexican style of lucha libre. She was the best at forming a real connection with the audience; her fans loved her from day one. They felt Bayley was one of them. She was also knowledgeable and passionate about the industry.

I worked with Sasha and Bayley in a variety of singles, tag team, and six-person matches. These were during non-televised NXT live events. My debut on NXT programming was right around the corner.

My NXT debut was against Bayley on July 18, 2013. Her character was a "super fan" turned NXT Diva who had an "attitude of gratitude." Before the match, my dad came to the ring and addressed the crowd. Then he introduced me to the Full Sail audience.

Since I was with my dad, it was okay I started the match with a signature Flair "WOOOOO!" Bayley did a great job leading me through. To make sure I had a strong debut showing for my debut, I used my athleticism and gymnastics background to perform maneuvers I did well and that looked good for the audience. And Bayley was the perfect opponent; she could do anything in the ring. My finishing move was to drive my opponent's face into the mat with a cutter-like position like Randy Orton's RKO, but when they were kneeling on the mat, I flipped over them rather than standing up like Randy's finisher. Bayley made sure she was right where she needed to be. I landed the move, and the referee counted one, two, three. It was special to have my dad in my corner for my first NXT match for TV and victory. I never thought I'd strut across the ring with my dad like I did with Reider when we were kids.

What I thought of the entire day leading up to the match with Bayley and the rest of the day after was simple: *Did Reider see my match?* I hope he did, because I felt like I was on my way.

That summer, I continued to gain experience working in matches with Sasha, Bayley, Paige, and Summer Rae in venues all over Florida. I turned on Bayley in a tag match against Sasha and Summer Rae and joined my first faction: the BFFs—the Beautiful Fierce Females.

When it came time to watch the heroes and villains of NXT, I had to understand what I was seeing. I studied so I could learn what made something good and what made something bad. Most important was the psychology the performers used to elicit the specific response they needed from the crowd. Training with my coaches and learning from the girls in the ring really helped me understand what went into putting a match together.

I learned a lot from my friend from FCW, Mike Dalton. In NXT, he created a character named Tyler Breeze who was a huge success. He explained the importance of certain character details, why a match was put together in a certain way, and what a particular ending is designed to do for the characters.

From the beginning, there were certain people whose work I admired. I could watch Bo Dallas's matches for hours. The way he'd take an opponent's offense and come back from it was awesome. Bo was another standout in training sessions and was an excellent NXT Champion.

C. J. Parker had great timing, humor, and personality all in one. He's someone else I learned a lot from watching.

The Vaudevillains were such a talented tag team. Gotch and English were meticulous in the way they approached their characters, created their move set, and told their stories in the ring.

Sami Callihan had one of my favorites personas. The dark side of his character was especially captivating when he spoke and moved in the ring.

Rusev was so intimidating and powerful. He could make the audience get behind any "good guy," hoping they'd beat him. All Rusev had to do was appear on camera. I always felt he didn't get enough credit for the charisma he had as the monster villain.

I was privileged to see so many things: Rusev coming into his own with Lana; Ambrose, Rollins, and Reigns becoming the Shield; the early days of Bray Wyatt and the Wyatt Family; and Big E. I enjoyed watching them work. I didn't fully appreciate having that opportunity until years later. It was an honor for me to see these performers progress in developmental and then go on to become huge stars on WWE's main roster.

Two unexpected things happened in the fall. Tom asked me for my hand in marriage. I said, "Yes." The year we were together was one of the happiest times of my life. We loved each other and were best friends.* Tom

---

*Ric: "I didn't like this guy either [laughs] . . . Tom was a nice guy. He needed to get his future in order before he and Ashley got married. I would've liked them to know one another longer before they got married. But with my marriage to Jackie, it seemed like I cor-

and I got married in a private service. I was truly happy when I said, "I do," in that small ceremony, compared to the terrible feeling I'd had when I married Riki in a wedding that had all the appearances of a perfect day.

Shortly after I said, "I do," to Tom, the doctor told me, "You can't." During a tag match with Sasha against Paige and Emma, my breast implant burst. I didn't realize it until the next day. The doctor said it had to be replaced immediately. And the worst part was that I'd be out for two months.

It was so difficult for me to be out because of an injury, especially for something like an implant popping, not a move I performed in the ring. It drove me crazy to have my activities restricted while I was recovering.

I didn't want to be on the sidelines anymore, in someone's corner, booked for the occasional tag team or singles match. I made a promise to myself I would come back stronger and with a tangible goal: to become a prominent member of the NXT Women's Division.

While I was out, I started to piece together all the things I'd been learning. The principles of developing a persona, building that persona into a character, and then knowing who you are as a performer, making that character come alive and making it real . . .

The facial expressions coupled with specific movements, the athletic component of our profession, which I had confidence in, they're all important. But it's one piece of a more intricate equation. It went beyond the concept of "good guy" versus "bad guy."

I couldn't wait to get back to the Performance Center. The arena at Full Sail was a replica of what it would be like on WWE's main roster. The stage, the ramp, the cameras, the lights, the ring—it was then I realized that once you walked through the curtain, the entire arena, not just the ring, is a performer's stage. The *entertainment* aspect of sports entertainment was something I needed to continue to learn. How to walk, how to hit your mark, how to pose, which way to look for the camera, makeup, hair, wardrobe—everything contributes to your performance.

---

nered the market in that area and couldn't say much. I just hoped the best for them and wanted Ashley to stay focused on what she was doing in NXT."

I started the new year cleared to return to the Performance Center. I was more dedicated to training than ever before. I noticed that my leaner build led to better mobility in the ring. By the end of January, I was awarded "Trainee of the Month." I dedicated myself to learning my character, learning the psychology of what to do and when and why, and knowing how to be Ric Flair's daughter.

I continued to be told not to evoke images of my dad. I just wasn't sure if fans expected it. Whether I was a villain or a hero, would fans expect Ric Flair's child to have the strength behind a reverse knife-edge chop that could knock a door off its hinges? Would the fans expect me to lift my opponent into a standing vertical suplex and keep her hanging in the air so long it would feel like time stood still? What about the figure-four leg lock?

I picked up where I'd left off with Sasha before I got injured. The BFFs were making a name for themselves in NXT and probably having a little too much fun doing it.

My character formed into what it was supposed to be: a supervillain, a physically domineering machine who destroyed her opponents.

Sasha and I became close friends away from the cameras. The BFFs worked very well because it was real. We were both disappointed with where we were in the developmental program. That frustration created a bond between us. We felt that if we didn't do something, we'd be confined to being enhancement talent. We both wanted to be the best. We wanted to be the next Emma-versus-Paige rivalry.

The villainous BFF duo acted out real emotions in front of the cameras. During this time, I was fortunate to work closely with Sasha. Sasha knew a lot about the wrestling business, and I learned a lot working with her. Sasha had loved wrestling since she was a kid, and she brought that drive with her to the Performance Center every day. Sasha pushed me to continue learning and to keep improving.

One of the things Coach Sara said during her work in developmental was, "It's not about being good for a girl. It's about being *good*. And you don't stop there." On NXT's first live special on the WWE Network,

NXT ArRival, two women showed how good they were, and this was just the beginning.

There was a level of excitement in the NXT locker room leading up to ArRival. The matches people were talking about beforehand were the two-out-of-three falls match with Cesaro and Sami Zayn, and the Ladder Match for the NXT Championship between champion Bo Dallas and Neville.

There was one match that stole the show, and that was NXT Women's Champion Paige versus Emma. I had so much respect for both of them. Their match was an emotional, hard-fought contest. It had people talking long after the event was over. People wanted to watch ArRival just to see that match. Fans wanted more matches that featured female athletes. That night, Paige and Emma set a new standard for female competition.

In the days and weeks following ArRival, you could feel a healthy competition start to set in between the male and female performers at the Performance Center. Everyone welcomed it. In the early days of NXT, we were all a team.

Over time, NXT became the place to watch incredible female wrestlers engaged in fiercely competitive matches with compelling story lines.

We were reminded in NXT that the WWE main roster was different, and things that worked in NXT might not transfer to *Raw* and *Smack-Down*. In this case, it was the opposite: the Divas on the main roster were relegated to the bottom of the card. The women on *Raw* and *SmackDown* were being presented as "fillers" between male-dominated segments. They had two- to three-minute matches that were often more comedic fodder than competitive showings of what they could really do in the ring.

The NXT Women's Division developed such a loyal following that those female presentations would not work in NXT. The audience wanted to see empowered females giving everything they had in highly contested matchups. They wanted to see women in meaningful story lines, not Bra-and-Panties Matches, or a Santa's Helper Battle Royal, or a food fight that ended up in a pool of chocolate pudding.

A couple of weeks before WrestleMania 30, I got the news that I would travel to New Orleans to walk on WrestleMania's wondrous stage.

No, I didn't make my main roster debut at WrestleMania. Hunter asked me if I'd be a part of his entrance when he came out to face Daniel Bryan. Sasha, Alexa Bliss, and I were under gold masks. We were goddesses who took off the King of Kings' battle gear before he went to war.

The feeling I had of walking out on that stage to Hunter's music was exhilarating. The energy, the enormity, and the pageantry of his entrance made me want to be a member of WWE's main roster even more than ever before. That night, I decided what my ultimate goal would be: to perform in a match at next year's WrestleMania.

When I returned to Orlando, I realized I was consumed by the thought of getting to the main roster. All I thought about was improving. My character development and learning curve dramatically increased to go at a much faster rate. In class, we'd be given scenarios to talk about. I was told to talk about Paige. She was the NXT Women's Champion. I had to talk about challenging her for her championship, that it would be mine and that nothing would stop me.

I started my monologue by stating, "I was going to come after the NXT title with an extra set of wings. I was going to win it for my brother. He was my angel."

I meant every word I said, and when I returned to my seat, I realized that I had the ability to channel feelings from my real life and express myself using a microphone. It wasn't about "Charlotte" being a "bad guy," or saying she's "genetically superior." It was about the bigger picture—that I was going to make it to the top for my brother, and he was going to be with me every step of the way. At that moment, nothing felt more real.

I continued to stress the importance of character development as it pertained to my own work at the Performance Center. I had the athleticism; I just needed more emotion. I needed to develop facial expressions so that what I felt transferred to the audience and told a compelling story.

I became obsessed with perfecting every aspect of my character. I didn't realize it then, but the timing was perfect because I earned an opportunity that changed the trajectory of my career and my life.

Paige made a historic debut on the *Monday Night Raw* that aired the night after WrestleMania 30. In NXT, it was customary when an NXT Champion dropped their championship to someone else, they'd get called up to the main roster. Paige won the Divas Championship that night on *Raw* and was still the NXT Women's Champion. The NXT title was vacated.

There was a tournament to crown a new Women's Champion. From the main roster, the tournament featured Layla, a former Women's and Divas Champion; Alicia Fox, a former Divas Champion; and Natalya, a former Divas Champion and third-generation performer from the famous Hart family.

I felt like I came full circle in the first round of the tournament. I faced Emma, the person I'd had my first match with in FCW. Emma was so smooth in the ring. With Sasha in my corner, we incorporated her into the match, so at the end, Emma mistakenly hit Sasha with the Cobra Strike, and I rolled Emma up to win the match. I'm sure it was unexpected from the audience's point of view, but I advanced to the next round of the tournament.

In the semifinals, I defeated Alexa Bliss. Alexa was a gymnast, an NCAA Division I cheerleader, and a competitive bodybuilder turned NXT Diva. Alexa had great agility and balance in the ring.

In our match, we complemented one another's skills well and used our height differential as a way to help tell our story. Alexa stood five foot one compared to my five foot ten. The match featured many reversals, and we kept up step for step with each other. In the end, my finishing move, now named "Bow Down to the Queen," was too much for Miss Bliss.

Natalya defeated Sasha in the other semifinal match, which meant the fans would see Natalya and me perform in the tournament finals, which was going to be featured on the second live NXT special, TakeOver.

I couldn't believe that from my beginning in FCW two years earlier, I was now in a match for the NXT Women's Championship with some-one of Natalya's caliber. I sat directly in the row in front of her during the 2012 Hall of Fame induction ceremony. She was my first match at an

NXT live event. I remember when I started in developmental, Reider told me, "Look at Natalya. That's who you want to be like." Now I was going to have my chance.

I remember that morning being on the treadmill in my favorite red Marvel cutoff T-shirt while Tom and my dad lifted weights on the first level of LA Fitness by my apartment.

I had just gotten my new music with my dad's entrance theme dubbed into it, and I can remember playing it over and over and over as I walked on an incline, hyping myself up for this match.

I had put together some ideas for the match with Coach Sara and Tyler Breeze. Nattie had come to the Performance Center the week before to roll around with me in the ring. She said she just wanted to see if I could move with her and listen. We didn't walk through anything; she just wanted to "play, play, play," as she called it. I looked up to Nattie. I respected her. I knew if I listened to her, we could have a great match.

When it came to the match, all I knew was that I wanted to prove everyone wrong. That I deserved to be in the position of winning the NXT Women's title and that I had progressed as a talent. That Hunter wasn't going with the wrong girl and that even though Paige vacated the title, Nattie and I were going to put a good match on. When I say I just wanted to put a good match on, I had no idea what I was capable of.

I just remember Nattie telling me, "Listen to me. I promise, it will be great." I took her words to heart. I wanted to gain her respect, but at the same time I had to listen, because I still didn't really know what I was doing. I just knew that she promised to take care of me!

I did a few things for that match. One, I prepared myself like never before. I envisioned how everything should happen from start to finish. It all revolved around feeling: how I should feel walking in, at different points of the match, and at the end. Before, I went through the motions I had memorized with little feeling or depth. I did exactly what Nattie told me. I listened to her, I let her guide me, and I poured my entire heart and soul into that match.

Nattie knew what this meant to me.* She knew what my family had suffered through. I told her I was dedicating this match to my brother, that I tried to envision what it would feel like to win the title, and that I teared up every time I thought about it and Reider. I couldn't believe I had made it this far. I wanted to do it for him.

Something special was announced for our match. My dad would be in my corner, and Nattie's uncle, legend Bret Hart, would be in hers. My dad and Bret worked together in WWE and WCW. Their relationship hit a rough patch because of things they both said about one another. When they saw each other backstage, they smiled and shook hands. You could tell how proud they were to be there.

It was special for us to have the match elevated in importance by having our legendary family members at ringside, but when the bell rang, Nattie and I made sure our work spoke for itself. This battle was about us and the NXT Women's Championship.

We wanted to establish a big-fight, championship feel to the match. Natalya, the storied competitor from an iconic bloodline, had the experience, poise, and grace of a champion. My character, Charlotte, was the brash, second-generation competitor on the rise.

It was important to show us going hold for hold and move for move to establish the groundwork for the intense story we were going to tell. We engaged in reversals of one another's moves, close pin-fall attempts, and going toe-to-toe with one another. This was the story of a true struggle. To the audience, perhaps both of us met our match?

The match seemed to be over when I was locked in Natalya's Sharpshooter, but when I rolled through to reverse the move into my version of the figure-four leg lock, the tables continued to turn. We raised the tension ever more when we slapped each other in the face while still being locked in the hold. We rolled out of the ring and hung off the apron

---

*Natalya: "I could relate to where Ashley came from. When I started my career, I wanted to prove myself. I didn't want people to think I was doing this because of my family name and that I expected an easy ride. For the match at TakeOver, Triple H believed in us. He told me to do what I wanted to do, that I was in charge. Then he said, 'You don't have a time limit.'"

while still locked in the hold. We wanted the audience to feel that both women were consumed with the thought of being recognized as the NXT Women's Champion.

Back in the ring, I regained the advantage. I picked up my leg and instead of locking in the figure four again, I committed the classic act of "adding insult to injury." I used Natalya's Sharpshooter against her. This time, I taunted her uncle Bret, who stood on the outside. This time, Natalya reversed the hold and was going to lock me in. At this stage in the match, it would've resulted in my character meeting her impending doom, but that night in Orlando, the story read differently.

I kicked out of Natalya's Sharpshooter attempt and hit my finishing move. The Full Sail University faithful counted as referee Charles Robinson's hand hit the canvas. I still couldn't believe that this time, I'd hear the audience say, "Three!"

Being announced as the new NXT Women's Champion was surreal. After my dad came into the ring, I needed to see Natalya. Having this moment with her meant so much to me. My dad and Bret hugged, and the four of us enjoyed a moment in the ring.

Nattie and Bret exited the ring. I celebrated with my dad. It was like we were the only two people in the arena. Both my parents always supported me 100 percent. They went to every recital, meet, competition, and game. For my dad to go from the stands at a volleyball game to my corner ringside was a thrill I couldn't quite grasp. We kept the celebration going right up the ramp. That's where it ended for the people in the audience. Backstage, the moment continued.

The first person I saw was Dusty in his camouflage jacket. I could see the pride radiating from every fiber of his being. I put my arms around him and cried.

The second person I saw was Hunter. He looked so proud. Hunter's watched me grow up since I was a little girl. He knew how special that moment was. He's always been a text or phone call away. That night, he was there in person. I wanted to show him what I was really made of and that NXT was my home. He wrapped his arms around me and put his hands on my face. It was like I was one of his daughters.

One of my favorite moments was when I went into the locker room and celebrated with the women I worked with every day.

The Divas Revolution started with two women at ArRival. It was up to every woman who trained at the Performance Center and performed on NXT cards to develop that foundation and make it stronger. We needed to make the most of every opportunity and build on that for the next time.

I was one of the women in the ring who celebrated Paige's winning the NXT Women's Championship a year before. Paige was an outstanding champion. Paige and Emma's match at ArRival elevated the prestige of the championship. Out of respect for them and respect for the women at the Performance Center who gave everything they had every day, I knew my work had to continue to improve.

After the show, Tom, Mom, Dad, and I went to the sushi restaurant at Dad's hotel in the airport. I remember taking pictures with the NXT title in the car on the way there. I was bursting with pride. It was sitting in my lap, and I kept thinking, *I did it. I really did it.*

Having dinner with the three of them after that match was rare and very special to me. They were all so proud. I actually think I surpassed my dad's and Tom's expectations.* I blew them away! It was a night I will never forget. I had no idea what the future would hold, but I had this night. It had a piece of my heart forever.

In one sense, this win represented how far I had come as a person and as a performer.† On the other hand, it served as my motivation to savor

---

*Sara Amato: "I noticed right away that Ashley was a standout athlete. What stood out to me was her heart. She was the hardest-working person at the Performance Center, and she was a showtime player. When the cameras were on and she was in front of an audience, she took it to another level. She was very special from the beginning. The NXT Women's Championship was an important milestone for her."

†Ric: "People don't understand when I say Ashley did this all on her own. I was not involved. John Laurinaitis asked her why wasn't she doing this at a dinner after my Hall of Fame induction with the Horsemen. I asked Paul to call her about it, and that was it. She did this by herself. I thought it was a great match and so important for Ashley's confidence.

this moment of victory and realize that I had a long way to go. I couldn't get to this point and walk away. This was destiny calling, and it symbolized another beginning in my young life.

I was on cloud nine. I felt I could do anything after that match. When I found a few quiet moments to myself, I couldn't do the one thing I wanted to: call Reider.

I wouldn't have been there were it not for him being my biggest advocate to give wrestling a shot. I went to dinner with him and our dad to speak with a WWE executive about what Reider needed to do. No one seated at that table knew how lost I was, how much pain I was in, and how much help I needed. Now, two years removed from that night, I was holding the NXT Women's Championship. It was so hard accepting that I couldn't call the one person I knew would've been there, the one person

---

That's the only way you get better is to keep working in the ring. Ashley had an incredible partner to dance with in Natalya. Nattie is so talented as a performer. I'll always remember what she did for my daughter. I couldn't have been prouder of Ashley that night. Seeing my daughter perform in that match was the biggest moment of my wrestling career.

There was a period where I wasn't able to be there with Ashley. In the fall of 2013, I entered a rehabilitation facility for alcohol. I also needed to process the suffering I was going through after Reid's death. The day I had to go in I called Melinda and completely cracked. I realized immediately that the lifestyle to which I had become accustomed was definitely not my new reality. I was living in a group facility with no air-conditioning. I shared a room with someone. I looked around my room and said, "This sure isn't a suite at the Ritz-Carlton." That wasn't the worst of it. I didn't know how anyone ate the food. A rule of the program was no phone calls but I snuck my phone and called Melinda every single day. She never missed one of my calls. I asked her to overnight me food and clothes. I wouldn't have made it through that time if I didn't have Melinda to speak to every day.

I think I got better because I wanted to get out of there so badly. There was also another reason: Wendy.

This was another time Wendy could've left. Instead, she was there for me every step of the way. She visited me every single weekend. Wendy's unconditional love and boundless positivity made me look forward to the weekend. She never made me feel like I was trapped somewhere or that I should feel ashamed for being where I was. Wendy was always upbeat and kept me in good spirits. This was another difficult time she helped me get through, and didn't expect anything in return. She did it because she loved me. Wendy needs to know I made it through one of the most difficult times of my life because of her."

I wanted to be there. I knew after that match I was going to live his dream for the both of us.*

Being a champion and what you do as a champion are two different things. I knew the challenges that were ahead. I looked forward to meeting them head-on.

For that night, I was walking on sunshine in legendary footsteps, ready to blaze my own trail.

---

*Ric's Legacy Talent agent, Melinda: "I've seen Ric emotional plenty of times but nothing like that day. He was crying so hard I couldn't understand what he was saying. It's hard to witness someone you are so close to break. Of course by the end of his stay he had made fans of every single person in there with him. Ric bought everyone cable TV for their rooms. I had to ship his WWE DVDs to all the guys in there with him. We still get fan mail from his rehab buddies to this day. Only Ric!"

17

YOU SAY YOU WANT A REVOLUTION

It was our time.

July 2015

After my match with Nattie at TakeOver,* my confidence grew by leaps and bounds. Nattie gave me the ability to believe in myself and to be comfortable in my own skin as a performer. She inspired me by showing what it was like to be a ring general and to be a genuine and unselfish person in this business.

Becoming the second Women's Champion in NXT history meant everything to me.

I wanted to enrich the prestige of the championship because of Paige's work as champion, my own goals as a performer, and because of what the championship meant during Paige's reign. I came a long way from the days of watching NXT tapings on the video screens in the classroom at the Performance Center. I wanted to bring my skill and dedication center stage and say, "Hey, you did that, and it was incredible. Now watch this." I wanted to up the ante, raise the bar, and continue the momentum— and not just be Ric Flair's daughter.

---

*Natalya: "That night, I wanted to make sure I gave Ashley the special moment she deserved. I think our match at TakeOver was when she broke through and found herself as a performer."

More than anything, it was all about the amazing work the women did in the Performance Center and what the championship meant to all of us. The way that was accomplished was through having great matches with every opponent I met in the ring.

It also included improving the areas I focused on before my match with Nattie: the strength of my character, the emotion behind what I said and did, and bringing the audience deeper into my performance. I didn't want to rely on my athleticism to execute impressive acrobatic moves; the moves did not mean anything in the larger sense of my character and the story I wanted to tell. I needed to further develop that ability and, as a villain, make the crowd despise me.

Despite focusing my attention on the many areas of my performance that did not revolve around athleticism, I started to incorporate some of my dad's moves and mannerisms into my character: chops, the knee drop, and of course, saying, "WOOOOO!" My finishing move's name appropriately changed to Natural Selection.

I wanted to work with Coach Sara on new maneuvers. A lot of moves I did were created when I'd play around in the ring with her and Norman Smiley, just trying new things. I was training in the ring with them when she suggested I try the figure-four leg lock. When the move was applied, she suggested I bring my body back into a bridge. Most people don't believe me when I tell them that Sara showed me how to apply the figure four—not my dad!

Once I performed the figure four with the bridge, I didn't know what to call it. Simon Gotch of the Vaudevillains, who was always so creative, was standing outside the ring and said, "You should name that the Figure Eight—twice as good as your dad's." And that was it. Something similar happened when Kassius Ohno saw my finishing move and said, "You should call that Natural Selection."

To be at the Performance Center, to perform on NXT cards and experience NXT's growth was incredibly rewarding. What was supposed to be a training ground for the future of WWE became its own brand. The weekly NXT program, which was supposed to give us experience performing in front of a television audience with scheduled live specials, became one of the most popular programs on the WWE Network. NXT Superstars had their own merchandise, trading cards, action figures; they were featured in the WWE video game. NXT was a legitimate, individual entity. People spoke about it as a third brand in the same breath as *Raw* and *SmackDown*.

To be someone who was highlighted on the NXT specials on the WWE Network, part of the NXT weekly show opening montage, and to be featured prominently on the NXT programs were indicators that my approach was working, but I had to continue learning and improving. I even received more requests from media outlets to do interviews. The pressure grew every week. I loved it!

I was so proud to be a part of this group of men and women who were committed to making NXT a success.

My first string of title defenses was against Bayley. Bayley became one of the most, if not the most, popular personality in NXT. The bond she shared with the audience became stronger every week. The fans felt a lot of sympathy for Bayley. They loved getting behind her and seeing her overcome the obstacles she faced.

I continued to perform in tag team matches alongside my BFF partner, Sasha. Around that time, I started to work with another incredible talent: Becky Lynch.

Becky is from Ireland. She's loved WWE from the time she was a child and has an incredible background. After being trained in wrestling by Finn Bálor, Becky performed in Europe, Canada, Mexico, the United States, and Japan. She studied Muay Thai in Thailand, was a personal trainer, got her degree in acting, and studied the art of the clown. Above all her talents, from the moment I met her, I knew Becky was a kind, genuine person. We became fast friends.

A story line was created on NXT TV where the BFFs would implode. Sasha and I beat Bayley and Becky Lynch in a tag team match. But when I didn't help her against Bayley, it marked the end of the villainous group and put Sasha and me on a collision course to do battle for the NXT Women's Championship.

Things were changing in front of the cameras and behind the scenes.

In the ring, the NXT fans began to support me after my match with Nattie. They started to respect me and my work. It meant a lot because those fans had seen me grow up professionally. To be respected for my work, especially when I was so new compared to many of my colleagues, made me feel good. On the other hand, this was not something I expected, especially since I was a five-foot-ten blond daughter of Ric Flair who proclaimed that she was genetically superior to everyone else. That didn't sound like the kind of performer who could endear herself to the fans or evoke feelings of sympathy.

I was excited to work with Sasha. I knew we were going to have great matches, but away from the cameras, something had changed.

After I won the NXT Women's Championship from Nattie, Sasha and I still traveled and trained together. But something was different.

Sasha took umbrage with the fact that the company made me the NXT Women's Champion. She felt that she deserved to have the match with Nattie and to be the one holding the championship at the end of the night. Sasha felt that she should've been crowned the NXT Women's Champion because of her talent and dedication and because she was more experienced than I was.

I understood why Sasha was upset and angry. She was an incredible talent, day in and day out. What I didn't understand was why she would end her friendship with me because of a decision someone else made, and in this case, a company decision.

It's not like I demanded to be champion or that I said I should be champion instead of Sasha. I always spoke about how much she helped me during our time in developmental, how much I learned from her, and how talented she was. I was proud to say Sasha pushed me as a performer and how much I admired her hard work and dedication.

A decision was made, and that decision involved me. Being angry with someone because of a decision the company made was something I just didn't understand. Some might say, "Well, that's easy for you to say when the outcome benefited you." I didn't know of any determination or outcome beforehand. I would've moved forward the same way, because I didn't make the decision.

We worked together throughout the summer and fall. As is the case with former tag team partners, Sasha and I had tremendous chemistry in the ring as opponents. It resulted in a great series of matches.

Sasha's resentment took a pointed turn during NXT's final episode before the December TakeOver special. I knew where the segment was going in terms of setting us up for our match. I didn't realize that she was going to take one of my DO IT WITH FLAIR T-shirts and cut it so it would say, DO IT LIKE A BOSS. I also didn't know she was going to say negative things about my dad. At one point she even referred to him as a "pathetic old man."

That's when I knew that the fire people saw from the Boss character had truly arrived—it was real. Sasha felt that she was overlooked. She thought she was passed over and underutilized. She thought she had to fight for what she believed in—that Sasha was the best.

I would've been fine with all those things. I just thought Sasha would've spoken to me about them first. The situation was disappointing, especially when I remember how we came up together. I never imagined that I'd become alienated from someone I had so admired professionally and someone I considered a friend. I thought we'd be working "together" in every sense of the word, but I was wrong.

As 2014 came to a close, I got a taste of life on the road with the WWE main roster. I performed in matches at WWE live events and in matches for arena audiences before WWE programming went on the air. Three memorable shows were from Columbia, South Carolina, Augusta, Georgia, and back home in Charlotte. They featured six Diva tag matches where I teamed with Emma and Alicia Fox against Paige, who was the WWE Divas Champion, and the Bella Twins, Nikki and Brie.

To help promote NXT's December 11 TakeOver special, I appeared on the December 8 episode of *Monday Night Raw.*

When I walked to the ring, I heard the crowd say, "WOOOOO!" I knew I was in Flair country, but that was from my dad's work. I didn't assume that the audience knew who I was. Whether you're a "good guy" or a "bad guy," you never want silence when you appear in front of an audience. There were two people in the crowd who knew me: my sister, Megan, and Reider's girlfriend, Whitney, were there to cheer me on.

I took control early in the match. I hit Nattie with heavy strikes and enjoyed returning to my villainous roots for the night by talking trash to my opponent, her husband, Tyson, who was in her corner, and the referee. I loved telling the referee, "I heard you the first time," when he'd order me to break a hold.

Nattie and I went back and forth, and one of the loudest reactions during the match was when I hit her with the signature Flair chop. We traded reversals for our finishing submission moves. On that night, Nattie's experience helped her roll me up for the pinfall victory.

The match was about two and a half minutes. Would I have loved more time for my match on *Raw*? Would I have loved to leave *Raw* victorious before NXT's major event? Of course. Anyone in my position would have. I was grateful for the opportunity to appear on the show. It wasn't about winning or losing my match; it was about making the most of the time I had to help promote NXT to the larger *Raw* audience. I was happy that the crowd reacted strongly during the match and that they were invested in what we did. As someone in NXT performing on the main roster, I also wanted to make sure that anything I was asked to do on the show, I did well.

Three days later, it was time for the match at NXT TakeOver: R Evolution. The atmosphere inside the arena was as intense as I had ever known. Half the crowd chanted, "Let's go, Charlotte!" The other half, "Let's go, Sasha!"

This was a head-to-head clash of two former best friends. That was what the audience believed. Away from the squared circle, they didn't know how true that was.

The intensity displayed in the match from the opening bell was more real than two women committed to a compelling performance. We both wanted to be the best. At all costs. Despite this match ending with a Natural Selection on Sasha from the top rope, our story was far from over.

At home, Tom and I worked hard to make time for each other. We completed our first Mud Run together. That Thanksgiving, we went to my grandfather's. For Christmas, I had time off and went to England with him to visit his family. I didn't realize it then, but that served as a harbinger of my life to come: I left his family's home early to do a WWE main roster Christmas tour.

As the NXT Women's Champion, the goal was to raise the bar every time I walked through the curtain, on the microphone during an interview segment, and in the ring. I think that as matches continued to get better, we showed we respected the men's work. They respected ours and knew we created an excitement for the NXT product. The guys never denied our passion. It was just a matter of wanting to be as good as the men. It took all of us working together and a lot of trust on NXT's part.

When I saw Paige, Emma, Summer Rae, and Lana make their debuts on the *Raw* roster, it was like the future was real. I could see a path to WWE through NXT if I continued to improve as a performer. That's what I wanted more than anything else, but it didn't happen for me when I thought it would.

My match at NXT TakeOver: Rival was a Fatal 4-Way against Sasha, Bayley, and Becky.

This meant the first person who scored a victory by pin fall or submission would be the winner. From a story perspective, this puts the champion—in this case, me—at an immediate disadvantage because the champion doesn't have to be the one who loses to lose the championship.

That's the type of suspense we want to sustain for the audience. For us, the storytellers, that's where the fun begins.

In the opening minutes of the match, I was out of action after Becky Lynch threw me into the LED board on the side of the ring. On TV, Becky and Sasha had a business association, not a friendship. The match showed how fragile that relationship was when Becky turned on Sasha after the Boss tried to order Becky around and found herself on the wrong end of a perfectly executed pump handle suplex.

Becky turned her attention to Bayley until Sasha returned to the fray. One of the things that impressed me about Becky was that she could perform the classic "ground and pound" European style just as well as executing a missile dropkick from the top rope.

When I returned to the match, Becky and Sasha were my targets. Sasha turned the tables and flattened Becky and me with a double knee in the corner.

The match continued at a fast pace. The crowd came unglued when Bayley brought me down with a top rope Bayleycanrana, which was followed up with a Bayley-to-Belly off the top rope.

The match was all but over until Becky interrupted the referee's count. The crowd was on a ride, and we weren't done yet. Coach Sara did a great job in putting this match together.

Sasha took everyone's heart rate right through the roof after she landed a dive outside the ring onto Bayley and Becky. I followed that up with a high-risk maneuver of my own and launched myself over the top rope onto my three opponents.

We wanted to show that all four competitors would pull out all the stops to be the NXT Women's Champion.

The night belonged to the Boss. Sasha had me locked in a crossface submission. She released it only to roll me up for a pin fall—and the victory.

After 259 days, my reign as NXT Women's Champion was over. Sasha was the new champion. It was her time to take the championship to a new level.

In that match, Bayley showed the aggressive side to her lovable character, and Becky emerged as a top contender for the NXT Women's

Championship. As for me, it was my time to prepare for the main roster—or so I thought.

While I hoped to get the call I had been waiting for, I heard about something that a WWE Diva said about me during a press interview.

Paige was asked what she thought about me and the possibility of me being called up to WWE's main roster. Paige said that I was good but that I needed more time and that Sasha was the complete package.

Everyone's entitled to an opinion. It disappointed me that someone I admired professionally, who was a WWE Diva with incredible equity with the fans, had made an assessment like that. Paige knew how hard I worked and how well my work was received. She knew I had been in the developmental program for two and a half years and knew what that was like. I understood everyone's experience level was different, including work on the independents, but I didn't expect her to say I wasn't ready for the main roster.

NXT's popularity continued to rise. For the first time, when NXT went on the road for a live event, it shot right past the Florida state line to the Arnold Sports Festival in Columbus, Ohio.

The next date that jumped off my calendar was March 27, 2015. The NXT live show in San Jose, California, during WrestleMania weekend. I had an NXT Women's Championship match with Sasha.

The crowd was electric before the match started. Chants of "This is wrestling!" filled the arena as Sasha and I exchanged holds, reversals, and used every inch of the ring and arena floor to tell our story.

When I chopped the Boss and a sea of "WOOOOOs!" came over the crowd, Sasha, as always, did a great job in turning the tables to keep the crowd on their toes. Chants of "Let's go, Sasha!" and "Let's go, Charlotte!" bounced back and forth to opposite sides of the arena.

After almost twenty minutes, Sasha ended it with her Bank Statement submission. Sasha and I tore the house down. The crowd showed their appreciation for our work in the form of a standing ovation.

When the crowd chanted, "Thank you, Charlotte!" I thought about how far I've come in such a short period of time. I couldn't figure out why I didn't debut on the *Raw* the next night after WrestleMania. By that point, I'd been on several live-event shows with the main roster. I felt I was ready. It became more of a challenge to remain positive.

The four of us—Sasha, Bayley, Becky, and I—developed a nickname reminiscent of when my father was in the ring. Because of our work, the fans referred to us as the Four Horsewomen.

At first, I was hesitant to embrace this because of mixed martial artist Ronda Rousey and her group of fierce fighters who were already called that, but I figured since my dad was a founder of the original group and I was considered a part of this one, it was okay.

The reason this meant a lot to me was because this was real. No one said, "Let's package these women from NXT together and call them 'the Four Horsewomen.'" It was something that happened naturally through the fans admiring our work and contributions to wrestling. When I realized that, I couldn't have been prouder to hold up my hand with that familiar symbol with three women I admired. We all fought hard every night for the progression of women's wrestling and for it to be featured and appreciated in the same light as the men's.

The four of us wanted the term *women's wrestling* to be used only to describe that females were participants in the matches and not an adjective used to describe a certain style of in-ring performance or story line.

Days turned into weeks, weeks turned into months, and I didn't hear anything formal about being called up to the main roster.* I heard rumors around the Performance Center that the Horsewomen were going to be called up together. I tried not to look online, but the talk on many sites posted similar stories.

NXT continued to tour outside of Florida: Sasha and I main-evented the first of two nights in Philadelphia. NXT then went to Pittsburgh, Cleveland, and Albany.

---

*Ric: "Ashley reminded me of me. When I started out, I was so eager to succeed and just wanted to know how I was doing. I remember hounding Harley Race and Terry Funk. 'Do you think I'll be the world champion one day? Do you think I have what it takes to make it? When do you think that would be?' I annoyed the hell out of them. Now I was getting a dose of my own medicine. Ashley wanted to make it to the main roster more than anything."

The buildings were packed, and everyone was in NXT shirts. With everything going so well, the fact that I wasn't brought up to the main roster started to weigh on me.

I felt that all my worries and anxieties were coming true. Was I not going to make it? WWE was known for having a "Divas" look. It resembled more glamorous swimsuit models and less of how I saw myself—a woman who was physically larger in stature.

Did I become part of the description of things that succeeded in NXT but would not succeed on the main roster?

I tried to keep things in perspective. One night when I came home from an NXT event, I heard through the grapevine that when I was training in Tampa, Riki impregnated a girl from his past. This happened almost a year to the date of his corrective surgery. Someone was watching over me. I thanked God again that I made it out and that I was free. I said a prayer for that woman and her child. Then I turned my attention to what was happening in my own home.

Tom and I did everything we could to make our schedules work, but it was work that always interfered. Tom was unhappy with where he was professionally. He wanted to do more with his wrestling talent. He continued to get independent bookings in England and receive high praise for his work. Soon after, Tom was hired by TNA Wrestling. I was very happy for him and knew he could be successful there. Our schedules continued to work against each other.

When I came home from the road, Tom was leaving. When I was leaving, he came home. Tom's travel schedule changed, his group of friends changed, and the little time we'd dedicated to each other before was now gone. We both devoted ourselves to our work, not each other. We started to drift apart. Going to theme parks and sushi Sundays felt like a world away.

A part of me felt like Tom wanted to go back to the partying lifestyle of old-school wrestling: living out of your suitcase, every night in a different town and a different good time after the shows. He used to say, "Wrestling's not wrestling anymore." I'd think, *It is to me*. We wanted different things. At that point, I felt that I had outgrown the relationship. I remembered that first call with Hunter and what he told me about relationships not lasting.

In interviews with people in sports and entertainment, I always heard that the life makes it very difficult to maintain relationships. They'd say, "Our schedules were different," and you wonder how that could be. I can attest that it does happen and can end a relationship. And we weren't even famous.

I went from one relationship to another. Looking back, that was not good for me. I needed time to heal from my relationship with Riki. I needed to process what went on in my life during that time and reestablish myself as a person. In many ways, because we were truly friends, Tom helped me do that. The romantic relationship should've waited, but things don't always work out that way. Life's not like it is in the movies.

A few weeks later, Tom and I officially went our separate ways. I shook his hand and said, "Thank you for giving me my life back. Thank you for being there for me when my brother died and for teaching me so much about wrestling." I felt like I had lost my best friend, but distance and recognizing that I wasn't happy with things—and being strong enough to end it—were the best things I had ever done.

I had to rid myself of the mind-set that someone else or someone else's perceptions of me would make me happy. I had to make myself happy first. If this was really my dream, I had to focus on myself. It was time for me to focus on me.

I moved out that morning. That night, I was in a tag team match with Bayley against Emma and Dana Brooke.

About a week later, I heard from Hunter. He wanted to check in to see how I was doing. He offered to help in any way he could.

He found out that my dad put his Hall of Fame ring on Reider's finger during his funeral services. A couple of months later, he sent my dad another Hall of Fame ring. He's always been there for me and my family. And it's not just us.

So many times, I've seen him go out of his way to help people. It's not for the cameras or a promotional appearance or a business function. For all the times people have asked him for help, I've seen even more instances when he's not asked; Hunter senses that someone might be going through something, or he sees that something has happened professionally or personally, and he reaches out.

Sometimes things happen when you least expect it. One of my favorite classes at the Performance Center was Terry Taylor's class. I learned so much about crowd psychology and the way to build a story. I was reviewing notes from that day's class when I received the news: the time had come—I was being called up to the main roster!

I didn't know all the details. I knew I'd be debuting on *Raw* in Atlanta, Georgia, and that I'd find out more when I got there. There were a lot of questions. The only thing I knew for sure was that I wouldn't be going to *Raw* alone.

After a lifetime of being backstage with my dad at wrestling shows and backstage at *Raw* over the last fourteen years, I was still nervous. I wasn't there as a guest. Now I was making my WWE debut.

The idea was that Becky, Sasha, and I would debut together in a segment opposing Team Bella, which consisted of WWE Divas Champion Nikki Bella, Brie Bella, and Alicia Fox. Becky and I were aligned with Paige as "good guys." We became known as Team PCB. Sasha joined Naomi and Tamina to make up Team B.A.D.

I was a bit concerned that I'd debut as a "good guy," because my character was created to be the supervillain. The NXT fans cheered for me because they had seen me develop and they respected me, which meant so much, but they didn't love the Charlotte character. I wasn't sure the WWE audience would find her appealing either.

My main concern was not debuting individually. I had dropped the NXT title in the Fatal 4-Way five months prior. Then Sasha and I had the great match at NXT San Jose. I became a "good guy" for that program with her, but after that, I felt I had lost momentum.

The idea for this debut sounded exciting. Being moments away from making my entrance, I was reminded that someone was missing: it was Bayley.

I felt for Bayley. The Four Horsewomen did it together; I felt that she should have been with us. I knew she was going to lead NXT and continue to evolve, but I wanted her to be a part of that night too.

My heart raced as I watched the segment from the monitor. Stephanie McMahon led the way on the microphone and introduced us one by one. I really felt like I had finally made it!

Once my music hit and I walked to the ring, I was overcome with the energy and electricity of the moment. I felt that the audience was ready for it, and so was I.

As the crowd chanted, "This is awesome!" Team Bella was surrounded. The battle lines were drawn. All the anxiety of making my debut and the self-doubt took its toll. This moment was proof that it was happening at the right time.

After more than a nine-minute debut segment on *Monday Night Raw*, the women from NXT emerged from a furious exchange in the ring and put the famous Team Bella into our respective submission moves.

The revolution made its way to WWE and kicked the door down. It was our time.*

In front of the cameras, we challenged Team Bella's glamorous triumvirate. Coming into WWE as rookies and developing a rapport with everyone, well, that was a different matter.

Before I debuted, someone called to tell me that I was being talked about negatively in the locker room. Forewarned is forearmed. I realized I had an uphill climb ahead.

After I debuted, a few people on the roster told me that my reputation in the locker room wasn't the best (no surprise). I figured, *That's the way it goes when you're new.* You have to give people time. In this profession, some people feel that new talent coming in is a threat to their position on

---

*Paul Levesque: "Ashley's part of a select group of women who are catalysts responsible for the dynamic way female competitors are presented to our audience. She needed to reinvent herself. She needed to create her own path and not be the second coming of Ric but be the first Charlotte."

the roster. Other performers are excited to have the opportunity to work with new people.

I knew that to people who didn't know me, sometimes I may have come across as a bit of a snob because I was quiet. That's because away from the cameras, I'm a shy person. I was also from a different roster of women. I knew that I just needed the opportunity to show my work ethic and let people see that I was a team player. Of course, I wanted to be in the title picture—who doesn't? But I wasn't going to be selfish or high maintenance. I just needed some time.

The women of NXT were given the platform to display their talents in a prominent way. The WWE Divas fought for those opportunities, but they weren't there. On an episode of *Raw*, there was a tag match that featured Paige and Emma versus the Bellas. The match ended in thirty seconds. The hashtag #GiveDivasAChance became the top-trended hashtag on social media for several days. That's what they dealt with every week. It was natural that there was some tension in the beginning.

I learned that because I was Ric Flair's daughter, it wasn't easy to reverse preconceived notions about me in the locker room. As the daughter of the Nature Boy, it was even harder dealing with criticism from the fans in the ring.

Another adjustment was the travel schedule. There was a real comfort level in the structure and regimen of the Performance Center. The WWE main roster was a whole different beast. I took for granted that, until NXT traveled out of Florida for events, we were in our own beds every night. We didn't have to work on Sundays, plus we had two weeks off for Christmas, and other holidays too.

I didn't know enough to value being developmental talent and having NXT pay for tour buses, hotel rooms, and catered food.

On the main roster, you sink or swim. WWE is a machine that runs twenty-four hours a day, seven days a week. You either move with it or it moves without you.

My itinerary was something like this:

- Fly out Friday morning
- Land at the airport
- Rent a car
- Find a gym
- Find a grocery store
- Pray that grocery store is a Whole Foods
- Make it to the arena by call time
- Work the event
- Drive to the next town
- Check into the hotel
- Wake up
- Work out
- Work the event
- Fly home Wednesday
- Repeat

That didn't include promotional appearances, photo and video shoots backstage at the venue, and press interviews.

For *Raw* and *SmackDown*, call time is 1:00 p.m. You're in a different city every night. We also finished up working in NXT. It was a grind, but there was something about it I loved.

For me, dieting was the hardest part because I was such a strict eater in NXT. I maintained that but learned to live a little!

What I was most thankful for during this time was that Becky was my travel partner. We navigated the main roster as well as the highways and byways of the United States together. We trained together and worked on honing our skills. Becky was the Thelma to my Louise. Getting used to the schedule was the most difficult part of the debut. And we didn't want to just debut; we wanted to make a difference.

In front of the cameras, I adjusted to being a part of Team PCB. We had singles, tag team, and six-person matches against variations of Team Bella and Team B.A.D. members. I didn't feel that I could lead a match the way I did in NXT. I didn't have Coach Sara and Norman Smiley. I knew the producers, but I had to start over to build that rapport and level of trust.

I felt a little out of place because Paige was a huge star with a great fan following. Becky came into her own as a hero. The fans adored her quirky wit, natural charm, and steampunk edge. Both women were phenomenal in the ring. I was Ric Flair's daughter who called herself genetically superior. That's so arrogant! I knew the company saw the bigger picture. I just felt out of place.

The way things progressed on TV, I emerged as the challenger to Nikki's Divas Championship.

Nikki was great from the moment we started working together. The members of Team Bella, as performers, debuted in WWE when the company was removed from competitive matches that Trish Stratus and Lita had, but before the company went to a PG rating, so the Divas were doing more provocative things on WWE programming. They only had a couple of minutes in the ring. The matches were not competitive. What the company had envisioned for female talent was different.

The women on the main roster wanted to go into that ring when the bell rang just like we did! All of a sudden, there were three NXT girls who were thrust into the spotlight. While they fought for opportunities to show what they could do in the ring, Nikki evolved into a top villain.

Until about a week before Night of Champions, I wasn't sure who would be the new Divas Champion.

Before the pay-per-view, I had a title match on *Raw* against Nikki. The Bellas performed their classic Twin Magic—where one Bella rolls out of the ring and the other rolls inside it. In the story line, I thought I pinned Nikki when I pinned Brie. The crowd went wild when they thought I was the new champion and Nikki wouldn't become the longest-reigning Divas Champion in WWE history. The story continued . . .

To make people detest Nikki even more, Stephanie McMahon announced that I couldn't win the title by pinning someone who wasn't the champion, and when Brie Bella touched me, it was considered outside interference. I won by disqualification, but I didn't win the championship.

Stephanie announced that my rematch was set for that Sunday's Night of Champions pay-per-view.

The day of the event, Becky drove us to the building. I wasn't sure how things were going to go.

Preparing for my first WWE championship match on a pay-per-view created an emotional day. Two of the most important people who believed in me and who were part of my journey to WWE weren't there.

I thought of my brother. I wondered if he could see me wrestle. My mom told me that she and Reider watched one of my first FCW matches online before he went to Japan. I don't count that. I wanted him there with me. I'm here because of him.

I was reminded of Dusty, who passed away three months before. I wondered what he'd say to me on the phone, me calling from the hotel in Houston and him speaking from his office at the Performance Center.

I didn't know who my character was. Why would the company choose me? Becky thrived in PCB and became the ultimate hero. Sasha had come off her two biggest matches thus far in NXT: dropping the title to Bayley in an all-time classic at NXT TakeOver: Brooklyn that August; followed by her Women's Iron Man Match with Bayley. Becky and Sasha had a ton of momentum. I felt like I was just Charlotte, Ric Flair's athletic, blond daughter. I didn't have any equity as a character.

When I won the Divas title, I didn't feel ready. I remember standing in the ring with it, proud of the moment and what it meant to me personally. I pointed up at Reider. As a talent, I didn't feel like a star. I didn't exude confidence.

Sasha was angry that she was not in the match with Nikki and that she was not leaving Night of Champions as the Divas Champion. At that point, Sasha was so good, she didn't need the championship. I needed it to elevate my persona. I felt that Sasha didn't understand that. Instead, she believed that the only reason I was in the match was because I was Ric Flair's daughter.

I didn't understand how she couldn't see that winning the championship elevated my character. Then we could have the high-quality matches we were known for, and she would win the title in grand fashion.

Nikki was a star. When Nikki Bella walked through that curtain, she owned the camera. If I was going to pick up where the longest-reigning Divas Champion in history left off, I needed that level of confidence to walk through the curtain.

I learned a great deal from Nikki, especially about the importance of presentation and the overall picture. By the time our rematch happened at Hell in a Cell, we had a strong working relationship. I felt like I had earned her respect. It was a good feeling.

The importance of my character really hit me when my music played in Atlanta for my match against Paige at the Survivor Series pay-per-view. I was the "good guy," and she was the villain.

The arena that had roared for me when I debuted there four months before was now resonating with boos. Just walking to the ring felt like an uphill battle. I kept second-guessing myself. What was right? What was wrong? The one thing I took away from that night was that the audience had a response. I had to go with it.*

After two months together, Team PCB splintered.

About a week before the TLC pay-per-view, I got news that put me in a state of shock: the company was pairing me with my dad full-time!†

---

*Ric: "During my career, there were certain guys who the fans loved giving their full support to during their climb to the world title. But once they got the championship and had to be the lead person to carry a story line and a championship, to have a thirty- or sixty-minute match, or have the quality of interviews where the fans are buying tickets, or watching a weekly TV program, or buying a pay-per-view based on what they said, the same enthusiasm wasn't there. It fell short. That's taken for granted, because when it's done properly, you don't notice it. People think anyone with a good physical appearance, or great athletic ability, or great interview skills can do all those things. To be the absolute best in this profession, you need to have all those things working together every night. That's why I talk about the 'total performer.' Ashley learned that the best way possible: on the job."

†Ric: "After Reid died, I went into a tailspin. I couldn't accept that my son was gone. I didn't know how to deal with the pain of missing him. I did something I shouldn't have done. For one year, I'd go to a restaurant or bar and begin drinking at eleven o'clock in the morning. I'd stay until it was closing time. I used alcohol to cope with the pain and feeling of guilt that took over. Over the years, so many people paid me the honor of saying I embodied everything they wanted to be. During that time, I became the example of what not to do. I was on the periphery of the business I felt so connected to in my mind and my heart.

My mind started racing. I didn't think of it as, *Oh, great! I get to work with my dad.* I thought, *Oh no! I'm working with my dad? I thought the title was supposed to help me develop! How am I supposed to make a name for myself? How can I match his skills on the microphone? How can I compete with his legacy?*

I had just started my WWE career. Was I going to have less TV time? Would I have less time on the microphone? It was another pivotal moment for me.

The company felt that pairing us together would help the audience relate to me as a "good guy." Fans would embrace the father-daughter relationship. But that didn't happen.

It was sink or swim. I wanted to rise to the challenge and see what obnoxious, arrogant, and despicable places I could take my character.

I was disappointed that someone like Sasha made posts on social media about being held back, implying that I had my position because of my dad. It was similar to what happened after I became the NXT Women's Champion. Her anger about the company's decision was projected onto me.

I turned the negativity into something I could use on the air. I transformed what people said about me into material and created the type of villain I wanted to be.

Going into December, my character started to enjoy taking shortcuts. Since I'm recognized as the daughter of the Dirtiest Player in the Game, this was a natural progression for my character.

My on-air friendship with Becky hung by a thread. During a match, I "faked" a leg injury. My dad distracted Becky, and I picked up the win. The crowd was disgusted. It was wonderful!

During *Raw*'s first episode of 2016, Becky and I solidified my villainy. In the match, when Becky let her guard down, I took advantage with a chop or right-hand strike. Of course, my dad did his part and hooked Becky's leg when she came off the ropes.

I was not myself. I was not ready to return to work with WWE on a consistent basis. I told myself enough was enough. I had children and grandchildren who needed me. I needed to return to being a meaningful part of their lives. The opportunity to work with my daughter every week was not something I ever expected."

When Becky rolled me up and held my tights for the victory, I got a taste of my own medicine, and I didn't like it. I assaulted her from behind. I hit Becky with my spear, and the boos bounced off the rafters.

At the Royal Rumble, there was a surprise. Sasha returned to WWE programming. To commemorate the occasion, the idea was for her to attack me after the match. Who would be my opponent at WrestleMania?

Sasha and Becky competed in a number-one contender's match. The first match ended with a double pin. No winner. The rematch ended when I interfered in the match. That meant the only way this could be settled was in a Triple Threat Match at WrestleMania.

While Becky and I pummeled each other in front of audiences, away from the ring, we were attached at the hip.

From traveling in PCB to our series of matches with one another, I learned to have fun while traveling with my partner in crime. I think the hardest part of this job is dealing with the travel. Finding someone you are compatible with on the road makes all the difference. We followed the same routine, and it worked. We always promised each other if one of us changed, we would call the other out and make sure she came back to earth.

Becky taught me so much as a friend and as a wrestler. I say it all the time, but she is that good a person. The run we had on live events in single matches turned out to be some of my favorite performances. We were finally getting into a rhythm, and everything was clicking. Having the opportunity to work with Becky those months leading up to Wrestle-Mania dramatically impacted my development as a performer.

The work my dad and I did together really took off. It reached a point where the fans booed us when my music hit—when I wasn't even in sight!

Every Monday and Tuesday morning, he'd ordered room service for me in the hotel: a six-egg-white omelet with vegetables. If Becky was riding with us, he ordered one for her one too. My dad knows I like to train and get sleep. He never tried to change my schedule. I think he wished I would relax more, but my mother told me he could never sit still either.

My dad and I had some laughs too. In a match one night, there was a point where he was supposed to take off the turnbuckle pad. The match was due to end when I drove my opponent into it. I hit my head on the post before that point. Instead of taking off the pad, he walked around the ring and checked on me. I said, "Why are you here? What are you doing? You have to take off the turnbuckle pad!"*

During my match with Paige in Germany, I looked at my dad at ringside. He had a huge smile on his face. And he was wooooing at random. He just loved being in my corner. He couldn't have been prouder or been having more fun.

My dad also enjoyed spending time with the guys in the locker room. He'd have everyone rolling with laughter, and he'd tell stories and give advice. He was right there at every show, watching every match on the monitor. On the European tour, he treated almost the entire roster to a night out. He was always the life of the party!

Working with him every week was the opportunity of a lifetime.†

I loved seeing my dad in his element. I thought because today's product moved faster that he wouldn't be in sync with the performance. Boy, was I wrong! He always said, "You'll know when you hear the crowd." That aggravated me because he always called it out there. His level of confidence and work standards were different from mine. Plus, we were father and daughter, so we butted heads now and then. But he was right!

We had so many questions heading into the final *Monday Night Raw* before WrestleMania. We found out the truth about a rumor that had been circulating for months.

Backstage, Stephanie McMahon and Hunter told us that at Wrestle-

---

* Ric: "She screamed at me right in the middle of the match. What was I supposed to do? I thought she was legitimately hurt. You know what she said to me the next day? She said that she was going to write down what I needed to do on the bottom of her boots. I couldn't believe it."

† Ric: "I couldn't describe the feeling of appearing on camera with Ashley. I was so proud of her hard work and how she developed into a top-flight performer in such a brief period of time. The only person I remember picking up our business so quickly was Kurt Angle. I never thought I'd work with her in this way. It was absolutely phenomenal."

Mania, the Divas Championship was going to be retired. I was going to be history's final Divas Champion.

Then they showed us the beautiful white, red, and gold championship that was going to be known as the WWE Women's Championship. To close the Divas chapter, Stephanie told us that women would no longer be called *Divas*. We were now going to be called *Superstars.**

The fact that the company changed the way women were described was a huge statement. I didn't have a problem with the term *Diva*, but to know that we were going to be called *Superstars*, just like the men, was monumental.

I didn't want our matches to be known as *women's matches*. I understood that the term was a way to identify the participants, but the audience needed to know that the match they were going to see was part of a deep story line, and the match was going to be as physical, as intense, and as compelling as a men's match!

Our course was set for Arlington, Texas. The greatest of all time was walking his daughter to the ring in front of an expected crowd of more than one hundred thousand people. I didn't even know how I got there.

The question that hung over me was, "Who would leave the largest WrestleMania in history as the new WWE Women's Champion?"

---

*Stephanie McMahon: "It was a company decision to change the way women were presented to our audience and to no longer refer to them as *Divas* but to call them *Superstars* just like the men. WrestleMania was the best place for WWE to showcase the strength of our female competitors and launch the Women's Evolution. The women deserved it."

18

DEFINING A GENERATION

I didn't dream of success. I earned it.

April 3, 2016

I woke up earlier than usual the morning of WrestleMania. I wanted to have a few minutes to myself before the day began. My family got into town on Thursday. I wanted to see everyone and spend time with them every night. I couldn't wait! I knew my dad was taking them out to great restaurants. I chose sleep.

WrestleMania week was filled with media commitments and promotional appearances. I had to prepare for my match. It was difficult just to find the time to get to the gym.

I also had a special robe made, and I had to try it on one last time before it was complete. I had gone to wrestling shows my whole life. WrestleMania was always special. I'd buy a new dress and get my hair and nails done. Today, I was part of the show and in a hotel ballroom. I was awed by the brilliant artistry of seamstress Terry Anderson. I couldn't wait for my dad to see this robe. I couldn't wait to walk into AT&T Stadium adorned in it.

When I thought about the fact that I was hours away from performing in a match at my first WrestleMania and that it would take place in front of more than one hundred thousand people, I asked myself again, *How did I get here?*

When I think of WrestleMania, I think of Reider, Megan, David, and me sitting in the front row for my dad's last match at WrestleMania XXIV.

It was just four years ago when I went to his WWE Hall of Fame induction for the Four Horsemen. That night in Miami, I was a month away from being in the hospital. I hated my life. I was lost. The only thing I looked forward to was working with my personal training clients. I was in perpetual pain. I didn't think I could live much longer.

When I thought about the path of a professional wrestler and what it takes, I realized that this is something that you're born to do. I could make every excuse to refute that: I was afraid to be a performer; I was petrified of public speaking; I wasn't pretty enough; I wasn't a Diva; when I was a kid watching anyone other than my dad wrestle, I was bored; I just wanted to be a wife and a personal trainer. But no. This was my destiny. Nothing has ever felt as natural to me as wrestling. Reider was the door; he put me on the path to realizing my life's work.

I arrived in Dallas for WrestleMania week on the third anniversary of Reider's passing. My brother left this world too soon, and that's because he was in pain. He couldn't fight anymore. But Reider was brave. From day one, he knew what he wanted to do with his life. He was proud to say that he wanted to become a professional wrestler. Reider was determined to make that happen. My brother lived life. Reider was outgoing, charismatic, charming . . . he was never afraid of who he was. I always played it safe. I always played by the rules.

For so many years, I thought I needed to be my brother's teacher. I thought I needed to save him. I looked out the window to my hotel room, and I was reminded that he saved me. It was Reider who taught me to be proud of who I was. My brother was the person who saved my life.

I looked at a message Reider sent me while he was in Japan. I saved it and read it all the time. He talked about doing conditioning drills in the mountains during his training. How he admired me, how he didn't give up running because of how hard I worked, and how he wanted to be just like me.

When I'm tired, when my body aches from performance after performance, and when I want to quit, I read that. I think of my brother. I can't fail. He didn't fail me, and I'm not going to fail him.

There's a part of me that hasn't accepted that Reider's gone. Sometimes I think that he's just on vacation and that when he comes back, I'm going to tell him everything that's been happening in my life; it's because of him that I'm here. Reider gave me my wings to fly to WWE.

Being one of the women who was featured every week in what became the Divas Revolution was a full-time job. I embraced every second of it. It was a once-in-a-lifetime opportunity to dedicate myself to my passion. I wasn't going to let that pass me by.

I was honored to be highlighted on every house show, every *Raw*, *SmackDown*, pay-per-view, and international tour. I didn't miss a single show or appearance. I didn't miss a step. I was damn proud of that. I wanted to prove that I was the right woman for the job because I was ready to do all the work and to work harder every week. I couldn't control someone criticizing me for how I looked or who my father was. No one could deny my ability to keep up with the schedule. I proved that being a top talent for the company is more than just performing in the ring. It's showing up in top form, every time, no matter the circumstances.

This is a profession where you're always learning.

I dedicated every moment in front of the camera, each second I was in front of the audience, to improving.

I was proud to be the WWE Divas Champion. I didn't want my championship reign to disappear into obscurity because the title was being retired. I didn't want to feel like I was just a placeholder until it was time to usher in the new era of the Women's Championship.

I thought about how little confidence I'd had when I debuted on *Raw* and felt I needed more direction. My transition to turning my character into a villain was slow and deliberate. It was impactful. I felt that was confirmed the night before at the Hall of Fame ceremony. I walked in wearing a black dress and styled my hair in a long ponytail. Once I appeared on screen making my way into the arena, the fans booed passionately. I smiled on the inside for a job well done. I said, "Let my haters be my motivators." In what other profession can you say your work is a success when thousands of people are booing at the mere mention of your name or the first sight of you in an arena?

I was so grateful for my time working with producer Fit Finlay. Fit was a generational wrestler during his career and was instrumental in developing my villainous persona—the vicious, ruthless queen of WWE. Fit also helped me get comfortable performing when I was first called up. One night before I went out on *Raw*, he said, "It's okay to be good."

I dedicated myself to my work in the ring, adding more layers to my character.

There was someone else who was crucial to my development. I would not have made it through my time on the main roster without my best friend, Becky.

For months, every Friday, Saturday, and Sunday, we locked up at live events. I learned so much from listening to her and to the crowd. I began to understand and feel the power we have as performers.

We bounced ideas off each other, laughed together, cried together (sometimes from laughing), and were angry, but we always had each other's backs. We wanted the best for each other. Imagine a friend who has something that you have dreamed about your entire life, but you still give her advice and want her to have that position and success. That's true friendship. Even if I was getting pushed and Becky wasn't, she was there for me. I can't wait for the day when I get to repay her.[*]

Becky and I had been texting and talking all week. She was my go-to person. My dad talked about the business and how lonely it can get. Thanks to traveling with Becky, I never felt that way. My dad turned to partying and the nightlife to deal with the loneliness of the road. Becky

---

[*] Ric: "I've always said, if you can leave this business and count on two hands the number of real friends you have, you're fortunate. Make no mistake about it: Becky Lynch is a special person."

and I had each other. We enjoyed gyms to work out in and mom-and-pop breakfast spots. We had a great list of places!

I thought of my dad . . . this was his return to WrestleMania. Since I started on the main roster, I developed a better understanding of his career and a deeper appreciation for his work as the last traveling NWA World Heavyweight Champion and everything he did when he returned to WWE in 2001.

Now that I found my true calling in being a wrestler, I remembered his final match at WrestleMania XXIV. I had only been in the business for four years. I couldn't imagine someone telling me that after my match at WrestleMania my career was over. My dad had to come to grips with that after more than thirty-five years of doing what he loved. During the time we worked together, I saw the unwavering passion he had for this business.

We had a press event at Reunion Tower. I was in a group with Stephanie McMahon, John Cena, Sting, Roman Reigns, Chris Jericho, and my dad. I walked around the room with the Divas Championship on my shoulder and talked about the women's wrestling movement. My dad was next to me, and AT&T Stadium was in the background. How did I go from driving to work every morning debating who I was and what I stood for to being center stage?

I enjoyed doing media appearances with my dad. I loved seeing him command the attention of an entire room. The week before Dallas, we had an appearance at Madison Square Garden during the Knicks game, and we did media in New York City the entire next day. He was truly my "parent in crime."

There were times when I felt overshadowed. It didn't bother me. He's my dad; he's the man no matter where he goes. I was proud to stand next to him.

He is not afraid to give his opinion. He was able to speak honestly and still say the right thing. I wish he didn't describe me in interviews as the best athlete in WWE. I'd rather prove that through my work, but that's my dad—always proud of his kids!

Ultimately, he is who he says he is. He has an incredible energy and lives every day like it's his last. I've never heard him say that he was tired, hurt, or sick. To be on top of this business for so long like he was requires a mental toughness that I've only come to appreciate in recent years.

During this journey as a member of the WWE roster, I constantly repeated his words to me: "Make sure you know who you are." That was an important reminder as I went into the largest WWE event of the year and what would be the most important performance of my life.

There were times of trepidation. There were moments of doubt. There were many sleepless nights, tears, aches, and pains leading up to this match.

Waves of uncertainty surrounded the outcome of the women's Triple Threat Match at WrestleMania. There was great debate within the company and even wider speculation online about who was going to win.

From our rise through NXT to debuting on *Raw* to me winning the Divas Championship . . . the dissolution of Team PCB . . . my matches with Becky . . . Becky breaking out as a top hero . . . Sasha's return at the Royal Rumble . . . to Sasha breaking away from Team B.A.D. . . . everything came down to one question: Who was going to win the Women's Championship at WrestleMania?

I didn't know the right way to feel. Becky and Sasha would make excellent champions. Maybe I just should've said, "Hey, I had a heck of a run as the Divas Champion. It's time for someone else to have a championship."

Who wouldn't want to win the championship—and a new championship? And on the most spectacular show of the year? Becky and I were able to speak candidly to each other without judgment. In a time of self-doubt, when I wondered if I would be the right choice, Becky was there for me. She had her own career to tend to. She had her own dreams, but she never stopped being my friend.

I asked myself a different question. *Why isn't being in the center image on the front of AT&T Stadium enough?* Clearly, that meant I had achieved a level of notoriety.

Then I realized that I wanted to win the Women's Championship because of the work that had changed the perception of the Divas Championship. It was a collective effort. I felt that my part in that effort showed that I would be just as good a choice as any for the Women's

Championship, especially since my character's change into a merciless villain was well-received by the audience.

I think people and especially some of the male Superstars felt that the women were strong athletes and strong in the ring but that we wouldn't go beyond a certain point in the card.*

It didn't matter how many times that week I saw it, I couldn't believe that Becky, Sasha, and I were in the middle of the picture that was draped across AT&T Stadium. Seeing my picture directly in the center of it reminded me of what I survived to reach that point.

We knew that after WrestleMania, the term *Diva* would be left behind. We were ready to seize the moment at WrestleMania and embrace our future as WWE Superstars.† To have my dad beside me made it perfect. That week, he bought Michael Kors watches for Becky and Sasha, to commemorate the special moment we would share at WrestleMania.

The first thing my dad and I did when we arrived at AT&T Stadium was go to ESPN's broadcast area. Jonathan Coachman interviewed us live on *SportsCenter*.

I looked down at the field from where we were. The stage was enormous. The ring was in the middle of the giant Texas star in the middle of the field. AT&T Stadium dwarfed anything I'd seen when I was at the Citrus Bowl in Orlando.

I rode in a golf cart to the women's locker room. There were two women's matches on the card. Before I knew it, the locker room was packed. All the women looked fantastic. Everyone proudly displayed their new ring gear, which was made specifically for WrestleMania, and the ladies were in the best physical shape of the year. You work all year to perform on WrestleMania's iconic stage.

---

*Ric: "I was happy that Ashley had such great people to work with in Becky and Sasha. Something that I used to have to do when I'd go to different territories was work with people I never worked with before in marquee matches. I knew the three of them were going to have the best match on the card."

†Becky Lynch: "Our goal was not to start a revolution or trend on social media. The women wanted to be viewed as equal to the men. We wanted to be known as great performers who were known for having great matches. The real revolution won't be a hashtag."

This was a special day for the members of the female locker room. The company arranged a group picture of all of us together. It was an important tribute to the women who contributed to the past, present, and future of WWE and the landscape of women's wrestling.

I met with Becky and Sasha to go over some final details for our match. We knew the pressure was on to perform. Our contest was between Brock Lesnar versus Dean Ambrose and the Undertaker versus Shane McMahon.

Hell in a Cell.

Becky, Sasha, and I had excellent training sessions for our WrestleMania match. I had complete confidence that my work with them would make this match spectacular. I wouldn't be where I am without them. A year before, we had Triple Threat matches all over Florida, sometimes in front of twenty-five people. Now, I was the villain and they were the heroes. This was a different match and a different story. I knew we were going to tear the house down in front of the largest WWE crowd of all time.

When we talked about the match, I went back to thinking about Dusty. He believed in each of us when no one else did. No matter where the road takes us in this business, we'll always have the bond of the work we did together. That helped put NXT on the map and caused a seismic shift in the way women are presented to the audience. It also paved the way for the establishment of the Women's Championship as the premier prize for female competitors in this business.

When you first walk through the curtain, it's the most defining moment of who you are. I start off with my dad's music playing. I need to be able to convince the audience that they're seeing the evil queen.

I saw someone on my way to the Gorilla Position: Paul Heyman. When I debuted, Paul reached out to me and shared a personal story. He could see what I was feeling about Reider and why I wrestled. Paul's story was not about losing a brother; it was something different. He talked about letting go of guilt and being able to relate to it. That always meant a lot to me.

I gave Paul a hug. He stared at me with a stern look and said something I'll always remember: "Go show the world why you're at the center of AT&T Stadium." My heart beat faster. Anxiety and nerves became excitement. I was ready.

Before the match, I met my dad to take pictures. I put my robe on and walked to him from a distance so he could see its stunning patterns. I felt like I was floating. I've never been big on costumes. I never loved the way anything looked on me as much as I loved that robe. My dad began to tear up.* It signified so many different things: his career; his legacy; my career and transformation into the queen; and bringing back an elegance to villainy as a larger-than-life character.

I surprised him: my robe had pieces of his robe from his final match with Shawn Michaels stitched into it.

We were at the Gorilla Position—Becky, Sasha, Snoop Dogg, my dad, and me. I couldn't imagine what the emotion was like for Becky and Sasha. This was what they had dreamed about since they were little girls. They did so much to get to WWE and live their dream. Becky and Sasha were products of hard work, dedication, resilience, and being true to themselves. I always admired their work ethic and was proud to share this with them.

Becky was the first to go to the ring. Her energy and connection with the audience made her the perfect person to kick things off. It's like she says; she's "straight fire."

The next was Sasha. The Boss looked fantastic going to the ring with her signature swagger. And for WrestleMania, Snoop Dogg, who was

---

*Ric: "I got emotional right there on the spot. I couldn't help it. I never thought it would be my daughter doing this. And she's done so well. I'm so proud of her. She's backstage at WrestleMania wearing a robe for her match that has parts of my robe from my match with Shawn Michaels? It was unbelievable. She just told me I couldn't cry during our entrance. I knew that part. There's a saying in this business about 'passing the torch.' I didn't pass anything to Ashley. She took the torch from me and ran as fast and far as she could with it. I'm not saying that because she's my daughter. I'm saying that because it's true and I know. With the exception of a few guys, over the last forty years, I've been in the ring with everyone in this business. I don't care who you are or what your name is. When you're the one in the ring, you have to deliver. Every night."

inducted into the WWE Hall of Fame the night before, performed a special version of her theme song. It was a grand entrance befitting the Boss.

At first, I thought, *How do you follow Snoop Dogg?* Then I did something I do each time before I walk through the curtain: I kiss my hand and point to the sky. After I did that this time, I looked at my dad from the corner of my eye. He didn't notice. I looked at the monitor and saw the stage and the path to the ring. That's when I realized this was the aisle he was supposed to walk me down *first*. All along. This was my destiny.

I heard Lilian Garcia's voice. My music hit. It was time to make history.

When I walked onstage at WrestleMania XXIV to receive my dad's Hall of Fame ring, my legs almost buckled. I didn't know how he had done this for so many years. This was eight years later. I was doing it with the greatest of all time beside me. I walked through the curtain with the most confidence I ever had.

I took my first steps in my robe onstage. I raised my arms and rotated 360 degrees. On this night, nothing felt more natural.

As I got closer to the ring, the enormity of the moment and the historical significance of the match became even realer. I stopped a second time to show the beautiful artistry of the robe for everyone to see, along with, for the final time, the Divas Championship. The splendor of the pyrotechnics and wonder of WrestleMania provided the perfect celebration of my father's legacy and my future.

When I entered the ring and saw WWE Hall of Famer Lita holding the new WWE Women's Championship, it was another instance of my coming full circle. Lita had been pivotal in my development as a member on the main roster.* The girl who had accidentally found her way into Lita's dressing room in England and was in the front row the night she

---

*Lita: "It was incredible to see Ashley emerge as Charlotte, because they're two different people. She was excellent at learning. She built on everything she learned and made it her own. Ashley's the most rewarding person I ever worked with. Those three women put on a match that was pure poetry. It had a main-event feel. I hope at some point they can look back and watch that match so they can reflect on it and absorb what a big moment in history it was."

and Trish Stratus main-evented *Raw* in 2004 never thought she'd be in the ring with her one day.

A Triple Threat Match is another match where the structure does not favor the champion. The champion does not have to be pinned or submit to lose. In this case, our story featured two top heroes against a villain. This time, I was ready to take the new crown. We were going to take the audience on a ride they never expected!

The crowd chanted, "Women's wrestling!" The three of us stood there—now WWE Superstars—and enjoyed the moment. The three women from NXT were in the middle of the ring at WrestleMania with more than one hundred thousand people on their feet waiting to see our match. They were waiting to see who would emerge victorious and be the WWE Women's Champion.

Our debut on *Raw* last July signified that it was our time. This moment meant that it was our time to take over.

The first act began with "the Lass Kicker" Becky Lynch and the Boss joining forces to take me down. That quickly proved to be temporary. They showed that Triple Threat matches are every Superstar for themselves and traded quick pinfall attempts to end the match early.

I put an end to that when I drilled Becky with a boot to the face. Then came a standoff between Sasha and me. The Boss showed the audience that she was ready to throw down. She blocked my offense and flew from the top rope with a Hurricanrana. After Sasha took off from the second rope, Becky followed that by giving me a German suplex. The two fan favorites spun the match so fast, going move for move, while I plotted my next strategy on the outside.

Triple Threats have the creative challenge of keeping all the participants involved throughout the match while giving the Superstars time to battle it out one-on-one.

Becky seized the moment and dove off the ring apron onto Sasha and me. It was time for Becky and me to take the chemistry we'd developed during matches at live events and raise the stakes on the grandest stage of them all.

All three of us had submission moves that could come into play at any time. Becky was the first to incorporate an offense that specifically targeted an opponent's arm just to let the world know that she could lock in the Disarmer arm lock at any time.

We kept the pendulum shifting as I teased going for my Figure Eight submission on Becky. Sasha returned and took the attack to me, only to be sent out of the ring courtesy of the Lass Kicker. Becky, making it clear that she was going to win the championship her way, continued to fire her high-powered offense. The crowd roared when she locked in her Disarmer submission move on me. Being trapped in the move in the center of the ring meant I had nowhere to go. As he was so adept at doing, my parent in crime on the outside got the referee's attention to buy some time.

Sasha broke up the hold to ensure that I didn't give up, thus giving Becky the victory. The Boss found herself back on the stadium floor. The tables continued to turn. I was able to regain control and blast my former best friend from behind. I stood over Becky and held her leg up an extra second. The more than one hundred thousand fans cheered, "WOOOOO!!" in unison, and that's when I knew it was time to lock in the figure four.

As the second act opened in dramatic fashion, the pages of this Women's Championship story continued to turn. Before I could bridge from the figure four into the Figure Eight, Sasha soared from the top rope with a perfect Five-Star Frog Splash that would have made her hero Eddie Guerrero proud. The crowd couldn't believe their eyes when my shoulder came off the canvas just before the referee's hand touched the mat for the third time.

Becky displayed her trademark resilience and tossed Sasha and me around the ring like rag dolls with her suplexes. Becky covered me. Sasha moved like a cat and broke up the pin to keep the match going.

When I rolled out of the ring, the fans waited to see Sasha and Becky once again go toe-to-toe. As they traded exchanges of great offense, both women showed the heart that makes them incredible performers.

The saga took a sudden turn when Sasha ducked a clothesline from Becky. Instead of going back at Becky, she launched herself through the ropes, flipped in midair, and sent me down to the floor.

Moments later, not to be outdone, Becky took flight. Just when everyone thought Becky was going to take out the Boss, Sasha pulled my dad into harm's way. Becky got a little payback after all the times my dad cheated her out of a victory. Our hearts were racing. We could feel the audience's flood of emotion. With both my opponents occupied, I climbed to the top rope. I wanted to do something I was told not to do in the NXT Fatal 4-Way match. At the time, that bothered me. Now I realized why. Doing it now, at WrestleMania, would mean the most.

My heart and mind were racing at light speed. It was time to show the world that I backed up the edict of being genetically superior. I launched myself off the top rope and took both my challengers down with a moonsault out to the floor.

AT&T Stadium echoed with chants of "This is wrestling!" As we entered the third and final act of the historic story of the first WWE Women's Championship, I was overwhelmed with intense, complex feelings.

I looked at my dad, took in that moment, and fed off the crowd. I grabbed both my opponents and declared, "This is my title!"

I dropped my challengers with a double version of my Natural Selection finisher. This should have been the end of the match. Becky escaped from my pinfall attempt. Sasha kicked out . . . Becky kicked out again . . . Sasha escaped . . . these women would not stay down. I exhausted all my options. The battle continued.

Becky fired back and drilled Sasha and me with a missile dropkick from the top rope. The Lass Kicker seized the moment and locked me in the Disarmer. I hung on for dear life. What looked like a clear path to victory became littered with roadblocks.

Sasha countered the Disarmer and had Becky cinched in her Bank Statement submission move. The fans shot to their feet to see the hero take the title home.

I took advantage of both competitors being down. I locked Sasha in the figure four, but she continued to fight back and reversed the move before I could bridge into the Figure Eight. Just when I thought the match was won, Becky pulled Sasha to safety.

Each woman locked in her submission during the match. It was impossible to predict a winner. As storytellers who took pride in their craft, that's exactly what we wanted.

We all endured incredible punishment. The drive to become Women's Champion witnessed the three of us in the middle of the ring. I chopped them with everything I had. They fired shots at me and then dropped each other.

The battle continued as the three of us were on the top rope. Sasha hung upside down from the turnbuckle in the Tree of Woe. Becky sent me flying with a Bexploder suplex from the top rope.

After reversing a suplex attempt from Becky, Sasha regained the advantage and had Becky locked in the Bank Statement. This was where being the child of the Dirtiest Player in the Game helped again. I made it into the ring and threw Sasha to the outside just in time.

I seized the opportunity to lock Becky into the figure four. I bridged into the Figure Eight. I held on with everything I had. My dad held Sasha on the outside. The Boss couldn't save the match this time. Becky held on for as long as she could, but the pain was too great.

It was all over. I wanted to grab Becky's hand and say, "Thank you." I sat on my knees for a moment. A tradition in the business was to never hold a championship until you became a champion. I didn't touch the Divas Championship until I won it at Night of Champions.

I waited for the championship to be handed to me so I could take a moment to hold it in front of me. I wanted to acknowledge the championship the way it deserved—to show the world what it meant to the women's division, to the sports-entertainment business, to the fans, and to me.

I was overcome with pride, holding that championship. I raised it over my head and pointed to my heart. I didn't choose this path. It chose me. My father was with me. He played an integral part in helping me throughout this journey. It would never have meant as much without him.

I know there will be more chapters in my future stories with Sasha and Becky. I'm grateful for that. As I held up the new Women's Championship,* I was honored to be the first woman to have the opportunity to define what the championship meant.†

It wasn't planned, it wasn't orchestrated. It happened naturally. The women of NXT rose to WWE Superstardom together. At Wrestle-Mania, we did what we had set out to do. Victory was ours. We had a great match, and we stole the show.

In the process, we became the guardians of women's wrestling. The history of women in our business that began with great names like Mae Young, Mildred Burke, June Byers, and the Fabulous Moolah and continued with Wendi Richter and Sensational Sherri, Alundra Blayze, Trish Stratus, Lita, and Beth Phoenix—and the legacies of all the women who gave everything they had to this industry—were now in our hands.

We were ready. It wasn't one woman who started this revolution; it was a group of driven women who worked together to propel it into an amazing transformation. We hoped that there was a little girl in the audience or at home watching TV who saw our performance and said, "This is what I want to do. This is my dream. I can do it."

We'll be able to take what we've done to a different level and set a new

---

*Paul Levesque: "This is the daughter of the greatest professional wrestler of all time. Ashley never had an interest in this. Reid's dream became her dream. Reid's passing brought Ashley's purpose to the forefront. To see where she landed is awesome. Everything she is, she earned."

†Sara Amato: "Ashley's the hardest-working, most deserving talent. She continues to evolve as a professional and dedicate herself to this business. Ashley's not only an amazing performer but an inspiring woman."

standard. We won't stop smashing ceilings. The dreams are to main event WWE pay-per-views and achieve the ultimate goal—headline Wrestle-Mania.*

Now that the glass ceiling has been shattered, the next generation of female competitors won't have to battle the skepticism, the questions about whether or not women can draw money in this business. They will have the opportunity to show that, yes, they can do it. The challenge they will have is to top it.

Backstage, my father and I shared a deeply personal moment. We hugged. This time together meant so much to both of us. Our relationship was stronger than it had ever been. He was there for me every step of the way.

Yes, I'm the daughter of Ric Flair. Yes, I'm an extension of the Nature Boy. I'm proud of that. I'm proud of who my father is, and I'm proud to honor him. I'm proud to take the Flair name to new heights as a woman.†

I went back to the locker room. I was told that WWE's corporate jet was waiting for me at the airport. I was flying through the night, straight to New York City, with newly crowned WWE Champion Roman Reigns, for an appearance on *The TODAY Show.*

---

*Paul Heyman: "Ashley was the perfect choice to establish the women's division and the new WWE Women's Championship. She has the intangible 'it' factor—a combination of look, talent, charisma, and the indescribable magic that occurs between a select few performers and the audience. It's the difference between a long-term, top-level, number-one Superstar and being someone who goes in and out of the main event. Ashley has the magic—the magic that can't be fully described even by people who've witnessed it their entire lives."

†Ric: "Through this once-in-a-lifetime opportunity to work with Ashley, I realized that doing other things in the business was not taking a backseat. It wasn't my career being minimized. Let's not get crazy; of course I can still go forty-five minutes in a match. The difference is now I don't feel lost if I'm not doing that. I'm secure with my legacy as a performer. I'm secure with myself as a person. I had to change the way I looked at myself in the context of the business. I moved on to another chapter in my career. I was grateful that I could still be involved in the industry I've loved my whole life. To be able to work with my daughter was a gift. For our relationship to return to a place it hadn't been in years was a blessing. After all we've been through, we're stronger than ever. I'm excited about what lies ahead."

I was told after the appearance on *TODAY*, I'd be back on the plane to Dallas in time to appear live on *Monday Night Raw* in the evening, where I'd be introduced as the new WWE Women's Champion. And my dad would be right by my side. It was our time.

And so it begins again . . .

PART V

DEDICATIONS

Dear Champ,

One of the brightest days of my life was when you came into this world. My greatest achievement in life was that I was your hero.

I think of your smile after you played jokes on all of us or did one of your famous imitations, the Disney character breakfasts you loved as a boy, and how the ultimate fudge brownie at Harper's was your favorite. Coming home and seeing the way your mom dressed you and how you and Ashley looked like twins always touched my heart.

Watching you become a standout athlete and pursue your dream made me so proud! What made me proudest, though, was the young man you grew up to be. Your love of family, the way you taught kids how to play sports, spending time with your nieces, and your affection for animals were just some of the ways you showed your thoughtfulness, kindness, and compassion.

It's difficult for me to put my love for you and what a privilege it was to be your father into words. Your spirit lives in all of us—your mom, Megan, David, and Ashley.

We celebrate your life every day. I feel your presence wherever I go.
I know that you're not gone but in a better place.
I love you, Champ.

Love,
Dad

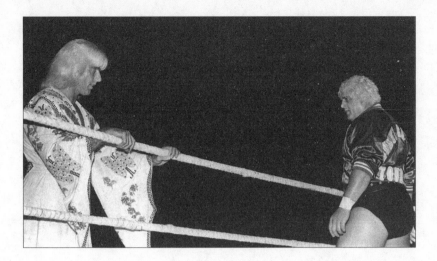

Dear Dusty,

It's difficult to find the words to describe how much you meant to me.

It feels like yesterday that we drove the dirt roads of Amarillo, Texas, that you took me to Japan as a young kid in this business, and that we stood in the center of the ring nose-to-nose as opponents.

Even when we had professional differences—and we had our share—I felt we still had a mutual respect for one another.

We had so much fun. We made a lot of money, and we spent a lot of money. We lived life exactly the way you said, "On the edge of a lightning bolt."

Some of my favorite memories were in recent years, looking back on our careers, talking about our kids, and discussing what was happening today. You were always better at the marriage thing than I was.

I never imagined that one day you'd protect and mentor my daughter Ashley the way you did for me.

I wouldn't be who I am today if it weren't for you. Your legacy will live on through your family and the generations of people you inspired to enter this profession. You encouraged them to "get a dream, hold on to it, and shoot for the sky."

No one embodied the American Dream the way you did—the biggest star of them all.

I love you, Dusty.
Ric

Dear Reider,

*I miss you. I miss you every day. I torture myself, not knowing
whether I told you how proud I was of you enough. I get angry knowing
that you never got to see me happy these last few years. I promise that
I am happy now, and it's all because of you.*

*Almost every day, I think about the letter you wrote me in Japan,
telling me you didn't give up because you thought about how hard
I worked. Now I get to write you that letter to let you know that I don't
give up because of you. You changed my future that weekend in Miami
when you told me that I should do this—that I should train to become a
wrestler. I regret so many things. I wish I could rewrite history. I wish I
had told you that I believed in your dreams because you were the one
who believed in this path. I am doing it now, Reider. Your dream is
coming true because I will continue to think about you when I want to
give up or when walking through that curtain seems too scary.*

I feel like I lost the only person who really understood me. I just hope you know how much I loved you. If I let you down sometimes, I'm sorry. It's funny. I always wanted to help you and give you advice, but in the end, you taught me the biggest lesson of all, and that was to have a dream. A goal. To live. Not to be trapped by what I thought and who I was. To believe in myself. You brought out all these things in me. If I had only known then that you were going to be the one teaching all of us now!

In Dusty's words from your favorite interview, "I've wined and dined with kings and queens, and I've slept in alleys and dined on pork and beans." Thank you, Reider. Thank you for everything.

I love you as big as the sky,
Winky

Dear Dusty,

We did it. I scroll through my phone to your number sometimes, wanting to text you. Every week when I get home from the road, I see the huge framed poster of you and my dad. It's surreal to think what an amazing role you played in both our lives and how you were a mentor to both of us at different times. You took a lost girl with no vision for the future and gave me the confidence to be whatever I wanted to be. You also instilled that confidence in Becky, Sasha, and Bayley. I can still hear your voice saying, "I love my Divas," with your one-of-a-kind lisp. When I debuted on the main roster, I still wonder, what would you have said to the promo class that Wednesday about Raw? What country song would you be playing loudly as we all took our seats before class? I know you would start off with "Did anyone see any good movies?" or "Who has the dirt?" We were your NXT kids, and you turned us into stars. Every big moment I've had up until now, before I walk through that curtain, I think about you. Can you see me?

I think about the week I came back after Reid's death and how you told me that it was a horrible thing but that you wanted me back. I think about the promo I gave when we moved from Tampa to the Performance Center in Orlando and you finally said I had it. You were the first person I hugged when I walked through Gorilla after my match with Nattie. I replay these moments all the time, wishing we were still having them. From the first day I walked through the doors at FCW, you never stopped fighting for me and believing I had potential. I remember after my very first match with Emma at FCW in Tampa, how you told the class how proud you were of me. Never hiding your feelings. You were never shy about acknowledging that you had known me since I was born or telling the class I was spoiled rotten in high school.

I always knew you felt where I was coming from in my promos. You never said it out loud, but I could see in your eyes that you understood whatever I was going through—just like a father would. I promise I will continue to reach for the brass ring. The world lost a little bit of magic when you left us, but your vision and hope for me, along with so many of my peers from NXT, have helped me make it to the big dance. And that's because you could find something special in all of us, something we never knew we had. Thank you for that, Dusty. I hope you are smiling somewhere knowing that your presence, knowledge, and magic will live on in all of us forever.

I love you, Dusty.
Ashley